LEASE or BUY?

Financial Management Association
Survey and Synthesis Series

The Search for Value: Measuring the Company's Cost of C
Michael C. Ehrhardt

Lease or Buy?: Principles for Sound Decision Making
James S. Schallheim

*L*EASE *or B*UY?

Principles for Sound Decision Making

James S. Schallheim

Harvard Business School Press
Boston, Massachusetts

98 97 96 95 94   5 4 3 2 1

Library of Congress Cataloging-in-Publication Data

Schallheim, James S., 1951–
    Lease or buy?: principles for sound decision making / James S. Schallheim.
        p. cm.—(Financial Management Association survey and synthesis series)
    Includes bibliographical references and index.
    ISBN 0-87584-558-4 (alk. paper)
    1. Lease or buy decisions.   2. Industrial equipment leases.
3. Lease or buy decisions—Accounting.   4. Industrial equipment leases—Accounting.   I. Title.   II. Series.
    HD39.4.S3   1994
    658.1'5242—dc20   94-10236
                                                                      CIP

To my parents, Edith and Paul,
for their love and support

Contents

Preface ix

Chapter 1: **Why Lease?** 1
Reasons for Leasing 3
Summary 15

Chapter 2: **Lessors and Lease Contracts** 17
Types of Lessors 17
Types of Leases 18
Types of Assets 23
Determination of Lease Payments 24
The Struture of Lease Contracts 30
Summary 37

Chapter 3: **Tax Rules for Leasing** 39
IRS True Leases 40
Other Tax Effects for Leasing 47
Alternative Minimum Tax 53
Motor Vehicle Leasing 54
Real Estate Leasing 55
Tax Advantages in International Leases 56
A Tax Law History: Safe Harbor Leasing 60
Summary 62

Chapter 4: **Accounting for Leases** 65
Definition of Capital and Operating Leases 66
Accounting for Capital Leases 67
Special Accounting Issues 75
Summary 91

Chapter 5: **The Concept of the Equivalent Loan** 93
The Equivalent Loan 93
Debt and Leases as Substitutes 99
Are Debt and Leases Substitutes? 100
Empirical Evidence 109
Summary 111

Chapter 6: **Net Present Value Analysis** 113
General NPV Analysis 113
Competitive Equilibrium in Leasing Markets 117
The Myers, Dill, and Bautista Model 119
Examples of Simple Lease Versus Purchase Analysis 120
Operating Costs and Salvage Value 125
The Differences Between Before-Tax and After-Tax Discount
Rates 129
Alternative Minimum Tax 130
Summary 134

Chapter 7: **Yields on Leasing Contracts** 135
How to Calculate Yields 135
Examples of Yields 137
What Determines Yields on Financial Leasing Contracts? 140
Empirical Analysis of Lease Yields 145
Lease Comparison with High-Yield Bonds 150
Summary 151

Chapter 8: **Residual Value Analysis: The Wild Card** 153
Residual Value Risk 154
The Portfolio Concept 157
Beta's Application to Residual Value 158
Residual Value Experience 163
Specialization or Diversification? 168
Options in Leases 168
Summary 176

Chapter 9: **Summary: Lease or Buy** 179
Use Net Present Value (Net Advantage to Leasing) Analysis 179
Do Not Ignore the Residual Value of the Equipment 180
Consider All Tax Consequences of the Lease 180
Follow the Accounting Rules for Leases 180
Consider All the Options in the Lease 181
A Complex Example 181
Summary 186

Appendix: Present Value Mathematics 187

References 195

Index 209

Preface

New financial analyst Pat McDonald is faced with her most difficult assignment so far at AdTech, a 23-year-old advertising and promotional firm. The chief financial officer has asked her to propose the least costly financing arrangements for acquisition of a new copier that would triple the duplicating speed of the company. The new machine is capable of duplicating in multicolors, collating, stapling, and binding. Pat estimates that the new machine would increase the firm's revenues because more promotional materials could be printed in-house, and productivity would increase. The price tag on the machine is $1,500,000, and Pat knows AdTech can borrow money at 9 percent.

What about leasing the duplicating machine? The seller of the machine suggests a five-year lease with payments of $370,000 per year. Is leasing equivalent to borrowing? What is the real cost of leasing? Perhaps the yield on the lease is greater than 9 percent. Does this mean the lease is more expensive than borrowing the money? Pat knows from her business school courses that yields on leases can be misleading. But how does she go about doing a net present value analysis?

Then Pat thinks about the special conditions that could make leasing attractive, such as the tax position of AdTech and the expected residual value for the new machine in five years. She also wonders about what kinds of options may be included in the lease, such as an option to purchase the new machine or an option to cancel the lease. Finally, Pat considers the accounting implications of the lease: Must the lease appear on the balance sheet and thereby increase AdTech's already high debt ratio? Is the lease a better bargain than purchasing the duplicating machine?

The answer to what Pat should do is found in this book. Its main purpose is to show how to perform lease versus purchase analysis. Chapter 1 explains the leasing market in terms of its size, membership, and products. In Chapter 2 the details of a lease contract, which may specify a host of provisions and options, are explored. There are important tax questions about leasing, and the answers are provided in Chapter 3. The accounting rules for leases that play an important role are the topic of Chapter 4. The question about the equivalence of debt and leasing is discussed in Chapter 5, which presents the latest advances from the academic literature. The nuts and bolts of lease versus purchase analysis are explained in Chapter 6. The answer to the questions about yield analysis posed above are provided in Chapter 7. Residual value and the value of options in a lease contract are the topics of Chapter 8. The combination of *all* of these factors in the lease versus purchase analysis is summarized in Chapter 9. An Appendix covers present value analysis for both readers unfamiliar with it and those who would find a review of the mathematics helpful.

To summarize, the purpose of this book is to:

1. Teach detailed lease versus purchase analysis.
2. Provide detailed information about lease contracting.
3. Describe the latest tax implications for leasing.
4. Supply information about the proper accounting rules for leases.
5. Educate the reader about the practical implications of the extensive body of academic research relating to leasing.
6. Cast all these topics within the central theme of a functioning economic market for capital and for leasing.

Acknowledgments

Many friends and acquaintances helped make this book possible. Michael Long, as editor of the Financial Management Association Survey and Synthesis Series, persuaded me, in a friendly way, to undertake this project in the first place. Mike encouraged my progress and provided valuable feedback in the early drafts of the book. Jim Johnson and Tony Memmo reviewed the manuscript, and their comments were extremely useful to me. I would also like to thank my friend and colleague, Ron Lease, for his advice and comments at the very early stages.

It has been a pleasure working with the professionals at the Harvard Business School Press. Nick Philipson has been a wonderful editor, always upbeat and supportive. I would like to thank Natalie Greenberg for her comments, which have improved the exposition greatly. I thank my secretary, Julia West, for her skillful assistance with typing the manuscript.

Two of my students, Jeff Hoffman and Brandi Hawley, provided research on the tax law as it applies to leasing. I am very grateful for their help and borrowed heavily from their research projects. I am indebted to Sudhir Amembal, Lynn Leary-Myers, and Jeff Negri of Amembal & Halladay for allowing me to attend their workshop entitled the '93 Tax Reform Conference.

A special thanks to Marianne Abueg for her comments, counsel, and unfailing support. Last, but not least, my loving thanks to my family, Barbara, Jason, and Leah, for their patience and forbearance.

Chapter *1*

Why Lease?

The important message to remember throughout this book is that leasing, like almost all other financial transactions in our economy, represents a market. When you are sitting in the office of a leasing company ready to sign a contract committing you to a series of monthly payments for many years into the future, it may be hard to imagine that a market is at work. Yet a market is at work in this setting that is just as real as the markets for tomatoes, televisions, or Treasury bonds. The leasing market brings together buyers of lease contracts, the lessors (also known as owners), with sellers of lease contracts, lessees (also known as users). From the economic perspective, the lessor is the purchaser of the lease contract just as the lender is referred to as a purchaser of the debt contract. Prices, or lease payments in this case, are determined by supply and demand as in any other market. Finally, the more competition in the leasing market, the more the customer, the lessee, will benefit in the form of lower lease payments.

Markets are shaped by many factors: the scarceness of the resource, the economic laws of supply and demand, the size of the market, the level of risk, and the competition. All these factors lead to the determination of a price. Here, price is a set of lease payments.

The leasing market is huge. For the past two decades, leases have provided the source of funds to acquire a large portion of all the capital equipment in the United States. The amount of dollars involved in equipment leasing in 1993 is estimated by the U.S. Department of Commerce to be $126.3 billion of the total investment in business equipment of $394.7 billion. Figure

1

1.1 illustrates the trends for the industry between 1986 and 1993. The record shows that equipment leasing has financed close to one-third of total business investment for most of the years 1986–1993. The level of leasing and proportion of leasing to total investment were increasing steadily until 1990. The impact of the recession can be seen in the numbers for 1991 and 1992, both for the amounts of equipment leasing and the total equipment investment.

Although the leasing market is very large, it is not unlimited. As in all markets, the element of scarce resources comes into play. The scarce resource in the leasing market is funds availability. If the leasing market is working efficiently, funds are allocated to their most productive use and most productive lessees. While lessees compete for funds provided by lessors, lessors also compete in financial markets for funds used in all types of credit operations. Thus the lessors compete for funds against other lessors and against all types of lenders, including banks, other financial institutions, insurance companies, and other creditors. While this competition limits the price that a lessor can charge for a lease contract, it is

Figure 1.1: Total Equipment Investment and Leasing

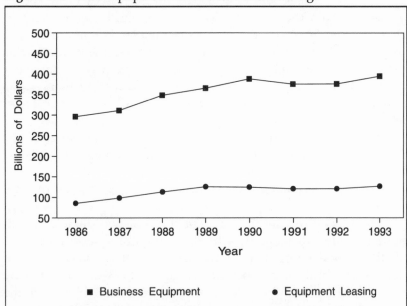

easy to see that the same competition allows a lessee to go elsewhere for funds.

All this competition leads to the determination of market prices by the process of supply and demand. The suppliers of leasing funds are the lessors; the demanders of leasing funds are the lessees. Competition among lessors (and other suppliers of credit funds) determines the supply of leasing funds in the market. The competition among lessees for leasing funds determines the demand for leasing funds. When supply and demand are equal, a price is determined, and economists define the market as being in "equilibrium." In the leasing market, equilibrium is represented by the consummation of a lease contract and the agreed-upon schedule of lease payments.

The last important element of the leasing market is determination of value. By value, we mean that the lease contract and its schedule of lease payments have a particular value today or *present value*. The present value can be thought of as the price at which the lessor is willing to sell the contract to another party. Alternatively, the value can be thought of as the price at which the lessor is willing to forgive the lessee all future obligations specified in the lease contract. In economic equilibrium, these two prices, the amount the contract will sell to a third party or the amount the lessee pays to rescind the contract, are the same.

Reasons for Leasing

The essence of leasing can be captured in a single sentence: *Equipment leasing provides customized financing with potentially unique tax features.*

Lease contracts can be written to provide the lessee with great flexibility in terms of the amount and timing of the lease payments. The ownership of the leased asset remains with the lessor in most leases. That is, the lessee does not "own" the asset after completing all the contracted payments, as a borrower would own an asset after meeting all loan payments. Yet the "use" of the asset by a lessee should not be affected by ownership.[1] Again, because ownership remains with the lessor, leasing is uniquely different from bor-

---

[1] The statement that the use of leased equipment is not affected by ownership requires qualification. Lease contracts must make provisions for adequate maintenance of the asset and prohibit abuse of the asset.

rowing; the lessor, unlike a lender, can deduct tax shields generated by the leased equipment. Not surprisingly, however, the Internal Revenue Service specifies rules for tax-oriented leases. If the lease qualifies under the tax guidelines, it is a *true lease;* otherwise the lease is a *conditional sales contract* under the IRS rules.

Under the operation of basic economic principles and the forces of competition, leasing and other forms of financing will have the *same costs* if the capital markets are *perfect.* Perfect capital markets exist when certain, somewhat idealized, conditions are met. These conditions are (1) there are no taxes; (2) there are no transaction costs, flotation costs, contracting costs, or brokerage fees; and (3) no single investor or firm can affect the market price of a security by trading in that security.[2] Under perfect capital market conditions, leasing is a matter of indifference; in other words, no reason exists to lease or not to lease (this is also called a zero net present value transaction). In order for these to be an advantage (or disadvantage) to leasing, perfect capital market conditions are *not* satisfied, and thus there are valid economic reasons for leasing.

As we begin to review the reasons for leasing, it is important to realize that there is more than one leasing market. One important segment of the leasing market, of course, is tax-motivated leasing. Another segment involves small leases to small firms with limited borrowing capabilities. Similarly, there is the "venture leasing" market for start-up firms that have limited access to capital markets. A large segment of the leasing market is motivated by residual value risk, or the avoidance of this risk, for assets such as computers or aircraft. Another segment is leasing across national borders. These cross-border leases exploit complex tax laws in two or more countries.

If you look at the advertisements and brochures distributed by leasing companies, you encounter a myriad of reasons for leasing. I have divided these advertised justifications for leasing into four broad categories: (1) tax savings; (2) pure financial cost savings; (3) transaction and information cost savings; and (4) risk sharing. Exhibit 1.1 lists popular reasons for leasing in these four categories.

There are two schools of thought concerning these reasons. The first is the efficient markets school. According to this line of thought, markets are competitive and efficient. Only solid economic reasons favor (or disfavor) leasing, and these reasons are based on violations

---

[2] Because leasing spans both the capital market and the real asset market, the perfect market assumption is that lessors have no special purchase price advantage or proprietary access to the leased asset.

Exhibit 1.1: Frequently Advertised Reasons for Leasing

Tax Savings
Leasing is advantageous for firms with excess tax shields Leasing is advantageous for firms with low earnings Leasing is advantageous for firms with low tax rates Leasing offers tax advantages Leasing may permit more rapid amortization than depreciation
Pure Financial Cost Savings
Leasing permits 100 percent financing Leasing permits off-balance sheet financing Leasing does not tie up capital Leasing offers lower initial outlay Leasing offers preservation of credit lines Leasing frees working capital for more productive use Leasing is a cheaper way to acquire equipment Leasing avoids some restrictions found in debt contracts Leasing may increase a firm's ability to acquire funds Leasing leaves normal lines of bank credit undisturbed
Transaction and Information Cost Savings
Leasing avoids the purchase transaction Leasing offers the convenience of making one payment Leasing may be tailored to the lessee's needs Leasing makes all costs known Leasing requires less record-keeping Leasing takes less time Leasing offers convenience and flexibility Leasing does not dilute ownership or control
Risk Sharing
Leasing avoids the sale of equipment no longer needed Leasing is good for short-term asset use Leasing offers protection against asset obsolescence Leasing permits hedging of business risk Leasing provides a hedge against inflation Leasing offers less risk and responsibility

of the perfect capital market conditions such as taxes, transaction costs, and other measurable costs. The second school could be called the psychological school of thought. Proponents of this school might argue that sometimes there is a "free lunch" in the marketplace, ready to be gobbled up by the clever and astute investor or manager. In addition, the market can be fooled occasionally by accounting tricks or misinformation. The market also overreacts to new information, leading to bubbles and busts. In sum, the market is driven by factors such as investor sentiment or psychology that can lead to pricing anomalies or worse, such as irrational behavior. I am clearly in favor of the efficient markets school, but admit that many anomalies exist that have not been explained, so far, by traditional economic reasoning.

Tax Savings

Much of the academic literature on leasing has concentrated on the tax savings. If both lessee and lessor face the same marginal tax rate, it is commonly argued, leasing does not provide any advantage from taxes (leasing remains a zero net present value (NPV) transaction). If lessee and lessor face different tax rates, there is a potential tax savings resulting from the lease transaction. The lessee and lessor can save at the expense of government tax revenues.

The tax savings argument becomes more complicated in a world of uncertainty about both future earnings and tax regimes. Chapter 3 discusses the past and current tax regimes. But it is important to remember that tax codes have changed and will surely continue to change over time. In addition, uncertainty about a firm's future earnings can be important in the decision to lease or purchase an asset. Chapter 5 considers the situation where the lessee and lessor may face the same tax rates, but uncertainty about future earnings makes leasing beneficial.

Pure Financial Cost Savings

The list of pure financial reasons for leasing can be divided into valid (efficient markets school) and dubious arguments (psychological school). Let's examine some dubious reasons first. Consider the case for "100 percent financing," a reason for leasing advertised by almost every leasing company in the world. From the economic perspective, it is easy to see that what this argument overlooks are the economic principles of substitutes and competition. As stated earlier in the chapter, leasing must be viewed in the context of competition and substitute products such as borrowing. If a firm qualifies for a lease with its so-called 100 percent financing, it also is possible that the firm can borrow 100 percent of the asset cost at some market-determined price or interest rate.[3] Yet 100 percent financing remains a popular advertising approach, especially to small lessee firms or for venture leases. The subject of Chapter 5 is the direct comparison of leasing to borrowing, specifically, the amount of the "equivalent loan" to leasing.

Another dubious justification for leasing is the off-balance sheet financing argument. (The accounting standards for leasing are the subject of Chapter 4.) One argument, from the psychological school, hinges on the notion that the capital markets will be "fooled" by the off-balance sheet financing. The debt ratio will appear smaller, making the lessee firm seem stronger financially.[4] Financial analysts, bank loan officers, and analysts for bond rating agencies, however, are trained to look for such off-balance sheet obligations as leases. For example, Standard & Poor's "uses a financial model that capitalizes operating lease commitments and allocates minimum lease payments to interest and depreciation expense."[5] It is unlikely firms can fool anyone except the most naive investors with accounting "smoke and mirrors." All the same, off-balance sheet financing remains an attractive selling point.

There may be valid economic reasons for off-balance sheet financing if the firm has a bond or other loan covenant that restricts additional borrowing but doesn't restrict leasing. Then leasing offers a way to circumvent restrictive bond or other loan covenants. It is simple to correct this loophole in the debt contract, however, and many bond or other loan indentures now place limits on leasing as well as borrowing. Another incentive for off-balance sheet classification of a lease is for tax purposes (taxes are the topic of Chapter 3). The lessee may be able to build a

---

[3] Bank financing usually requires a down payment of 20 percent to 40 percent of the asset cost. Yet a down payment can be borrowed from other sources, or the entire asset cost may be borrowed from non-bank institutions.

[4] A debt ratio can be calculated numerous ways. Variations of debt, sometimes including leasing, make up the numerator. The denominator is made up of total assets, total value, or equity and variations thereof. In the example that follows, two debt ratio calculations are illustrated.

[5] Standard & Poor's, "Operating Lease Analytical Model," *Creditstats*, October 21, 1992, p. 10.

stronger case that the lease is a "true lease" as classified by the Internal Revenue Service (IRS) if the lease is not reported on the balance sheet. Tax accounting and financial accounting, however, are separate items. The notion of off-balance sheet financing is not a legitimate economic justification for leasing according to the efficient markets school, but it remains popular among the psychological school proponents.

To illustrate the off-balance sheet nature of leasing, let's consider the simple example of OFF-B Corp. OFF-B Corp. has total assets of 1,000 (500 in current assets and 500 in fixed assets). OFF-B Corp. has a debt-to-asset ratio of 40 percent, thus giving the firm debt of 400 and equity of 600.[6] Next, consider the market value of OFF-B Corp., remembering that market values can differ substantially from book values. (Market values capture future earnings, while book values report the past.) Suppose that the market-to-book ratio for equity is 1.5, so the total equity value of the firm is 900 (1.5 × 600).[7] Assume that the market values of the current assets and the debt are the same as the book values (not a bad working assumption).

Given these numbers, OFF-B Corp. has the following simplified balance sheets in both book values and market values:

OFF-B Corporation
Book Value

Current Assets	500	Debt	400
Fixed Assets	500	Equity	600
Total Assets	1,000	Total Claims	1,000

Market Value

Current Assets	500	Debt	400
Fixed Assets	800	Equity	900
Total Value	1,300	Total Value	1,300

Notice that the market value of fixed assets has been increased to 800 to balance the balance sheet in market value terms. Also, in

---

[6] The debt-to-asset ratio is simply total debt divided by total assets.

[7] The market-to-book ratio is the market price of equity (often, per share) divided by the book value of equity or net worth (again, can be done per share).

market value terms, the debt-to-value ratio is 30.8 percent compared to the debt-to-asset ratio of 40 percent.[8] This example is also useful to illustrate the difference between book and market values and the importance of making the distinction.

Now OFF-B Corp. is going to lease an asset with a book and market value of 200. The lease will not appear on the balance sheet (off-balance sheet financing) for financial reporting purposes or book value. The new balance sheets will appear as follows:

OFF-B Corporation
Book Value

Current Assets	500	Debt	400
Fixed Assets	500	Equity	600
Total Assets	1,000	Total Claims	1,000

Market Value

		Debt	400
Current Assets	500	Lease	200
Fixed Assets	1,000	Equity	900
Total Value	1,500	Total Value	1,500

The book value balance sheet of OFF-B Corp. remains unchanged. But the market value balance shows an increase of 200 for the new leased asset. The market value balance sheet also shows an important change in the *combined* debt and lease ratio from about 31 percent before the lease to 40 percent with the lease.[9] Although the actual market value balance is not computed often, sophisticated investors, financial analysts, and bank loan officers will incorporate this information into their analysis and decisions concerning the lessee firm.

---

[8] The debt-to-value ratio is calculated as the book value of debt divided by the total market value of the firm. The total market value of the firm is often calculated as the book value of debt plus the market value of equity.

[9] Here, the combined debt and equity ratio is the debt plus leases divided by total value.

Impact on Earnings

In a similar vein to the off-balance sheet argument, leasing is often advertised as "increasing earnings." The reason that earnings can be increased with leasing versus purchase is that lease payments are likely to be less than interest payments and depreciation in the early years after the asset acquisition. Thus accounting earnings will be greater when an asset is leased rather than purchased. At the same time, cash flow may be greater for purchase rather than leasing. Cash flow is more important than accounting earnings to the financial health and market value of the firm.

A simple example will illustrate the illusionary impact of lease payment versus depreciation and interest on the earnings versus the cash flow of the firm. Suppose the revenues of EARNUP Company are $10,000, the lease payment is $5,000, depreciation and interest (on a purchase) are $6,000 and $1,000, respectively, and the loan principal repayment (on a purchase) is $4,000. The income statements for EARNUP Company if it leases and if it purchases the asset would appear as follows:

EARNUP Company

Income with Leasing		Income with Purchase	
Revenues	$10,000	Revenues	$10,000
Expenses		Expenses	
Lease	5,000	Depreciation	6,000
		Interest	1,000
Income before Tax	5,000	Income before Tax	3,000
Taxes (35%)	(1,750)	Taxes (35%)	(1,050)
Net Income	$3,250	Net Income	$1,950

This simple example clearly shows that net income for EARNUP Company is much larger under leasing ($3,250) than under purchase ($1,950).

Financial markets capitalize cash flow or *economic* earnings, not *accounting* earnings. So a comparison based on accounting earnings is incomplete. A cash flow (from operations) calculation adjusts the net income by adding back non-cash expenses and subtracting non-cash revenues. Net cash flow is the operating cash flow less investments in fixed assets and working capital. In the EARNUP example:

EARNUP Company

Cash Flow with Leasing		Cash Flow with Purchase	
Revenues	$10,000	Revenues	$10,000
Expenses		Expenses	
Lease	5,000	Depreciation	6,000
		Interest	1,000
Income before Tax	5,000	Income before Tax	3,000
Taxes (35%)	(1,750)	Taxes (35%)	(1,050)
Net Income	$3,250	Net Income	$1,950
Add: None	0	Add: Depreciation	6,000
Subtract: None	0	Subtract:	
		Loan Repayment	(4,000)
Net Cash Flow	$3,250	Net Cash Flow	$3,950

Now the picture has changed dramatically! The purchasing option shows a larger net cash flow ($3,950) than the leasing option ($3,250).

Some interesting details remain in this example. The net cash flow calculation under purchase shows the "add back" for depreciation. This step is performed in all cash flow calculations. The next step, the subtraction of the loan repayment, is necessary because this represents the investment in the fixed asset. For the leasing option, the lease payment builds in the investment cost of the fixed asset as well as the return on investment to the lessor firm.

The purpose of this example is not to suggest that purchasing always generates more cash flow than leasing (the numbers for EARNUP Company are made up, after all). It does not! Rather, the purpose is to show the importance of cash flow over accounting earnings. Also, the example shows that accounting net income can be misleading or illusionary. "Increased earnings" is also a dubious reason for leasing because it assumes that the capital market, investors, or lenders can be fooled by inflated book earnings. This motivation can be exacerbated if managers are compensated on the basis of accounting or book earnings.

Other Financial Reasons

One benefit to leasing does not show up in the advertisements by leasing companies. This valid economic reason for leasing involves the costs of financial distress and bankruptcy (a topic that advertisers naturally avoid). If a lessee defaults on the terms of a lease contract, the lessor, as owner, is often able to repossess the asset with minimal legal costs. Furthermore, the Bankruptcy Act allows the appointed trustee to continue lease payments, while all other debt faces a payment moratorium. Therefore, in financial distress and bankruptcy, a lease can have higher priority than other forms of debt. A lessee firm that may be unable to borrow using traditional debt may be able to obtain a lease because bankruptcy laws give the lessor an advantage. In fact, this financial default and bankruptcy advantage to leasing may be one of the main reasons leasing is so popular in small-business financing. Also, the bankruptcy advantage of the lessor can lead to lower lease rates.

Other dubious reasons for leasing from the psychological school include the preservation of capital and credit lines and the liberation of cash and working capital. These reasons are especially convincing to managers of businesses and government agencies who are given limited capital acquisition budgets but have slack in operating budgets. The importance of these reasons for leasing cannot be denied. The creation of artificial capital constraints by firms, however, may cause managers to choose more costly lease financing over less costly borrowing. As discussed in Chapter 6, the choice of leasing or purchasing should be made on the basis of net present value and not for reasons of arbitrary self-imposed budget limits. Nevertheless, these reasons for leasing may have relevance in the highly political environment of the public sector (or large bureaucratic corporations, for that matter).

Transaction and Information Cost Savings

Reasons for leasing that include savings in transaction, contracting, and information costs can have valid economic content. These reasons are purely speculative, however, because no evidence has documented that transaction costs for lease contracting are lower than for debt and purchase contracting. If the lease payments include some type of maintenance agreement, sometimes called a *service lease* or a *full service lease*, transaction costs play a larger role. The service lease may offer maintenance services at lower transaction cost than a purchase with a separate maintenance contract. In addition, the maintenance services may be tied into the lease payments with a metering system. For example, many copy machines base the lease payment on the number of copies produced. When the copy machine breaks down, both the lessee user and the lessor owner suffer. Therefore, the metering coupled with the maintenance service provides appropriate incentives for both parties of the lease contract. In other words, the lessee pays more when the equipment is used more, while the lessor will face decreased rental income if the equipment is not repaired quickly.

Another part of lease contracting concerns asset abuse or "wear and tear." If it owns the asset, the owner/user has the incentive to take proper care of the asset because the residual or salvage value belongs to the user. If the asset is leased, the lessee/user has an incentive to spend less on maintenance because the residual belongs to the lessor/owner.

There are several ways to handle the potential asset abuse problem. First, the lessor can charge a larger lease payment to cover the losses from asset abuse. Second, the lessor can provide maintenance through a service lease as described above. Third, the lessor can cover specific asset abuse problems through provisions in the lease contract. For example, automobile leases almost always specify certain mileage limitations in the contract, and aircraft leases have engine hours limitations. If the mileage or engine hour limit is exceeded, a specified penalty applies.

Finally, the asset abuse problem can be mitigated by the use of options in the lease contract. For example, an option to purchase the asset at a fixed price at maturity provides the lessee with an incentive to maintain the asset properly.

Risk Sharing

The last category of reasons for leasing involves risk sharing. The most important and unique element of risk sharing for leasing is the residual value risk. The residual or salvage value is the amount the asset is worth—its market value—at the maturity of the lease. A lessee who is unwilling or unable to assume the residual value risk can transfer that risk to the lessor. As always, it is important to remember that the lessor is willing to assume this risk only at a price. The lessor will adjust the lease payment to cover the residual value risk. There are many examples, however, where the lessor has a comparative advantage in the disposal of used equipment. The lessor may be able to sell or release this equipment at a higher price than the lessee. The lessor's advantage in the secondary market for used equipment will help reduce lease payments.

One prime example of a company that specializes in selling and releasing one type of equipment is GPA Group Ltd., an aircraft lessor. Since the company's founding in 1975 in Shannon, Ireland,

GPA has concentrated on trading used planes, primarily to start-up airline carriers. By the late 1980s, GPA had become a major purchaser of new aircraft, and the firm planned to establish a fleet of 600 aircraft. In 1989, however, the sale of used planes accounted for about 35 percent of pre-tax profits, while the lease-only activities accounted for another 35 percent of pre-tax profits. GPA became extremely profitable during the period 1987–1990 by specializing on the short-term, off-balance sheet operating lease. It is important to remember, however, that specializing in one asset market exposes the lessor to additional risk as the fortunes of the market ebb and flow. By 1993, GPA was in severe financial difficulty because of the worldwide recession in the airline industry.

Risk sharing also involves the concept of diversification. A small business can become very concentrated in a limited category of capital equipment. To avoid this concentration, the small firm can lease capital equipment, saving funds for the owners to invest in the capital markets to obtain broader diversification. This motive for leasing, however, is a benefit only to the extent that leasing offers asset diversification at lower cost than other methods of financing.

Another advertised reason for leasing is that it permits hedging inflation and business risk. This "advantage" to leasing seems to rest on the notion that lease payments are fixed. Given the high interest rates of the early 1980s, however, lessors are more cognizant of interest rate risk and will protect themselves. This protection takes the form of higher rates (read: lease payments) or variable-rate leases that fluctuate with prevailing interest rates. Leasing as a "hedge against business risk" simply because the lease payments are fixed is another dubious reason for leasing.

Leasing, however, does offer the flexibility of uneven payments. For example, many firms would like lower lease payments early in the contract and larger lease payments later. Leasing offers this flexibility, although it should be noted that term loans can also be constructed in a similar manner. If lease payments are tied into asset use by way of a metering agreement, leasing may offer a hedge against business risk. When use is high, lease payments will be higher; when use is low, lease payments will be low. Lease contracts for stores in a shopping center frequently let a portion of the lease payment fluctuate with store sales.

Finally, as I explain later, leasing can offer a hedge against the loss of tax shields. When the lessee firm's earnings are low, tax shields will have relatively little value. If the tax shields can be transferred to a firm that can use them, and thus value them more, the lessee firm can benefit from leasing.

Employee Leasing

One of the interesting areas of "leasing" that has arisen in recent years is employee leasing. Firms, particularly small ones, can lease a portion of their staff from employee leasing companies. This may be unusual, but the same factors discussed above—taxes, transaction costs savings, and risk sharing—are the motivating forces for this market.

Employee leasing was motivated by tax regulations. In the 1970s, a loophole in federal tax law made employee leasing advantageous for high-income professionals who wanted to exclude lower-paid workers from company pension plans. The Tax Recovery Act of 1986 closed this loophole.

Currently, employee leasing is motivated by cost savings and risk sharing. Small firms have problems with access to reasonable health care benefits for employees. Employee leasing companies can provide better health care benefits at lower cost because their employment pool is larger (risk sharing). In addition, workers' compensation may be less expensive for the employee leasing company than for the small firm if the accident rate is less for the leasing company (again, risk sharing).

Other factors involve transaction costs. Employee leasing firms can provide payroll and withholding tax accounting and check writing functions, perhaps at lower cost than the small firm can provide itself (economies of scale). The reduction in paperwork is also attractive to small businesses, as is the fact that pension plans are also provided by the employee leasing firm.

Summary

This introductory chapter has presented leasing in the context of an economic market. In order for a business to use equipment to provide a product or service, the equipment does not need to be owned; it can be leased. *Equipment leasing provides customized financing with potentially unique tax features.* The answers to the question "why lease?" are abundant. This chapter reviews popularly advertised reasons for leasing that seem to lack economic content, such as 100 percent financing, off-balance sheet financing, increased earnings, and preservation of credit lines. Proponents, members of the psychological school of thought, find these reasons genuine. The decision maker simply needs to question these motivations with some skepticism, but may find them acceptable if convinced of their validity. Valid economic reasons for leasing, according to the efficient markets school (in addition to tax savings), include the flexibility of lease contracts; savings in financial, transaction, and information costs; valuable options in the lease contracts; and risk-shifting opportunities with leasing.

Chapter 2

Lessors and
Lease Contracts

The word "lease" is used to describe every possible contract from short-term rental of an asset for a few hours or days to a long-term lease that may last for 20 or 30 years. To bring some order to this complex market, this chapter examines types of lessors, categories of leases, types of assets leased, and determination of lease payments, and provides examples of the language contained in lease contracts.

Types of Lessors

Lease contracts can be written by a variety of firms (or occasionally, individual investors). There are many independent leasing companies. Many banks have leasing divisions or subsidiaries. There are leasing divisions or "captive" leasing companies of larger corporations. Sometimes an equipment manufacturer has a leasing division or subsidiary.

The Equipment Leasing Association (ELA) publishes an annual *Survey of Industry Activity.*[1] Exhibit 2.1 illustrates the percentage of each type of lessor as reported by the ELA survey of 688 member companies. The percentages reported show that independent leasing companies and financial services firms constitute over one-half of the ELA membership. While banks represent almost 30 percent of ELA membership, this percentage says nothing about the dollar volume of the leasing business. Banks and other financial institu-

---

[1] ELA was formerly the American Association of Equipment Lessors (AAEL).

tions probably account for between one-third and one-half of the total leasing business in terms of dollar volume. As ELA members, captive leasing companies make up 10 percent of the industry. These companies include leasing subsidiaries of manufacturers, which may lease any kind of equipment besides the equipment manufactured by the parent corporation.

The numbers in Exhibit 2.1 show that a multiplicity of potential lessors exist. For the potential lessee, this means that choices are plentiful and competitive. "Shop around" is good advice to any potential lessee.

Types of Leases

Before complex tax laws and accounting rules were enacted, finance professionals often divided leases into two categories: financial and operating. Although the distinction is often blurred, operating leases were short-term relative to the life of the asset, while financial leases were longer-term. Operating leases frequently included "ownership" services provided by the lessor such as maintenance agreements, insurance coverage, property tax, and other fee payments. Financial leases, as the name implies, were more financing-oriented, leaving the lessee responsible for most of the ownership services.

The accounting profession uses two categories to differentiate leases: capital leases, which must appear on the balance sheet, and operating leases, which appear only in footnotes to the balance sheet. The accounting profession seems to have borrowed the term

Exhibit 2.1: ELA Membership and Survey Response by Type of Lessor

Type of Lessor	Total 1992 ELA Membership
Bank	30%
Financial Advisor:	9
Broker/packager and investment banker	
Captive	10
Independent, financial services	51
Total	100%

Source: Survey of Industry Activity 1992, Equipment Leasing Association of America.

"operating lease," the off-balance sheet lease, to stand for leases where ownership, in more than name, resides with the lessor. In attempting to distinguish operating leases from capital leases, however, the accounting rules have left many loopholes for exploitation by both lessees and lessors. Chapter 4 discusses these accounting definitions and their use and abuse in greater detail.

The 1992 *Survey of Industry Activity* reports, for the 246 firms responding to the survey, that the cost of equipment under lease for direct financing was $65.5 billion (48 percent), for leveraged leases $50.1 billion (36 percent), and for operating leases $21.6 billion (16 percent). From the finance perspective, the most pronounced economic difference between financial leases and operating leases concerns lease maturity, residual value risk, and tax treatment. Although financial and operating leases are often recognized as distinct contracts, most leases actually fall on a continuum between a strictly financial and a strictly operating lease.

Financial Leases

Financial (or direct financing) leases are sometimes called *net leases*, where: (1) the lease payments are calculated to repay the full cost of the asset, and (2) the lessee pays all property taxes, sales taxes, user taxes, fees, maintenance, and insurance.

The tax aspects of financial leases have a direct bearing on the terms and provisions of the lease. While we discuss the tax aspects of leases in Chapter 3, it is sufficient at this point to remember that in order for a financial lease to qualify as a *true lease* in the eyes of the IRS, certain constraints are placed on the provisions of the lease contract terms.

Condition (1) for *net financial leases* violates the IRS rules for a *true lease*. If a transaction is not a *true lease*, the lease payments are not tax-deductible to the lessee. Nor is the lessor allowed to deduct depreciation and other tax shields associated with ownership. To avoid this outcome, the lessor will assume a residual or salvage value for the leased asset and reduce the lease payments accordingly. This adjustment introduces an element of risk not usually associated with financial contracts, namely, residual value risk, which describes the unknown value of the asset at the maturity of the contract. The detailed analysis of residual value risk is the topic of Chapter 8.

The disposition of the property at maturity of the lease contract also varies greatly, even within the category of financial leases. The equipment can be returned to the lessor at maturity. The option to purchase the asset for its "fair market value," or the right of first refusal, however, is almost always available to the lessee. Some financial leases offer a purchase option at a fixed price, thereby creating a "call option" that adds value to the lease.[2]

Financial leases also may offer renewal options. The option to extend the lease for a given period of time may be offered in the original contract for stated payment amounts. The lease extension may allow the lessee to cancel at any time without penalty. Renewal terms vary greatly, often as a function of the asset's residual value. Renewal terms sometimes are negotiated at the maturity of the lease contract.

Operating Leases

Operating leases are an important segment of the leasing market. They represented over 15 percent of the leasing market in the 1992 ELA Survey.

The operating lease does not have an exact definition, although the accounting profession has used the term to define leases that are not required to appear on the balance sheet. For the purposes of this discussion, the economic differences between financial and operating leases are more important. We define an operating lease as a lease whose residual value plays a major role in determining the rate of return that the lease provides to the lessor.

One distinguishing feature of the operating lease is its *relative* short-term maturity. The operating lease has a contract term that is usually much shorter than the economic life of the asset. Shorter maturity means that the lessor is responsible for the disposal of the used equipment sooner. More frequent releasing or sale of used equipment raises the transaction costs of operating leases compared to financial leases over the life of an asset. Therefore, operating leases are most frequently found for assets that tend to maintain higher residual values. For example, operating leases are found frequently in the transportation industry, covering such assets as aircraft, over-the-road trucks and trailers, and railroad rolling stock.

The importance of the residual value to operating leases is critical. A prime example of inaccurate estimation of residual value

---

[2] The holder of a call option has the right, but not the obligation, to *buy* an asset or security at a *fixed* price (exercise price) at the maturity of the contract (for a European option), or at any time before maturity (for an American option).

risk is seen in leasing insurance provided by Lloyds of London. Lloyds provided lease cancellation insurance for computer operating lease contracts. In essence, Lloyds insured the residual value of the computers against the risk of obsolescence during the cancellation period of the operating leases. When IBM introduced a new generation of computers about 1977, Lloyds suffered its largest loss (at that time), estimated to be around $250 to $350 million. Two of the most prominent firms involved were Itel Corporation and OPM Leasing Company; that, despite Lloyds insurance coverage, they filed for bankruptcy as a result of the new IBM computers entering the market.

Operating lease contracts, particularly for manufacturer or captive lessors, frequently require that the lessor maintain and insure the leased equipment. These responsibilities usually fall to the lessee in a financial leasing arrangement, which is then called a *net lease*. Leases that include some form of maintenance agreement are called *service leases*. Responsibility for maintenance of the leased equipment has raised interesting issues in the finance literature, such as asset abuse and metering agreements.

Another important economic distinction between operating and financial leases is the cancellation policy. The financial lease cannot be canceled, without penalty, during the life of the contract. The operating lease sometimes contains a cancellation option. This option offers the lessee the right to cancel or terminate the lease before the contract expiration date without penalty. If the cancellation option is exercised, the equipment is returned to the lessor who now must decide on the disposal of the equipment (by sale or releasing). Operating leases often include options in addition to the cancellation option, for example, an option to renew or extend the lease or an option to purchase the equipment.

In summary, the economic features that differentiate the operating lease from the financial lease are: (1) residual value risk, (2) transaction costs, (3) maintenance commitments, and (4) contract options. Consequently, the pricing of the lease terms for an operating lease should differ substantially from a financial lease.

Leverage Leases

The leverage lease differs from the financial lease by the direct involvement of a third-party lender. The third-party lender supplies most of the funds used to acquire the specific asset of the leverage lease. The debt generally is non-recourse borrowing by the lessor. From the lessee's perspective, the third-party lender is not particularly important unless a lower rate is available relative to other types of leases.

Leverage leases can be very complex and require extensive documentation. Instead of a single lessor and a single lessee, the leverage lease lessor and lessee can be a set of firms and/or individual investors. Similarly, the third-party lenders can be a consortium of banks, insurance companies, and/or private investors. In one example of a very large leverage lease, in 1973 Anaconda agreed to lease a new aluminum reduction mill from a consortium of five banks and one commercial finance company. The mill cost $110.7 million. This is a leveraged lease because part of the required cost of the plant was raised by borrowing $72 million from three insurance companies, which acquired a chattel mortgage on the mill and first claim to the lease payments. The lenders, however, have no claims against the lessors if Anaconda defaults and the principal and interest due cannot be recovered.

Sale-and-Leaseback

The sale-and-leaseback arrangement calls for the sale of an asset that the lessee firm already owns to another party, with the simultaneous agreement that the asset will be leased back from the new owner. The lessee receives funds that reflect the current market price of the asset while using the asset in its production process. The new owner or lessor assumes all the rights and benefits of ownership, including the tax benefits of depreciation, tax credits, and any residual value. The sale-and-leaseback instrument may contain a variety of supplemental contractual provisions, but the core of the arrangement is the transfer of the legal ownership of an asset or group of assets from the user enterprise to another firm at an agreed-upon price.

The largest sale-and-leaseback arrangement in the United States was completed by Midland Cogeneration Venture in 1990. The purpose of the venture was to salvage an abandoned nuclear power plant in Midland, Michigan, and turn it into a gas-fired plant producing electricity and steam for the Midwest and Canada. The $2.3 billion transaction includes $536 million, 12-year debt financed by 30 lenders. The 25-year lease is also a complex *leverage lease* involving 7 equity partners, 10 lessors, 4 trustees, and 13 different law firms, in addition to the 30 lenders. The lessors formed a consortium called Deerpath Group with an investment of $207 million. Notes totaling $1.2 billion (with an option for $300 million more) provided major financing for the cogeneration project. The entire deal involved signatures on 337 separate documents!

Contract Options

Lease contracts may include several options. These potential options include options to: (1) purchase the asset, (2) renew the lease, and/or (3) cancel the lease.

The option to purchase the asset at the maturity of the contract may be for a stated fixed price or for the "fair market value" of the asset. The fair market value purchase option, which is allowed by the IRS for tax-oriented true leases, does not have value because the lessees always have the option to purchase an asset for its market value. A fixed-price purchase option does have value. If the market price of the asset is higher than the fixed-price purchase option at maturity, the lessee gains the difference in value. The option does not force the lessee to purchase the asset, so if the asset is less valuable at maturity than the fixed-price option, the lessee can walk away without penalty. It is important, however, to realize that the value of the purchase option to the lessee is simultaneously an opportunity cost to the lessor. The lease payments will be higher to reflect the value of the purchase option.

The same point applies to other types of options such as an option to extend the maturity of the lease or an option to cancel the lease. All these options add value to the lease and will command a higher price in the form of higher lease payments.

Types of Assets

Leasing companies usually lease a wide variety of assets, but some companies specialize in a single asset type. The types of assets that are leased are truly varied, including such unusual items as telephone equipment buried in the walls of a building, a "removable" building such as a grain silo, and computerized entertainment robots sometimes found in pizza parlors. "Employee leasing" is another unusual area that has become popular in recent years.

Exhibit 2.2 reports the percentages in each asset category for the years 1988–1992. The categories show the wide spectrum of assets that are leased. One common feature, however, is the tangible nature of these assets.

The percentages in Exhibit 2.2 show that the leasing industry does not concentrate in any one type or category of assets. In fact, only the category of office machines consistently represents more than 10 percent of the new leasing business for the five years reported.

Determination of Lease Payments

Lease payments are determined by numerous factors:

1. The lessor's cost of funds.
2. The risk of default by the lessee.

Exhibit 2.2: Types of Assets for Direct Financing Leases (percentage of new business based on asset cost as weighted average)

Assets	1988	1989	1990	1991	1992
Agricultural	1.0	1.0	1.1	1.5	1.3
Aircraft	7.1	6.6	8.6	9.1	6.1
Computers					
Mainframes	10.1	10.0	8.0	8.5	8.7
Peripherals	5.0	3.8	4.8	5.3	5.2
Small systems	5.1	6.1	7.0	7.8	7.5
Software	—	—	1.0	1.2	1.1
Construction	8.0	8.9	10.5	6.9	7.1
Container	0.2	0.4	0.2	0.2	1.1
Electrical power	0.3	0.3	0.2	0.2	0.5
Furniture, etc.	3.3	5.4	6.1	3.0	5.2
Industrial	3.8	2.7	4.9	2.5	2.8
Manufacturing	5.3	6.5	5.0	5.4	6.0
Materials handling	2.0	1.9	1.2	1.2	2.0
Medical	4.3	5.7	5.7	4.3	6.7
Office machines	10.6	12.8	14.7	10.3	10.6
Project, multiasset	0.1	1.1	0.7	1.0	0.5
Railroad	0.9	1.1	1.2	1.3	1.3
Telecommunications	9.8	6.3	4.8	8.5	8.5
Trucks and trailers	12.0	11.0	7.8	8.7	9.2
Water transport	0.3	0.4	0.3	0.7	0.9
Other	10.8	8.0	6.2	12.4	7.7
Total	100.0	100.0	100.0	100.0	100.0

Source: Equipment Leasing Association, *Survey of Industry Activity*, 1988, 1990, and 1992.

3. The service and processing costs.

4. The type of leased asset as well as the economic depreciation and obsolescence risk associated with that asset.

5. The value of the tax benefits to the lessor.

6. The options offered in the contract.

7. Maintenance and service provisions.

8. The degree of competition in the market.

Lessor's Cost of Funds

The lease payments must be sufficiently high to capture the lessor's cost of funds. Costs of funds are not stable over time or across lessors. As prevailing interest rates change, so will the lessors' costs of funds. All interest rates tend to move together, and these changes can be highly volatile over time. For example, the short-term U.S. Treasury bill rate averaged 14.7 percent in 1981 compared to 3.5 percent in 1992. Costs of funds will differ from lessor to lessor. For example, the leasing subsidiary of a bank holding company is likely to have a lower cost of funds than an independent leasing company.

Fixed-lease payments must incorporate interest rate risk. The lessor is vulnerable to changing interest rates and will price this risk into a fixed-lease payment schedule. If the lessee is willing to assume interest rate risk, variable lease payments can be set to reflect prevailing interest rates.

Risk of Default by the Lessee

The financial condition of the lessee is an important factor in the determination of the lease payments. Because financial statements do not always reflect a firm's true condition, a precise measure of the lessee's financial strength is always difficult to ascertain. The lessor will consider several measures of default risk based on traditional financial ratios to get an approximation of the lessee's financial position. These ratios are used by lenders to evaluate default risk and have been shown in prior research and practical application to have power in predicting bankruptcies.

Information about the lessee firm becomes extremely relevant when considering default potential. Finance theory suggests that when lessors have adequate information about the financial condition of lessees, lease yields accurately reflect default potential. Lease payments will be lower for financially strong lessees, all other factors being equal. In the absence of adequate and reliable financial information, the lessor will assume the worst, and the lease payment will be commensurately high.

To protect against the potential losses resulting from default, lessors often require prepayments in the lease contract. Frequently used prepayments are two monthly payments due at the origination date of the lease contract. Of course, this means that the last two months of the lease contract do not require payments. Almost all lease contracts require prepayment of at least one payment (in other words, each monthly or periodic payment is prepaid), and in some extreme cases prepayments for as many as six monthly payments have been required.

Another protection for the lessor is a security deposit. A bank could require that a lessee firm deposit a certain sum of money in a certificate of deposit held by the bank as security until the maturity of the lease or another prespecified condition is met. Letters of credit are also used as security deposits. Personal guarantees by the principals of the lessee firm can also be collateral for leases, especially in the case of a start-up firm or a firm without tangible assets. A personal guarantee requires individuals to pledge their own personal assets in the case of default by the lessee firm. In general, third-party guarantees and the pledging of other assets can be the difference between approval to lease and no credit approval.

Service and Processing Costs

In a lease contract, transaction costs are per-unit costs such as writing the contract, specifying the security agreement, identifying the asset, negotiating the terms of the lease, and other legal fees. Many of these costs are fixed and independent of the characteristics of the lessor, lessee, or the leased asset. Therefore, transaction expenses are expected to decline proportionately as the cost of the asset increases. These expenses are recaptured over time by the lessor through the periodic lease payments.

For example, suppose the transaction costs are $200 per lease. If so, the transaction cost as a percentage of the cost of a $1,000 asset is 20 percent. But the same $200 is only two-tenths of 1 percent of an asset that costs $100,000. Therefore, for leases on higher-priced assets, transaction costs are a less significant component of the lease payment; for leases on lower-priced assets, transaction costs will be a more significant component of the payment.

A type of transaction cost frequently found in the leasing market is the brokerage commission. Although this is a fee paid by lessors to their own in-house sales personnel or to outside lease brokers, lessee firms should be aware of these fees because the amounts will be recovered by the lease payments. In-house sales commissions are typically less than outside lease brokerage commissions. The range for average commissions is from less than one-half of 1 percent of the cost of the asset, for in-house commissions, to about 2 percent or more for outside brokers.

Type of Asset and Residual Value Risk

The type of leased asset will influence the size of the lease payments, particularly as the asset type affects the residual value and obsolescence risk associated with that asset. For example, lessors have learned, often through painful experience, to assume almost no residual value for computers. Computers have a huge obsolescence risk because of constant technological innovations in the computer industry. An opposite example is railroad rolling stock. Boxcars suffer almost no economic depreciation over long periods of time. In fact, over certain periods the fair market value of a boxcar has been higher at the end of the lease than at the beginning of the lease.

Residual value risk clearly differs across asset types. The uncertainty of the residual value will be priced and incorporated into the lease payments. It is important, however, to understand that realization of the residual value does not occur until the end of the lease. These factors make the pricing of the residual value risk very difficult. This topic is addressed in Chapter 8.

Use of Tax Benefits by the Lessor

In the true lease arrangement, only the lessor is allowed tax deductions for depreciation. Otherwise, the lease is a conditional sales contract, and the IRS treats it like a loan. Other tax benefits, such as investment tax credits (when allowed by the tax code), may be taken by either party to the lease contract. The lessor will adjust the lease payment to reflect all, some, or none of the tax benefits. The degree of adjustment is determined by the strength of the lessor in the bargaining process and the degree of competition among lessors. Because one of the attractions of leasing includes tax advantages, however, we expect that the lessee will benefit, in the form of lower lease payments, from the tax shields taken by the lessor.

Suppose that after a lease contract commences, the lessor loses expected tax benefits. How can the lessor be protected? Lease agreements generally provide for tax indemnities, especially when the lessee is benefiting from the tax shields taken by the lessor. Some tax events that require protection are: (1) loss of *true lease* status, (2) change in the income tax rate, (3) change or disallowance of depreciation deductions, and (4) other changes in tax laws or tax status. These events can occur even though an advance tax ruling is obtained. Tax indemnities may be found even in small leases, where the contract language is basically "boilerplate." In very large tax-motivated leases, the tax indemnities could be a matter of considerable negotiation, with an obvious impact on the pricing of the lease.

Options Offered in the Contract

Lease contracts offer a variety of options. These include options to purchase the asset, to renew the lease, and to cancel the lease. Naturally, the presence of one or more of these options will affect the amount of the lease payments.

An additional option concerns the periodicity of the lease payments. Lease contracts are most often written in terms of monthly payments, but quarterly payments are common, and semiannual and annual lease payments exist. Leasing promoters often claim that leasing allows the lessee to avoid a substantial down payment for a loan. It is difficult to find, however, an actual lease where no payment is made in advance. Finally, lease payments can be written with flexible payment schedules. For example, a start-up company may wish to have lower fixed payments early in the contract and higher payments toward the end of the contract.

Maintenance and Service Provisions

Operating leases sometimes provide for the maintenance and service of the leased asset. A service lease offers maintenance services whose cost is included in the periodic lease payment. Maintenance services may be tied into the lease payments with a metering system such as the number of copies made on a copy machine or the number of miles driven for an automobile or truck. In this case, lease payments are directly linked to the asset's use.

Degree of Competition in the Market

Competition plays a pivotal role in lease payment determination. Entry into the leasing market is relatively easy for independent leasing firms as well as financial institutions such as banks. Ironically, independent leasing firms sometimes face the possibility that a bank, which supplies funds to the lessor, will, in turn, enter the market as a competitor. This situation is particularly worrisome to the independent leasing firm because the bank often has access to the financial statements, operating procedures, and customer list of the lessor. This highlights the competitive nature of the leasing market. No firm has to settle for the lease payments offered by one lessor. Again, "shop around" is good advice to any potential lessee.

Target Pricing

Most lessors "target" price, adding a profit margin to the sum of their money, service, processing, and risk costs.[3] From the lessor's perspective, McGugan suggests that the terms of a typical lease may be computed as follows: (1) an annual service or processing charge is added to the amount of the asset acquisition price; (2) an expected residual value is determined for the maturity date of the contract; (3) the difference between the asset price plus fees and the residual value represents the amount to be amortized or repaid over the term of the lease; (4) the total asset price plus fees is multiplied by a per month "income factor"; and (5) any per month use, sales, or property taxes and insurance amounts are added to arrive at the contracted lease payment. In essence, this pricing formula is quite simple: compute asset cost, adding fees and transaction costs and subtracting any residual value, and then multiply by an income factor to obtain monthly payments. In fact, many lease officers in leasing companies make this calculation.

The McGugan pricing formula, however, is missing a few important components. How is the income factor computed? Income or lease factors are determined by the eight economic factors we have discussed: (1) the lessor's cost of funds; (2) the risk of default

---

[3] Vincent J. McGugan, "Competition and Adjustment in the Equipment Leasing Industry," Research Report #51, Federal Reserve Bank of Boston, 1972.

by the lessee; (3) the service and processing costs; (4) the type of leased asset as well as the economic depreciation and obsolescence risk associated with that asset; (5) the value of the tax benefits to the lessor; (6) the options offered in the contract; (7) maintenance and service provisions; and (8) the degree of competition in the market. Only the third factor, the service and processing costs, is mentioned specifically in the pricing formula. The remaining seven factors must be considered by both lessors and lessees when negotiating the terms of the lease payments.

The Structure of Lease Contracts

A lease contract has several sections, which can be divided into eight general categories:

1. Terms of the lease payments.
2. Equipment procurement and delivery.
3. Use, maintenance, and insurance of equipment.
4. Expiration or termination of lease, return of equipment.
5. Warranties.
6. Default and remedies.
7. Financial information.
8. Miscellaneous.

Each section is discussed below, with samples of the language found in actual contracts.[4]

But first, it is interesting to ask: *Who writes the fine print in the lease contracts?* The first answer that comes to mind is that the lessor writes the lease contracts because it is the lessor that presents the written contract to the lessee. From an economic perspective, however, think about the lessee being the "writer" of the lease covenants. What if no, or very few, restrictive covenants were written into the contract? Then the lessor would be forced to charge a very high lease rate (very high payments) to cover the increased risks. The lessee benefits from a lower lease rate because he or she agrees to

---

[4] These examples were gathered from several leasing entities that wish to remain anonymous. The language repeated is generalized and modified from the specific contracts studied.

covenants that restrict the possible adverse behaviors by the lessee (adverse from the lessor's viewpoint). From this perspective, the lessee can be considered the "writer" of the lease covenants.

Terms of the Lease Payments

The terms of the lease payments cover such matters as the dates the lease payments are due, the periodicity of the payments, expiration or maturity date of the contract, and terms for renewal of the contract, if any. The payment terms set the purchase option amount if fixed or specify "fair market value" (FMV), usually, if not fixed.

The payment terms also include provisions for late fees or interest rate charges for late payments. The following language is typical of that covering a late fee:

> If any rental or other amounts payable hereunder shall not be paid within ten (10) days when due, Lessee shall pay to Lessor, as supplemental rental, an amount equal to five percent (5%) of such amounts, plus interest on such amount until paid at the rate of eighteen percent (18%) per annum.

As illustrated above, lease contracts often refer to the lease payments as rent. These payments are due in "advance" or "arrears" as specified by the contract. A lease is noncancelable unless the terms of early cancellation or termination are expressly provided.

Equipment Procurement and Delivery

The lessor (unless also the supplier, or unless the lease includes maintenance) usually absolves itself from any responsibility concerning the installation or performance of the equipment. A certificate of delivery and acceptance may state:

> By execution of this delivery receipt the above named Lessee confirms delivery of the equipment described below and that the equipment is found to be completed and/or installed in conformity with any relevant purchase order issued by either the Lessee or the Lessor on behalf of the Lessee. The undersigned further certifies that the aggregate purchase price of the equipment is correct as shown below.

After receipt of the certificate, the lessor will complete payment for the equipment. The lessor retains legal title to the equipment.

Use, Maintenance, and Insurance of Equipment

Lease contracts clearly specify the lessee's obligations concerning the use, maintenance, and insurance of the equipment. An example is:

> Lessee shall not (a) use, operate, maintain, or store equipment improperly, carelessly, or in violation of any applicable law or regulation of an governmental authority, (b) abandon any equipment, (c) sublease any equipment or permit the use thereof by anyone other than Lessee without the prior written consent of Lessor, which consent shall not be unreasonably withheld, (d) permit any equipment to be removed from the location specified in the Schedule without the prior written consent of the Lessor, (e) affix to or place any equipment on any other personal property or to or on any real property without first obtaining and delivering to Lessor such waivers as Lessor may reasonably require to assure Lessor's ownership and right to remove such equipment free from any lien, encumbrance or right of distraint, or any other claim that may be asserted by any third party, or (f) sell, assign or transfer, or directly or indirectly create, incur, or suffer to exist any lien, claim, security interest, or encumbrance of any kind on any of its rights hereunder.
>
> Lessee, at its own expense, will repair and maintain the equipment to keep it in as good a condition as when delivered to Lessee, ordinary wear and tear excepted, but, in any event, to the same extent that Lessee would, in the prudent management of this properties, maintain and repair comparable equipment owned by the Lessee.

Expiration or Termination of Lease, Return of Equipment

The typical lease calls for the lessee to return the equipment upon expiration of the lease. An example is:

> Upon expiration of the lease term, Lessee will immediately return the leased property in as good a condition as received, less normal wear, tear, and depreciation, to such place as is then specified by Lessor, carefully crated, shipped freight prepaid and properly insured.

Additional provisions for penalties for late return of equipment may be stated.

Many leases offer the lessee the right to purchase the equipment at maturity of the lease or during the term of the contract. Often a schedule is provided in the contract of the amounts for the purchase of the asset at prespecified dates throughout the life of the contract. Bargain purchase options or bargain renewal options are stated clearly in the contract. Many contracts, however, allow the lessee to purchase the asset at *fair market value* at maturity. Fair market value is defined in this example:

> The fair market value of any item shall be the value upon which an informed and willing seller and an informed and willing buyer (other than a used equipment or scrap dealer) would agree, each under no compulsion to buy or sell. Fair market rental value for any item shall be the value upon which an informed and willing Lessee (other than a Lessee currently in possession) and an informed and willing Lessor, each under no compulsion to lease, would agree.

As stated, this definition also applies to fair market rental value for renewal options. To reach agreement on fair value options, provisions in contracts may specify:

> Fair market value or fair market rental value is to be determined by agreement between Lessor and Lessee, and if they cannot agree, by an independent appraiser selected by Lessor but acceptable to Lessee. The cost of appraisal shall be borne by Lessee.

Warranties

The lessor typically warrants that during the term of the lease, if no default occurs, the lessee's use of the equipment will not be interrupted by the lessor ("quiet enjoyment"). Warranty of the equipment itself is not provided by the lessor, as the following implies:

> Lessee acknowledges and agrees that (a) equipment is of a size, design, capacity, and manufacture selected by Lessee, (b) Lessee is satisfied that the same is suitable for its purposes, (c) Lessor is not a manufacturer thereof or a dealer in property of such kind, and (d) Lessor has not made, and does not hereby make, any representation, warranty, or covenant with respect to the title, merchantability, condition, quality, description, durability,

or suitability of any such unit in any respect or in connection with or for the proposes and uses of Lessee. Lessor hereby assigns to Lessee, to the extent assignable, any warranties, covenants, and representations of supplier with respect to any unit, provided that any action taken by Lessee by reason thereof shall be at the expense of Lessee.

The exception to this lease covenant applies, naturally, to the manufacturer lessor.

Default and Remedies

A default and remedy clause is one of the most important lease covenants and can be found in every contract. At the outset, the conditions for a default are defined. If a lessee defaults, two actions are usually required. First, the lessee must return the equipment. Second, all remaining lease payments are due, although some adjustment is made for the remaining market value or rental value of the returned asset. Here is a detailed example of a default clause:

A. The following shall constitute Events of Default hereunder:

(i)   Lessee shall fail to make any rental payment when due, and such failure shall continue unremedied for ten (10) days;

(ii)   Lessee shall fail to maintain required insurance;

(iii) Lessee shall fail to make any payment other than rental or shall fail to perform or observe any obligation, covenant, or condition under this Agreement, and such failure shall continue unremedied for ten (10) days after notice from Lessor requiring performance;

(iv) Any representation or warranty made by Lessee herein, in any Schedule or in any document in connection herewith, shall prove to be incorrect at any time in any material respect;

(v)   Lessee shall become insolvent or bankrupt or make an assignment for the benefit of creditors or consent to the appointment of a trustee or receiver, or a trustee or receiver shall be appointed for Lessee or for a substantial part of its property without its consent and shall not be dismissed within sixty (60) days, or bankruptcy, reorganization, or insolvency proceedings shall be instituted by or against Lessee and, if instituted against Lessee, shall not be dismissed within sixty (60) days; or

(vi)   Lessee shall fail to perform or observe any obligation under any other agreement with Lessor or any other creditor.

B. At any time after the occurrence of an Event of Default, Lessor may, at its option, do any one or more of the following:

(i)   By notice in writing terminate any lease or all leases, whereupon all rights of Lessee to use the equipment shall cease;

(ii)   Proceed by court action to enforce performance by Lessee of this Agreement and/or recover damages for the breach thereof;

(iii)   Whether or not the applicable Lease is terminated, cause Lessee, and Lessee hereby agrees, to promptly deliver such Equipment to Lessor, at any hour, without notice to Lessee, and without liability except for malicious acts by its agents, enter Lessee's premises or other premises and take possession of or render unusable any item and attachments thereon, whether or not the property of Lessor;

(iv)   Upon return or repossession of any Item, retain, use, re-lease or sell at public or private sale any such item and attachments thereon;

(v)   Recover all rental and all other amounts due and payable hereunder then accrued and unpaid, and also recover, as liquidated damages and not as a penalty, the present value of (a) the fair market value of each item at the expiration of the applicable term as estimated at the time of default and (b) all remaining rentals that would have accrued through the end of the term (each discounted at the rate of ___ percent (_%) per annum) minus the then fair market value of such Item.

C. In addition to any amounts recoverable by Lessor, Lessor shall be entitled to recover

(i)   All expenses and collection costs that Lessor shall have incurred by reason of any Event of Default, including but not limited to salary paid to and expenses incurred by employees and reasonable attorneys' fees including attorneys' fees on appeal,

(ii)   Interest on any amount payable under any lease at the rate of ___ percent (_%) per annum, both before and after judgment, and

(iii)   If applicable, an amount sufficient, in Lessor's opinion, to compensate Lessor for loss of tax benefits in connection with such Event of Default.

D. Lessor's remedies shall be cumulative and shall be in addition to all other remedies at law or in equity. Lessee waives any requirements of law that might limit or modify any of the remedies herein to the extent permitted by law. No express or implied waiver of any Event of Default shall be a waiver of any subsequent Event of Default. Lessor's failure or delay in exercising any rights shall not be a waiver of any such right upon the continuation or recurrence of any Event of Default. Any single or partial exercise of any right by Lessor shall not exhaust the same or be a waiver of any other right.

Financial Information

The lessor requires periodic financial information from the lessee, as in the following example:

> Lessee shall keep its books and records in accordance with generally accepted accounting principles and practices consistently applied and shall deliver to Lessor its annual audited financial statements and such other unaudited financial statements as may be reasonably requested by Lessor.

Miscellaneous

Lease covenants may include many other provisions. After all, one of the attractions of the lease contract is its flexibility. Some other provisions of the lease contract include taxes, applicable law, modification of the lease, notices, and repairs and alterations of equipment. Another provision often found in lease contracts is a security deposit and/or a personal guarantee by the firm's owners. For example, the following specifies security deposit conditions:

> If Lessor has required a security deposit from Lessee, Lessor may, but shall not be obligated to apply the security deposit to cure any default of Lessee, in which event Lessee shall promptly restore the security deposit to the full amount specified in the Agreement. Upon termination of this lease and all renewals, if Lessee has fulfilled all the terms and conditions, Lessor shall return to Lessee any remaining balance of the security deposit actually made by Lessee.

Leases may contain debt-like covenants concerning limitations on dividend payments, limitations concerning other debt, and specification of certain financial ratios. Although many participants in the leasing market argue that leases tend to have far fewer restrictive convenants than loans, no study has carefully examined this issue.

Summary

This chapter has explored the types of lessors, categories of leases, types of leased assets, and determination of lease payments, and has given some samples of the language contained in lease contracts. The active types of lessors include independent leasing companies, financial services firms, banks and other financial institutions, and captive (or subsidiary) leasing companies, including the subsidiaries of manufacturing firms. Also, leasing brokers play an important role in the leasing market. The types of leases include financial, operating, leverage, and sale-and-leaseback. A myriad of different types of assets are found in lease contracts. One element common to these assets is their tangible quality, although there are exceptions. Employee leasing is an example of an unusual type of "asset" to lease.

Lease payments generally are determined by eight factors: (1) the lessor's cost of funds; (2) the risk of default by the lessee; (3) the service and processing costs; (4) the type of leased asset as well as the economic depreciation and obsolescence risk associated with that asset; (5) the value of the tax benefits to the lessor; (6) the options offered in the contract; (7) maintenance and service provisions; and (8) the degree of competition in the market.

Finally, a lease contract can be divided into eight general categories: (1) terms of the lease payments; (2) equipment procurement and delivery; (3) use, maintenance, and insurance of equipment; (4) expiration or termination of lease, return of equipment; (5) warranties; (6) default and remedies; (7) financial information; and (8) miscellaneous.

This chapter should give the decision maker a good idea about the types of contracts in the market, the elements important for the pricing of these contracts, and the type of language written into the lease contracts.

Chapter *3*

Tax Rules for Leasing

One of the main economic factors, if not *the* main economic factor, that favors leasing is the tax law. A leasing contract provides the opportunity for a low tax-paying firm to transfer tax shields to a high tax-paying firm where the value of the tax shields is higher. The low tax-paying firm or lessee will benefit by paying lower lease payments. If tax shields can be transferred through the lease contract, a lease must satisfy the tax rules for leasing established by the Internal Revenue Service. If the tax rules for leasing are not satisfied, then the lease is considered a *conditional sales contract* and is treated like any other term loan or installment purchase contract. Before 1981, a lease had to meet the IRS requirements for a *true lease* in order for the lease payments to be tax deductible to the lessee. After 1981, the tax rules for leasing were greatly modified, and in 1982, 1984, and 1986 the tax rules, including those for leasing, were modified extensively once more.

If a lease is a *true lease* for tax purposes, the lessor recognizes the rental income in gross income and will be able to deduct depreciation and applicable investment credits.[1] Any expenses paid by the lessee are considered to be additional rental income. The lessee considers the lease payments as rental expense, fully deductible from taxable income. If a lease is characterized as a *conditional sales contract*, a gain or loss is recognized by the lessor, which may be a capital or an ordinary gain, depending on the character of the asset

---

Note: I am indebted to Eric Hoffman and Brandi Hawley for help in researching and writing this chapter.

[1] Section 61(a)(5) of the Internal Revenue Code. All references to sections are for the Internal Revenue Code, unless proceeded by "Regs.," which indicates a section of the Treasury regulations, which are interpretations of the code.

in the lessor's possession. The lessee in this case is allowed the depreciation deduction, interest expense implicit in the lease, and any investment credits.

In this chapter, we examine the tax laws applicable to leasing. Ever-changing tax laws offer unique market opportunities, and leasing is one of the contracts frequently employed to take advantage of these opportunities. First, I discuss the important IRS rules that qualify a lease as a *true lease*. Other implications for leasing discussed in this chapter include rental expense, depreciation, tax credits, and other tax rules (e.g., the alternative minimum tax). Special rules for motor vehicle leases are also presented, as is a brief discussion of real estate leasing tax rules and of international leases that exploit special tax rules, both domestic and foreign.

At the end of the chapter, I return to the theme that leasing is an economic market. What happens when one of the forces that shapes the leasing market—taxes—is changed? How does the market respond? In the final section, we can learn the answers to these questions by examining the story of Safe Harbor leasing.

IRS True Leases

Lease or Sale

To determine whether a lease is a *conditional sales contract* or a *true lease*, the IRS and courts look at the various facts and circumstances surrounding the lease.[2] The lease characterization is quite important because the tax treatment depends on its representation. The description of a lease was originally made under the provisions of the 1955 Revenue Ruling 55-540,[3] which focused on the intent of the parties as seen by lease agreement and circumstances at that time:

> Whether an agreement, which in form is a lease, is in substance a conditional sales contract depends upon the intent of the parties as evidenced by the provision of the agreement, read in light of the acts and circumstances existing at the time the agreement was executed. In ascertaining such intent no single test, nor special

---

[2] *Frank Lyon Co v. US,* 435 US 561 (1978), 98 S Ct 1291, 78-1 USTC ¶ 9370, 41 AFTR2d 78-1142. Criteria for the type of lease evolve from this court case. Also listed are the various court reporters where the decision may be found.

[3] 1955-2 C.B. 39. Revenue Rulings are IRS responses to particular fact situations. They are normally abbreviated "Rev. Rul." and are most commonly found in bound editions called "Cumulative Bulletins" (abbreviated "C.B."). Rev. Rul. 55-540 indicates that this was the 540th revenue ruling of 1955. 1955-2 C.B. 39 indicates that this revenue ruling is found in the second cumulative bulletin for 1955 on page 39.

combination of tests, is absolutely determinative. No general rule, applicable in all cases, can be laid down. Each case must be decided in the light of its particular facts.[4]

Intent of both parties to the lease must be considered.[5] Under Rev. Rul. 55-540, evidence of sale was determined by looking at various factors such as transfer of title, rent in excess of fair value, an identifiable interest component in the rental payment, or the presence of a bargain purchase option. For example, in *Day v. Commissioner* (of the IRS),[6] the transfer of water rights under a tract of land, where the transferee intended to extract all water under the land, is indicative of a sale. Similarly, when a lessee sells a portion of leased property without the lessor's objection, a sale would also be indicated.[7]

This characterization process was changed with the issuance of Revenue Procedure 75-21 in April 1975.[8] This Rev. Proc. set forth the guidelines to be used for advance ruling purposes for the lease/sale determination.[9] It was later supplemented by Rev. Proc. 75-28 (1975-1 C.B. 752), which identified the information that taxpayers must provide to receive advance rulings. The earlier Rev. Rul. focused on the characterization of a lease as a sale. The later Rev. Procs. look at when the lessor has economic interest sufficient to characterize that party as the lessor for tax purposes.

Rev. Proc. 75-21 sets forth six guidelines for advance rulings to determine true ownership and lease validity. These rules remain in effect and should be followed carefully by decision makers who desire tax-deductible lease payments. These rules are outlined in Exhibit 3.1.

Minimum At-Risk Requirement

This guideline requires that at inception and throughout the lease term the lessor must have an investment equal to at least 20

---

[4] Rev. Rul. 55-540 (1955-2 C.B. 39).

[5] *Breece Veneer & Panel Co v. Commissioner*, 232 F2d 319 (7th Cir. 1956), 56-1 USTC ¶ 9485, 49 AFTR 895.

[6] 54 TC 1417 (1970).

[7] *Graves v. Commissioner*, TC Memo May 14, 1952, 11 TCM 467, ¶ 52,143 P-H TC Memo.

[8] 1975-1 C.B. 715. Rev. Procs. are also published by the IRS and are primarily to inform taxpayers of its requirements.

[9] Advance rulings are taxpayer submissions of the facts of a particular situation so that the IRS can inform the taxpayer how it will treat that situation.

Exhibit 3.1: Guidelines for Advance Rulings

1. Minimum at-risk requirement
2. Minimum estimated residual value
3. Minimum remaining life for asset
4. No bargain purchase option
5. No loan from lessee to lessor
6. Lessor must demonstrate expectation of profits

percent of the total acquisition cost of the property, as defined by Section(§) 1012.[10] The investment made is considered to be only the consideration paid and the personal liability of the lessor. The lessor must have net worth sufficient to cover such obligation. This investment must be unconditional, with no provisions for return, although provision for reimbursement from outside groups for failure of the equipment to meet quality standards is permissible. The investment must be maintained at all times throughout the lease term, with the sum of the lease payments to be made never to exceed the excess of the initial investment over the 20 percent minimum investment plus the cumulative pro rata portion of the projected profit. Profit is defined by §4.02(5)(d) of Rev. Proc. 75-28 to be the excess of the payments to be made by the lessee plus the residual value over the payments to be made by the lessor in connection with ownership of the property.

Minimum Estimated Residual Value

The second requirement of Rev. Proc. 75-21 is that the leased property must have a reasonably estimated residual value equal to at least 20 percent of the initial cost of the property at the end of the lease term. The lease term is defined in §4(2) to include any extension periods except those before which the lessee may renegotiate rental payments.

At the beginning of the lease, the lessor can obtain an appraisal confirming the estimated residual value of 20 percent or more of cost at the end of the lease term. For pricing purposes, the lessor might use a residual value of less than 20 percent on the basis of liquidation value or quick sale price, for example. This fact, if it

---

[10] §1012 defines the basis of a property to be its cost.

applies, does not invalidate the 20 percent estimated residual value for tax purposes.

Minimum Remaining Life for Asset

The third requirement for advance ruling states that the remaining life of the property at the end of the lease term equal the longer of one year or 20 percent of its originally estimated life. The Internal Revenue Service requires the lessor to make representations that these requirements have been met.

No Bargain Purchase Option

There may also be no bargain purchase option (for any member of the lessee group), nor may there be any requirement that any party purchase the property at any price. To prove the validity of the lease, the lessor must be required to dispose of the property at the end of the lease term, thus bearing the risk of ownership. In similar fashion, the lessee is restricted from providing any of the cost of the property or the cost of any improvements made to such property (with the exception of those readily removable from the property or routine maintenance). Rev. Proc. 79-48 (1979-2 C.B. 529) discusses the severability of improvements made. If the lease does not prohibit the lessee from paying for improvements, the lessor must recognize as income the value of such improvements.

No Loan from Lessee to Lessor

The fifth requirement for advance ruling purposes is that no member of the lessee group may lend the lessor the money necessary to purchase the leased property, nor may the lessee group guarantee loans the lessor incurs to purchase such property. This does not preclude other members of the lessee group from guaranteeing the performance of the lessee.

Lessor Must Demonstrate Expectation of Profits

Last, the IRS requires that the lessor be able to demonstrate the expectation of profits to be derived from the lease. Tax benefits from such transactions are not considered to be "profits" sufficient to demonstrate that expectation. But residual value of the equipment does count as part of the "profit." Rev. Procs. 75-21 (§4(6)) and 75-28 (§4.07) provide formulas for profit determination to be used to demonstrate the profit expectation for advance ruling submission. Figure 3.1 gives a simple flow-chart representation of the IRS guideline criteria.

With Rev. Proc. 76-30 (1976-2 C.B. 647), the IRS relayed its intent not to give advance rulings for limited-use property. Determination of limited use depends on the "commercial feasibility" of further leasing the property at the end of the original lease term to another unrelated group. Specific determination is made through reference to §4.09 of Rev. Proc. 75-28, which sets forth three criteria to consider for a ruling: (1) the capability of further leasing at the end of the original lease term; (2) the usefulness of that property at that time to anybody other than the initial lessee group; and (3) the necessity of dismantling or moving the property to return possession to the lessor.

Case Law

Judicial interpretation of a *true lease* is based largely on the intent of the parties to set up a transaction in a particular way, as seen in *Oesterreich v. Commissioner*,[11] not on the way the parties attempt to characterize the transaction. The courts have applied a number of tests to determine the intent of the parties.

The first of these tests is the relationship between the sales price of the property and the rental payments. If the rental payments over a relatively short period of time are at least equal to the sales price of the property plus interest, the courts have generally found fit to reclassify a "lease" as a sale.[12] Although this type of structure is generally found in conjunction with a bargain purchase option, this second element is not necessary for reclassification.[13]

A second test the courts have used examines the relationship between the exercise price of an option and the anticipated fair market value at time of exercise. If the option exercise price is excessively low, the evidence supports the true character of the transaction as a sale rather than a lease.[14] This determination is made with regard to the facts at the time the contract is formed,

---

[11] 226 F.2d 798 (9th Cir. 1955).

[12] *Home News Publishing Co. v. Commissioner*, 28 T.C.M. 753 (1969).

[13] *Mt. Mansfield Television, Inc. v. U.S.*, 239 F. Supp. 539 (D. Vt. 1964), aff'd per curiam, 342 F.2d 994 (2d Cir.), cert. denied 382 U.S. 818 (1965).

[14] *M & W Gear Co. v. Commissioner*, 446 F.2d 841 (7th Cir. 1971).

Figure 3.1: Classification Criteria for a True Lease or a Conditional Sales Contract

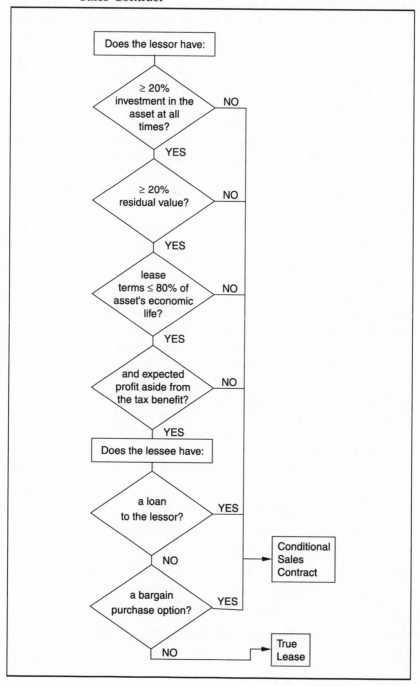

rather than at the time of option exercise.[15] The rationale behind this treatment is that the low option exercise price gives the lessee economic incentive to exercise the option and is indicative of the intent of the parties to transfer ownership at the end of the lease term. In cases where the option exercise price is correlated with fair market value, courts have not reclassified the lease in question.[16]

Courts also examine the relationship between the option exercise price and rental payments. When the former is relatively low in comparison to the latter, the relationship may indicate the existence of a sale rather than a lease.[17] When the length of the lease (with any renewals through option exercise), however, is still relatively short in relation to the economic life of the leased property, a relatively low option exercise price does not necessarily indicate a sale.[18]

A last factor that the courts tend to emphasize is the presence or absence of tax avoidance motives. This is particularly true when the leased property is of a type not normally leased or suitable for leasing,[19] which may indicate the intent of the parties to disguise a sale as a lease for tax purposes. Courts are placing increasing emphasis on the presence or absence of non-tax, legitimate business purpose motives to make the lease/sale determination.[20] Transactions may be recast as "sham" if they do not meet either a business purpose or economic substance test.[21]

The IRS has also attempted to recast leases by looking at the business of the lessor to determine the presence of financing, rather than leasing, arrangements.[22] The courts have generally rejected this mode of attack. The courts will reason that although evidence of sale may be seen in particular transactions of a lessor, if the incidence of these transactions is low in relation to the total number of pur-

---

[15] Rev. Rul. 55-540, 1955 CB 39.

[16] *Benton v. Commissioner* (1952, CA5) 197 F2d 745, 42 AFTR 229, 52-1 USTC ¶ 9367.

[17] *Est. of Starr v. Commissioner,* 30 T.C. 856 (1958), rev'd on other grounds, 274 F.2d 294 (9th Cir. 1959).

[18] *Lockhart Leasing Co. v. U.S.,* 446 F.2d 269 (10th Cir. 1971), aff'g 54 T.C. 301 (1971).

[19] *Midwest Metal Stamping Co. v. Commissioner,* 24 T.C.M. 1533 (1965).

[20] *Frank Lyon Co. v. U.S.,* 435 U.S. 918 (1978); *Goldwasser v. Commissioner,* T.C. Memo 1988-523.

[21] *Rice's Toyota World v. Commissioner,* 81 T.C. 184 (1983), aff'd in part, rev'd in part and rem'd, 85-1 USTC ¶9123 (4th Cir. 1985).

[22] *Northwest Acceptance Corp. v. U.S.,* 500 F.2d 1222 (9th Cir. 1974), aff'g per curiam, 58 T.C. 836 (1972).

ported leases, the evidence presented is not strong enough to recharacterize an entire business as being engaged in sales rather than leasing. Factors influencing the court include: the absence of bargain purchase options, the ability of the lessee to profit from the transaction without exercise of a purchase option, and the fact that a lessor purchases the equipment with no right of return.

In summary, the IRS and the tax courts allow the classification of a *true lease* if the lessor assumes the burdens and benefits of ownership. If the lease is classified as a *true lease,* the lease payments are tax-deductible to the lessee and count as taxable income to the lessor. The lessor benefits from depreciation tax shields and interest deductions. The latter applies because the source of lease financing is primarily debt. If the lease is classified as a *conditional sales contract,* the lessee is entitled to the depreciation and interest tax shields.

Other Tax Effects for Leasing

Rental Payments

From the lessee's point of view, rental payments under the terms of a *true lease* are ordinary and necessary business expenses and are deductible, provided that the lease payments are: rent, incurred or paid during the taxable year, required for the continued use of the property, for property used in a trade or business of the taxpayer, and for property that the taxpayer has neither title to nor equity in with respect to the payments made (§162(a)(3)). Rental payments made to related parties must be at arm's length and reasonable, or the deduction may be disallowed.[23] In related-party transactions where rent is fair and equivalent to the rent that would be paid to other market participants, the rental deduction has been allowed.[24]

In most cases, accrual basis taxpayers deduct rental payments in the year the liability is incurred, and cash basis taxpayers take the deduction in the year the rent is paid.[25] In the case of extremely large discrepancies in payments, however, the taxpayer may be required to prorate total payments to be made over the entire rental

---

[23] *Sparks Nugget, Inc. v. Commissioner,* 458 F.2d 631 (9th Cir. 1972), cert. denied, 410 U.S. 128 (1973); *Potter Elec. Signal & Mfg. Co. v. Commissioner,* 286 F.2d 200 (8th Cir. 1961).

[24] *Kansas City Southern Ry Co. v. Commissioner,* 76 T.C. 1067 (1981); *Hyde v. Commissioner,* 33 T.C.M. 502 (1974).

[25] Regs. §§1.461-1(a)(1) & (2).

period.[26] Rev. Proc. 75-21 sets forth two tests to be used to determine whether a deferred or prepaid rental issue will be raised. This will not be an issue if the taxpayer can demonstrate that either (1) the rental for any one year is not more than 10 percent above or below the average rental over the lease term, or (2) the first test is met for the first two-thirds of the lease term, and for the remaining term average rental is between 50 percent and 100 percent of the average rent during the first period.

Section 461(h), added by the Tax Reform Act of 1984 (TRA), limits the deduction of accrual basis taxpayers to the period in which actual economic performance takes place. For leases, this means that the lessee may not take a deduction until the property is actually in use. Exceptions to this are provided when the item meets the all-events test during the year (liability is fixed and determinable), economic performance occurs within a reasonable period after the close of the taxable year (must be within eight and a half months), the item is recurring and is consistently treated as deductible by the taxpayer in the year the all-events test is met, and either the item is not material or treating it as deductible in a particular year will lead to a more proper matching of revenue and expenses (§461(h)(3)).

Section 467—Uneven Rental Payments

Also added with TRA 1984 was §467 of the code regarding deferred or prepayments (i.e., uneven rental payments) for the use of property or services. Normally these payments have some element of interest, but are treated by the code as being just rent. Congress added this section to cover leases with terms of longer than one year and having total payments of more than $250,000, in which either rent for one calendar year is not due until after the close of the succeeding year or there are differing rent payments to be made in various years. The rationale behind this addition may have been prevention of perceived abuses when cash basis lessors (reporting revenue in the year received) enter into stepped-rent lease agreements with accrual basis lessees (deducting rent as level payments over the lease term) with the intent of having both parties receive favorable tax treatment.

---

[26] Rev. Rul. 60-122, 1960-1 C.B. 56.

Section 467 rental agreements may apply to leases with nearly level rental payments. For some leases, payment for part of one calendar year is to be paid after the close of the following year, or rental payments under the lease are to be increased over the term of the lease (§467(d)(1)). Any lease where an even rent payment is not d·1e for each period of the lease agreement is a §467 lease, although §467 does not apply to cases where the sum of all cash and any other consideration given is not more than $250,000 (§467(d)(2)).

The lessee takes a deduction equal to the total of the rent accrued per §467(b) and interest on unpaid amounts from prior years. The lessor reports the same amounts as income. Section 467(b) dictates that the rent amount accrued in a period shall be the amount allocated to that period per the rental agreement, unless an amount allocated to one period is not payable until after the close of that period. In that case, the present value of the delayed rent payment is used in calculation of the total at a rate equal to 110 percent of the applicable federal rate per §1274(d) (§467(e)(4)).

When the lease does not specify the amount to be allocated to a particular period, §467(b)(2) dictates that a "constant rental amount" be allocated. This type of rent leveling is accomplished by determining the amount that, if paid equally at the end of each period, would have an aggregate present value equal to the aggregate present value of the payments required by the lease (§467(e)(1)). As with the case of specified allocations, this amount is added to interest on amounts accrued in prior years but not yet paid.

This method is also to be applied to "disqualified leaseback transactions and long-term agreements" (§467(b)(3)(A)). A disqualified leaseback is a §467 lease in which the lessee or a related person (per §465(b)(3)(C)) had a material ownership interest in the property within a two-year period prior to the leaseback (§467(e)(2)). A long-term lease is a §467 lease with a required lease term greater than 75 percent of the federal statutory recovery period for such property (§467(b)(4)(A)). In either of these cases, the transaction will be disqualified only if it provides for increasing rents, and the Commissioner of Internal Revenue determines that there is a primary tax avoidance motive (§467(b)(4)(B)). Exclusions to this are provided in various cases, including situations where rent is tied to lessor receipts or where rent is tied to price indices (§467(b)(5)).

When property being leased under a §467 agreement without rent leveling is sold prior to lease expiration, that property will normally have an increased value because of the future rental payments to be received. Therefore, §467(c) provides for recapture to prevent this increase from being realized as capital gain, rather than ordinary income. In cases of non-disqualified §467 leaseback or long-term leases (§467(c)(2)), the amount to be recaptured as ordinary income shall be equal to the lesser of the excess of the amount realized over the adjusted basis of the property or the excess of the amount that would have been taken into account had the rent been leveled over the amount actually taken into account per §467(a).

Depreciation/Cost Recovery

With the passage of P.L. 97-34 (ERTA) in 1981, Congress added the accelerated cost recovery system (ACRS) to replace the previous systems of depreciation being used for tangible personal property. ACRS provided two methods of depreciation calculation. At the taxpayer's option, the amount of depreciation could be calculated by either multiplying the unadjusted basis of recovery property by a set percentage over a set period of time or taking straight-line depreciation over an optional recovery period. The Tax Reform Act of 1986 significantly changed these provisions, leading to the renaming of this cost recovery system as the modified accelerated cost recovery system (MACRS). ACRS divided depreciable property into five categories based on such characteristics as lifespan and type of asset with recovery periods of between five and fifteen years. The recovery periods for realty were changed in 1984 and 1986, with the Tax Reform Acts of those years, and in 1986, with the Imputed Interest Simplification Act. Property excluded from ACRS includes pre-1981 acquisitions, post-1981 reacquisitions of pre-1981 purchases from related parties for the purpose of gaining ACRS deductions, and property being depreciated under other allowable methods (former §168(e)). Although the original legislation called for the phasing in from 150 percent declining-balance depreciation to 175 percent declining-balance depreciation to 200 percent declining-balance depreciation between 1981 and 1986, this phase-in was repealed with TEFRA in 1982. Property basis was also affected by TEFRA, which mandated that such basis be reduced by one-half of the investment and energy credits taken for the regular 10 percent credit. If the taxpayer elected not to take the full credit available, no basis reduction would be made for the reduced credit taken (TEFRA §205(a)(1)).

MACRS cost recovery is significantly different. Asset class lives for this system are found in Rev. Proc. 83-35 (1983-1 C.B. 745), although modifications were made to this with §168(e) of TRA 1986. Under this section, personal property is grouped into 6 class lives of 3, 5, 7, 10, 15, and 20 years, depending on the type of asset being considered. The class lives are accelerated, giving the taxpayer the opportunity to recover cost fully over a shorter period of time. For example, the 7-year class includes property that was classified under the pre-1981 asset depreciation range (ADR) to have a class life of at least 10 but less than 16 years. MACRS cost recovery allows 200 percent declining-balance depreciation to be taken on items with class lives of between three and ten years, switching to straight-line when that method allows a greater deduction (§168(b)). The taxpayer may elect to use straight-line depreciation for property with class lives of between 3 and 20 years.

These rules apply to assets placed in service after 1986, with appropriate grandfather clauses for property for which there were contracts for purchase or construction before March 2 of that year. Taxpayers had the alternative to elect early adoption for items placed in service after July 31, 1986. An alternative depreciation system using ADR class life is also provided for (§168(g)).

Possible complications may be involved in the disposition of property subject to depreciation recapture under §§1245 and 1250. These sections call for the characterization of part of the proceeds upon disposition of property as ordinary income, so the taxpayer may not reap the double benefit of income reduction both through cost recovery allowances and capital gain treatment on sale.

Investment Tax Credit

Although repealed in 1986, the investment tax credit (ITC) was once an important factor in leasing decisions. Depending upon lease characterization, this credit went to either the lessor or lessee. The ITC was intended to stimulate economic activity and employment through increased capital equipment acquisition. The ITC had the effect of lowering the cost of acquired equipment because the tax credit was a dollar-for-dollar reduction in a firm's tax liability. In fact, hardly a year passes that a member of Congress does not consider implementing a new ITC to stimulate economic activity.

Leasing provided an opportunity for a firm to receive benefits from the ITC when the firm could not otherwise take advantage of the ITC. That is, if the lessor firm could use the ITC when the lessee could not, the lessor passed along the savings in the form of lower rental payments. In addition, the Internal Revenue Code permitted either party to take the ITC in a *true lease* agreement.

The Tax Reform Act of 1986 provided transition rules for property placed in service after 1985. These exceptions applied to transition property and to qualified progress expenditures, for transition, or other property (§49(b)). Transition property is defined by §49(e) to include property under prestanding binding contracts, property under construction for which financial commitments had been made, and property as part of other real property for which financial commitments had been made. To be considered transition property, such property must be placed in service by set dates, which depend upon the class life of that property. Reductions of the regular ITC available are made for property placed in service in taxable years beginning after June 30, 1987, with pro rata reductions made for property placed in service during a taxable year straddling July 1, 1987 (§49(c)). Similar reductions must be made to other credits receivable through the ITC.

Even though the ITC no longer exists, it is not forgotten. The probability that a new ITC will exist in the future is not insignificant.

Passive Activity Loss Rules

TRA 1986 enacted §469, which limits the use of passive activity losses and credits. A passive activity is any in which the taxpayer does not materially participate and includes all rental activities, regardless of the participation of the taxpayer. These rules apply to individuals, estates, trusts, closely held C corporations, and personal service corporations (§469(a)(2)). Closely held C corporations are those in which at any time during the last half of the taxable year, more than half of the stock is owned by five or fewer individuals (§469(j)(1)).

Section 469 dictates that passive activity losses may offset only passive activity gains, while passive activity credits may be used only to offset the tax attributable to other passive income. Closely held C corporations may use passive activity losses to offset active income, but may not use it to offset portfolio income. Taxpayers may carry forward disallowed losses, which may be used to offset future passive income or may be deducted in full when the taxpayer disposes of all interest in that passive activity in a taxable transaction (§469(g)).

Interest

The passive activity loss rules also affect the deductibility of interest. In general, interest expense incurred in obtaining leased property is deductible to the lessor. For post-TRA 1986 acquisitions, however, this amount is limited to net investment income (§163(d)). Additionally, §163(d)(3) excludes from the calculation of investment interest any interest amount considered in the calculation of passive activity gain or loss. As all rental activities are passive, this disallows the deduction as investment interest of amounts paid in connection with rental activities. During the four-year phase-in period, any passive loss allowed reduces investment income available for offsetting of investment interest for that year (§163(d)(4)(E)).

Alternative Minimum Tax

The 1986 Tax Reform Act adds another complexity to the leasing decision: the alternative minimum tax (AMT). The tax is imposed at a rate of 20 percent for corporations, compared to the regular corporate tax rate of 35 percent (§55(b)). It is an alternative tax because, after computing both a regular tax and AMT liabilities, the corporation pays the higher of the two. Leasing may be attractive to the low-tax-rate corporate lessee subject to the AMT.

The AMT's fundamental goal is to prevent individuals and corporations with substantial economic income from using preferential deductions, exclusions, and credits to eliminate their tax liability. The tax code uses the terms "adjustments" (§56) and "preferences" (§57) to refer to differences between regular taxable income and alternative minimum taxable income (AMTI). Adjustments differ from preferences only in that adjustments involve a "substitution" of a special AMT treatment of a specific item for the regular tax treatment, while a preference involves the "addition" of the difference between the special AMT procedure and the regular tax procedure. Because accelerated *depreciation* is one of the major tax adjustments but lease payments are not, leasing could become attractive to the corporation that faces the AMT.

Accelerated depreciation in excess of 150 percent declining-balance (ADR midpoint life) is an example of a tax preference. An example of tax adjustment is the difference between the adjusted net book income and alternative minimum tax income before adjustments. For 1993, adjustments are multiplied by 0.75 before they are added to the taxable income in order to compute the AMTI (this is called "ACE" or adjusted current earnings). After 1993, no adjustments or ACE are added back to taxable income.[27]

The tax to be paid is the larger of 35 percent of the regular taxable income (without tax adjustments or tax preferences) or 20 percent of the AMTI. If the regular taxable income for a corporation is very large, the AMT will not apply. For the lease or buy decision, the AMT can make a difference if the amounts involved are significant relative to the AMTI. Examples in Chapter 6 illustrate application of the AMT to the lease or buy decision and net present value analysis. The impact on NPV can be very large for firms subject to the AMT, but the impact can be uncertain because of the uncertainty about future earnings and the future tax status of the firm. In other words, the number of years a firm is subject to the AMT will determine the NPV advantage, if any, to leasing.

Motor Vehicle Leasing

Motor vehicle leasing is subject to special rules because of the unique nature of that type of lease. Auto leases normally contain a terminal rental adjustment clause ("TRAC"), which states that, on termination of the lease, the lessee is required to pay the lessor the difference, if positive, between the expected value, as used to calculate payments for the lease agreement, less the actual wholesale value of the vehicle. If the difference is negative, in that the actual value is greater than the expected value, the lessee keeps the gain. Therefore, the TRAC effectively shifts the risks and rewards of ownership to the lessee.

This matter was taken up by the IRS, which wanted to prevent dealers/lessors from being able to receive depreciation allowances and ITC credits for property that they bore no risk of ownership. Initially, the Ninth Circuit agreed, and provided that any motor vehicle lease including a TRAC was not a lease at all, but must be reclassified as a conditional sales contract.[28] This matter was on appeal in 1982 when Congress provided in TEFRA (§210) that the IRS could not reclassify auto leases containing TRACs as sales con-

---

[27] In 1987, 1988, and 1989, the adjustment between book income and alternative minimum taxable income was multiplied by 50 percent and was known as the "BURP" (book untaxed reported profits) preference. ACE preference applies to the tax years 1990–1993. After tax year 1993, no preference adjustment (no ACE or BURP) is made.

[28] *Swift Dodge v. Commissioner*, 692 F.2d 651 (9th Cir. 1982), rev'g 76 T.C. 547 (1981).

tracts. This did not apply to leases for personal purposes, nor did it apply to leases in which the lessor had obtained the property through non-recourse debt.

With TRA 1984, Congress amended §168(f) (since changed to §7701(h)) to include special rules for motor vehicle leases containing TRACs, maintaining that a TRAC is not sufficient for the recharacterization of a lease as a sale. These provisions apply only to "qualified motor vehicle operating agreements," under which the amount of lessor's personal liability plus the fair market value of any property used as security must be greater than or equal to the amount borrowed (§7701(h)(2)(B)). Additionally, there must be a statement from the lessee that the vehicle subject to the agreement is to be used in the trade or business of the lessee and that the lessee has been advised that it will not be treated as the vehicle's owner for tax purposes (§7701(h)(2)(C)). The lessor may have no knowledge that the lessee has provided false information (§7701(h)(2)(D)).

Real Estate Leasing

The leasing of real estate (§1250) is substantially different from that of equipment or personal property (§1245). Much of this difference is due to the favorable treatment allowed by 1981 ERTA, which reduced income and capital gains rates, introduced ACRS depreciation and the class lives that went with it, and changed investment and rehabilitation credits for real estate. These were the primary reasons for the attraction of the tax shelters of the early 1980s. Congress saw this and responded, as seen by the change in recovery period mandated by TRA 1984.[29]

Additionally, TRA 1984 enacted IRS §467, as discussed previously, which introduced the concepts of the time value of money and rent leveling to leases. Many other changes were also made, particularly in relation to tax shelters and the reporting requirements that go with them.

The TRA of 1986 changed treatment of real estate leases even further. The changes closed the loopholes that caused tax shelter proliferation, going so far as to hurt the whole real estate industry. Some of the changes included the introduction of passive activity loss rules, repeal of the investment tax credit, reduction of the

---

[29] S. Rep. No. 169, 98th Cong. 2d Sess. 460–461 (1984).

rehabilitation tax credit, modification of the ACRS cost recovery system, and elimination of special capital gains rates. The effects of these measures can still be seen today, as the real estate industry struggles to be profitable and the savings and loan industry faces increasing insolvency, in large part because of problem real estate loans.

Rent payments are considered to be amounts ". . . received or accrued for the occupancy of real estate . . ." (Regs. §1.61-8(a)). This may include fixed monthly payments as well as any payment contingent on the sales or income of the lessee. It may also include any payments made by the lessee on behalf of the lessor, including mortgage payments, maintenance and repairs, insurance, or taxes (Regs. §1.61-8(c)).

Rent is to be included in gross income, per §61(a)(5). Year of inclusion will vary, depending upon whether the taxpayer is on an accrual or a cash basis. Accrual basis taxpayers must include rent in income when the amount due is fixed and measurable; cash basis taxpayers must include rent payments in income when they have actual or constructive receipt of such payment. Advance rentals must be included in income at the time of receipt regardless of the lessor's accounting method (Regs. §1.61-8(b)).

Rent payments made for business (but not personal) property are deductible to the lessee when paid (§162(a)(3)). Once again this is tied to the method of accounting. Advance rentals must be capitalized and amortized over the remaining lease term. Rentals of property split between home and office use may qualify for deductions under the home office rules (§280A(c)(1)). As with equipment leasing, no deduction is available for rent when a lease is recharacterized as a sale (although cost recovery allowances may be available to the lessee).

The acquisition of a lease presents unique problems. The value of the leasehold acquired by a lessor may not be amortized, although the costs of acquiring the lease (e.g., fees and commissions, necessary renovations) must be capitalized and amortized over the lease term (Regs. §1.162-11(a)). Similarly, the lessee also capitalizes and amortizes these expenses over the lease term.

Tax Advantages in International Leases

Several more complex lease structures are gaining popularity, particularly in the international leasing area. Among the most prominent of modern lease transactions are cross-border/double-dip transactions, FSC leases, and Japanese leveraged leases.

Double-Dip Leases

Cross-border leases, or "double-dip" transactions as they are often called, allow two parties to receive the tax benefits of ownership simultaneously. The double-dip lease depends on two conditions: (1) the tax laws of many foreign jurisdictions provide large tax benefits to property owners, and (2) foreign law notions of tax ownership may differ substantially from those of the United States. The double-dip transaction combines foreign tax savings with U.S. tax benefits to reduce the financing costs of the total lease transaction. Double-dip leases could be considered a form of tax arbitrage.

A double-dip lease works as follows. A U.S. firm enters into a lease with a foreign lessor. The foreign lessor's return is based primarily on the tax benefits in its jurisdiction. This lowers the rental payments required by the lessor. More tax savings are derived when the definitions of tax ownership and the definitions of a true lease differ between the U.S. and foreign jurisdictions. The difference makes it possible for the foreign lease to be deemed a loan in the United States. As a result, a U.S. entity can claim the U.S. tax benefits of ownership at the same time the foreign lessor is claiming ownership in its local jurisdiction.

Double-dip transactions are unique. Here is one example.

1. A British firm receives a 20 percent equity contribution from an equity contributor and a loan for the remainder of the equipment cost from a lender. Each of the parties is from the United Kingdom.

2. The British firm purchases a Boeing 747 airline and leases the plane to a U.S. airline.

3. The U.S. airline assigns its rights under the lease to a lessor (an owner trustee in this scenario) and leases the equipment back from the owner trustee.

4. The owner trustee receives an equity investment of 20 percent from a U.S. investor and borrows the remaining 80 percent of the aircraft price from lenders.

5. The U.S. owner trustee assigns tax benefits of ownership to the U.S. equity investor and assigns rental payments to the lender.

6. The owner trustee pays the airline a consideration payment of 100 percent of the airplane's value.

7. The airline deposits a defeasance of approximately 95 percent of the original lessor's cost with a British bank. The bank becomes responsible for all rental payments to the original equipment lessor.

In double-dip transactions, the original lessee (the party leasing the equipment from the foreign entity) may not be the party who becomes the actual lessee. Often, the owner trustee in the transaction leases directly from the foreign entity and subleases the equipment. The original lessee may also be a party to the transaction, only to receive 100 percent of the equipment cost as consideration from the U.S. owner trustee while paying perhaps 95 percent of the equipment cost to defease its responsibility. The lessee realizes a front-end profit of 5 percent of the equipment cost!

Foreign Sales Corporation Leases

Another lease structure is known as the foreign sales corporation (FSC) lease. FSCs are leveraged leases under which all or a portion of the rent from the transaction qualifies as "foreign trading gross receipts" and is entitled to partial exemption from U.S. taxation under §921. In 1984, Congress enacted FSC legislation in an attempt to increase U.S. exports. FSC tax incentives were intended primarily to benefit sales of exports, but leasing was also covered by the legislation. An FSC selling or leasing U.S. manufactured assets overseas realizes a U.S. tax exemption for a portion of the income generated from the transaction. In turn, the lessor can share a portion of these tax savings with the lessee in the form of lower lease payments.

The legal requirements and fees for these FSC leases can be staggering. $1 million in legal fees would not be unusual. Therefore, the leases must be very large (almost all are aircraft leases).

Japanese Leveraged Leases

Another recent lease innovation is called the Japanese leveraged lease. In this transaction, a Japanese owner receives tax depreciation allowances equal to 100 percent of the cost of the equipment it wishes to purchase and lease. Again, the benefit to the user comes when the owner shares these tax benefits with the lessee in the form of reduced lease payments.

In the Japanese leveraged lease, the lessee has the option to purchase the equipment at the end of the lease, an option it will inevitably choose. When the purchaser and lessor is a Japanese legal entity, the lessee can acquire equipment for a purchase price that is reduced by the value of the Japanese tax shields for depreciation (allowing a profit for the Japanese entity). This reduction in purchase price generally falls in the range of 5 percent to 7 percent. Because of this price reduction, the Japanese leverage lease can be a more cost-effective method of financing the purchase of equipment (Chapter 6 shows how to quantify this savings).

The Japanese leveraged lease must meet certain requirements. In order for the Japanese firm to obtain the tax benefits of ownership, the lease must meet certain guidelines:

1. Equity investment must not be less than 20 percent of the total equipment cost.

2. The lease term must not be more than 120 percent of the useful life of the equipment.

3. The asset must have a high level of second-hand marketability.

4. The total taxable income for the lease accruing to the lessor must be less than 1 percent of the total equipment cost.

5. The lessor may not have negative taxable income in excess of 50 percent of the lease term.

6. The amount of the tax to the lessor may not exceed 160 percent of a designated amount. This amount is calculated on the assumption that (a) the lease period is equal to the life of the equipment, (b) the option given to the lessee to purchase the equipment will be 10 percent of the asset's purchase price, and (c) the rate of return to the lessor from leasing the equipment is 5.5 percent.

7. The lease agreement cannot fix the option purchase price at above 45 percent for aircraft cost or 10 percent for other equipment cost.

The lessors in Japanese leveraged leases are usually special-purpose companies whose only activity is the lease transaction in question. Equity participants usually form an association with the lessor, which is called a *"Tokumei-Kumiai"* or a limited partnership. A *"Kumiai-in"* is defined in the lease to be "any person (or business entity) entering into a *Tokumei-Kumiai* Agreement with Lessor in relation to Equipment and any registered assign of any such Person."

The *Kumiai-in* are often small- to medium-sized Japanese firms that are motivated to participate because of the tax shields. High Japanese tax rates provide strong motivation. For example, one Japanese leveraged lease stated "the combined effective tax rate applicable to the Lessor and *Kumiai-in* for fiscal years ending on or after March 31, 1992, is approximately 51.4 percent."

A Tax Law History: Safe Harbor Leasing

The tax treatment of leasing is dictated by case law (decisions handed down by the courts) and by the IRS rulings discussed in this chapter. For a brief period of time, however, many of the IRS guidelines for a *true lease* were greatly relaxed. With the Economic Recovery Tax Act (ERTA) of 1981, Congress added Section 168(f)(8) of the Internal Revenue Code, which was an attempt to adopt formal rules for leasing. This code section created an elective "safe harbor," assuring parties to leases characterized as a *true lease* access to the transfer of investment tax credits (ITC), accelerated cost recovery system (ACRS) depreciation allowances, and energy credits between the parties. Safe harbor leasing essentially allowed the sale of these benefits by a party unable to use them.

1981 ERTA

Under the provisions of the safe harbor section of the code (§168(f)(8)), if the safe harbor requirements were met, the lessor would be considered the owner of a leased asset for federal income tax purposes, and thus would receive the tax benefits (e.g., cost recovery, ITC) of ownership. This could occur even if the lessee had the actual economic benefits of ownership. The parties to the lease contract then had the ability to choose who the ultimate beneficiary of the favorable tax treatment would be.

The provisions of safe harbor leasing provided relief from Rev. Proc. 75-21—that is, there were no requirements that the lessor enter into the lease with the expectation of profit other than tax benefits provided, or that the lessor bear any of the risks and rewards of ownership. If the lease met the requirements of §168(f)(8), the lessor was treated as the owner of the property for federal income tax purposes, *even though* (1) the lessor's profits from the transaction depended largely or even wholly on tax benefits, (2) the lessee retained ownership for state and local law purposes, (3) the property could be limited-use property, (4) the lease involved lessee financing, or (5) the lease contained a nominal or fixed-price purchase option exercisable by the lessee at the end of the lease term.

These leases were quite popular, particularly in the sale-and-leaseback form. A study by Stickney, Weil, and Wolfson analyzed the benefits to General Electric from its active participation in safe harbor leasing. One conclusion is:

> Through tax-transfer leases, General Electric paid its lessees about $350 million in 1981 for benefits estimated to be worth on the order of $500 million. . . . These transactions contributed to GE's being able to arrange its tax affairs to receive a refund of $104 million from the U.S. Treasury.[30]

As *The Wall Street Journal* said at the time, "in the hands of the critics of tax-benefit-transfer leasing, the disclosure of its value to GE is likely to become a political Molotov cocktail."[31] Using this method to transfer tax benefits became so prevalent that Congress closed the loophole the very next year with TEFRA.

TEFRA Changes

Safe harbor leasing was changed in 1982 with adoption of the Tax Equity and Fiscal Responsibility Act (TEFRA). TEFRA modified the treatment of leases entered into after July 1, 1982, and eliminated the safe harbor provisions for leases entered into after December 31, 1983.

For transactions entered into before 1984, substantial changes to existing provisions were made. Limits were placed both on the

---

[30] Clyde P. Stickney, Roman L. Weil, and Mark A. Wolfson, "Income Taxes And Tax-Transfer Leases: General Electric's Accounting For A Molotov Cocktail," *Accounting Review* v. 58(2), 1983, p. 439.

[31] S. R. Schmelel, "GE's Huge Tax-Leasing Benefits Expected to Heighten Controversy Over 1981 Law," *The Wall Street Journal*, March 15, 1982, p. 12.

tax benefits available in any year due to safe harbor leasing (§168(i)) and on the amount of property that a lessee could lease through safe harbor leases (§168(f)(8)(D)(ii)). Additionally, the maximum lease term was reduced (§168(f)(8)(B)(ii)), the ITC credit was required to be used over a five-year period (§168(i)(3)), the ACRS cost recovery deductions were required to be used over a longer period than was originally provided for (§168(i)(2)), and the maximum amount of interest that the lessee could charge the purchaser-lessor was reduced (§168(i)(5)). TEFRA also modified the at-risk rules of §465 by allowing eligible lessors to determine their amount at-risk by reference to the amount by which the lessee was considered to be at risk. These rules were, in most cases, intended to apply to leases commencing after July 1, 1982. Transition rules allowed extended benefits for some industries; leases for property depreciated using percentage depletion, however, were required to adopt the rules at the earlier date of February 19, 1982.

TEFRA also affected non-safe harbor "finance" leases, through provisions allowing lessees to be given the right to purchase the property for not less than 10 percent of the property's original cost, and allowing property specifically for one user (limited-use property) to receive lease tax treatment. The Tax Reform Act of 1984 delayed the adoption of the finance lease provisions for four years until 1988, and then they were never instituted because of their repeal with the Tax Reform Act of 1986. Thus finance leases were repealed effective January 1, 1987, except for certain very limited property eligible under certain prior transition rules.

The role that leasing plays in transferring tax shields from the party that cannot use the tax shields (the lessee) to the party that can (the lessor) is seen very convincingly in the history of safe harbor leasing. The safe harbor leasing provisions were so effective in reducing the cost of transferring tax shields that Congress eliminated the provisions in just one year.

Summary

Taxes are one of the primary economic forces that motivate leasing. Lease contracts allow the transfer of valuable tax shields from one party, usually the lessee, to the other party, usually the lessor. If tax shields can be transferred through the lease contract, however, a lease must satisfy the tax rules for leasing established by the IRS. If the tax rules for leasing are not satisfied, the lease is considered a *conditional sales contract* and treated like any other term loan or installment purchase contract.

In this chapter, we first looked at the guiding rules for a *true lease*. Other tax effects include rental expense and depreciation. The alternative minimum tax, special rules for motor vehicle leases, and real estate leasing tax rules also are discussed. International leases that exploit special tax rules, such as cross-border/double-dip transactions, FSC leases, and Japanese leveraged leases, are explained. A brief history of the safe harbor tax law demonstrates the market response to changes in the tax rules that apply to leasing. Decision makers need to be aware of these opportunities as they are created by ever changing tax laws.

Chapter *4*

Accounting for Leases

A lease may appear on the lessee firm's balance sheet (a capital lease), or off the balance sheet (an operating lease). This chapter describes the accounting rules for classifying these two types of leases and demonstrates the impact of lease classification on key accounting ratios. The focus is on the lessee firm. An almost symmetric set of rules applies to the lessor firm, but I do not focus on the lessor's accounting rules here.[1]

Prior to the publication of the *Statement of Financial Accounting Standards (SFAS) No. 13*, "Accounting for Leases," by the Financial Accounting Standards Board in 1976, most lessees accounted for leases as operating leases. By doing so, they avoided reporting the leases on their balance sheets as liabilities. Publication of *SFAS No. 13* codified the accounting profession's decision that many lease contracts represent fixed obligations identical to secured debt contracts and should be reported on the balance sheet.

What are the economic and market implications of this accounting decision? There are two schools of thought. The first school, the efficient markets school, argues that almost all these accounting decisions are irrelevant. The off-balance sheet placement of leases is really just "smoke and mirrors," and competent financial analysts will see through this treatment of leases. The other school, the psychological school, argues that there is value to off-balance sheet financing. The arguments related to these two schools are discussed in this chapter.

---

[1] Readers interested in the accounting rules for lessor firms may refer to almost any intermediate financial accounting textbook.

Definition of Capital and Operating Leases

SFAS No. 13 provides the detailed criteria for specification of a lease contract as either a capital or operating lease. Four criteria apply to lessees; a capital lease is defined as a lease that meets *any one* of the four criteria.

1. Transfer of Ownership. If the lease agreement transfers ownership to the lessee before the lease expires, without payment of additional compensation to the lessor, the lease is considered a purchase financing arrangement, similar to an installment purchase.

2. Bargain Purchase Option. The lessee can purchase the asset for a bargain price when the lease expires. A bargain purchase option requires comparing the option's purchase price to the leased asset's expected residual value at the maturity of the lease. If the purchase option is well below the expected residual value, the lessee is unlikely to pass up the savings; the probability is high that the lessee will buy the asset at maturity.

3. Seventy-five Percent of Economic Life. The lease lasts for at least 75 percent of the asset's expected economic life. A bargain renewal option, that is, an option to renew the lease at a rental rate below the expected fair market rental at the time of the exercise of the option, is considered to lengthen the lease life used in this determination.

4. Ninety Percent of Asset's Value. The present value of the *minimum lease payments* is at least 90 percent of the asset's fair value. The minimum lease payments are defined by *SFAS No. 13* to mean "the payments that the lessee is obligated to make or can be required to make in connection with the leased property." Periodic payments account for the majority of the minimum lease payments; other components include such items as the bargain purchase option or bargain renewal option payments. Some leases also contain additional provisions that are included as minimum lease payments, such as a guaranteed residual value by the lessee or a penalty payment for failure to renew if it is expected that the lessee will pass up the renewal option.

For criterion number four, determination of the appropriate discount rate at which to discount the lease payments is very important.[2] *SFAS No. 13* states that the lessee is required to compute the present value of the minimum lease payments using the lower of the lessee's incremental borrowing rate or the discount rate used by the lessor (also known as the implicit rate computed by the lessor) if known or determinable by the lessee. The lessee's incremental borrowing rate is defined by *SFAS No. 13* as "the rate that, at the inception of the lease, the lessee would have incurred to borrow the funds necessary to buy the leased asset on a secured loan with repayment terms similar to the payment schedule called for in the lease."

If any *one* of the four criteria is met, the lease is considered to be a capital lease. If none of the criteria is met, the contract is accounted for as an operating lease. Figure 4.1 gives a simple flow chart representation of these criteria.

Accounting for Capital Leases

The Basic Example

To explain the accounting methods, an example is most useful. I use the same example throughout this chapter (and in later chapters too), although some of the basic terms will change to illustrate special accounting problems. On January 1, 1994, ABC Warehouse Stores and Pacific Leasing Company sign a lease agreement for a forklift calling for annual payments of $10,000 per year for five years. Here is information applying to this basic lease agreement:

1. The non-cancelable lease payments of $10,000 per year for five years are due at the end of the year.
2. If purchased, the forklift would cost $40,000. It has an estimated economic life of five years, and has no residual value.
3. ABC Warehouse Stores' marginal borrowing rate is 10 percent.
4. ABC uses straight-line depreciation for similar equipment that it owns.

This lease must be capitalized according to criterion number four because the present value of the lease payments at 10 percent

---

[2] Discounting (also known as capitalizing) the lease payments is an application of the basic principles of present value mathematics or the time value of money. The Appendix to this book reviews present value mathematics.

Figure 4.1: Classifying Operating and Capital Leases

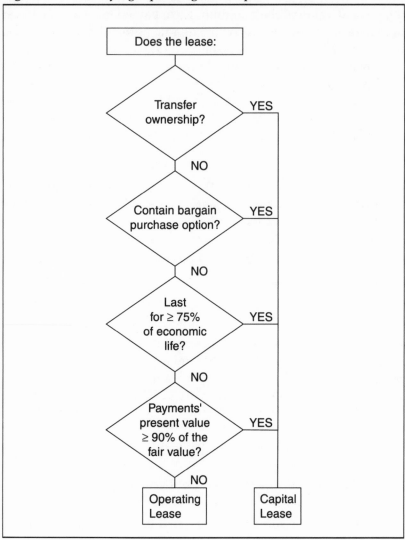

is $37,907.87,[3] which exceeds 90 percent of the equipment value (0.90 × $40,000 = $36,000). The life of the lease is more than 75 percent of the life of the asset, which would also require this lease to be a capital lease according to criterion number three. The valua-

---

[3] This calculation is the present value of a $1 annuity for five years at 10 percent interest times the $10,000 lease payment (3.790787 × $10,000).

tion of the leased asset and the related liability is $37,907.87. Table 4.1 shows the amortization schedule for the lease payments based on the present value of lease payments at the 10 percent interest rate.

ABC's journal entries for the first year, based on this lease agreement, are:

January 1, 1994 (to record the lease)

Leased Asset	37,907.87	
Lease Liability		37,907.87

December 31, 1994 (to record first lease payment and to recognize interest and depreciation expense)

Lease Liability (see Table 4.1)	6,209.21	
Interest Expense (see Table 4.1)	3,790.79	
Cash		10,000.00
Depreciation Expense— Capital Leases	7,581.57	
Accumulated Depreciation— Capital Leases ($37,907.87 ÷ 5 years)		7,581.57

Other entries will be similar, with the exception of the lease liability and interest expense figures, which change each year according to the numbers in Table 4.1. At the end of the five-year lease,

Table 4.1: ABC Warehouse Stores' Lease Amortization Schedule

Date	Annual Lease Payment	Interest (10%) on Unpaid Balance	Reduction of Lease Obligation	Lease Obligation
1/1/94				$37,907.87
12/31/94	$10,000.00	$3,790.79	$6,209.21	31,698.65
12/31/95	10,000.00	3,169.87	6,830.13	24,868.52
12/31/96	10,000.00	2,486.85	7,513.15	17,355.37
12/31/97	10,000.00	1,735.54	8,264.46	9,090.91
12/31/98	10,000.00	909.09	9,090.91	0.00
	$50,000.00	$12,092.13	$37,907.87	

the amount capitalized is fully amortized, and the lease obligation is totally discharged. If not purchased, the equipment is returned to the lessor, and the leased equipment and related accumulated depreciation accounts are removed from the books. If the asset is purchased at the termination of the lease, say, for $3,000, the following entry would be recorded:

December 31, 1998 (to record purchase of leased equipment)
Equipment (37,907.87 + 3,000.00)	40,907.87	
Accumulated Depreciation—Capital	37,907.87	
Leases		
Leased Asset		37,907.87
Accumulated		37,907.87
Depreciation—Equipment		
Cash		3,000.00

Accounting for Operating Leases

Suppose that the lease illustrated above did not qualify as a capital lease, and thereby would be accounted for as an operating lease. The journal entry to record the rental payments of $10,000 would be as follows:

December 31, 1994–1998 (to record operating lease payment)
Rent Expense	10,000.00	
Cash		10,000.00

No entries are made to the balance sheet for the operating lease. Rent expense is reported naturally on the income statement. In addition, it is important to note that disclosure in a footnote to the balance sheet is required for all operating leases that have non-cancelable payments extending over more than one year.

Table 4.2 presents an example of the footnote disclosure of leases. It is a note from the 1992 annual report of Ameritech. Ameritech had total capital lease obligations of $24.7 million at December 31, 1992.

Comparison of Capital and Operating Leases

At first glance there appear to be major expense differences between capital and operating leases. Over time, however, the same total expenses will occur for the capital lease as for the operating

Table 4.2: Footnote Disclosure of Leases Ameritech, December 31, 1992

Lease Commitments		
The company leases certain facilities and equipment used in its operations under both operating and capital leases. Rental expense under operating leases was $196.3, $213.0, and $209.8 million for 1992, 1991, and 1990, respectively. As of December 31, 1992, aggregate minimum rental commitments under noncancelable leases were approximately as follows:		

Years	Operating	Capital
1993	$92.7	$12.1
1994	78.6	10.2
1995	54.8	8.2
1996	46.0	4.9
1997	37.3	3.3
Thereafter	220.1	10.6
Total Minimum Rental Commitments	$529.5	49.3
Less: executory costs		4.7
interest costs		11.1
Present Value of Minimum Lease Payments		$33.5

lease. There is a timing difference: Under the capital lease, the charges are higher in the earlier years and lower in the later years.

Table 4.3 shows the year-by-year expense charge for the two methods for the forklift lease of ABC Warehouse Stores. The timing difference is illustrated in the last column. In the first year, the capital lease has expenses that exceed the equivalent operating lease by over $1,300. In the last year, the operating lease expense is more than $1,500 higher than the capital lease expense. If an accelerated depreciation method had been used, the differences between the amounts in each year would have been even larger in the earlier and the later years.

The differences between capital and operating leases are highlighted by this example. For the capital lease, an asset and related liability of $37,908 is reported on the balance sheet; no asset or liability is reported under the operating method. The reporting of a capital lease rather than an operating one causes: (1) an increase in the amount of reported debt, (2) an increase in the amount of total assets, and (3) a lower income in the early years of the lease,

Table 4.3: ABC Warehouse Stores Comparison of Capital and
Operating Lease

	Capital Lease			Operating	
Year	Depreciation	Interest	Total Expense	Lease Expense	Timing Difference
1994	$7,581.57	$3,790.79	$11,372.36	$10,000.00	$1,372.36
1995	7,581.57	3,169.87	10,751.44	10,000.00	751.44
1996	7,581.57	2,486.85	10,068.42	10,000.00	68.42
1997	7,581.57	1,735.54	9,317.11	10,000.00	(682.89)
1998	7,581.59	909.09	8,490.68	10,000.00	(1,509.32)
	$37,907.87	$12,092.13	$50,000.00	$50,000.00	$ 0.00

resulting in lower retained earnings. Thus the debt-to-equity ratio
using the capital lease method will always be higher than under
the operating lease method. In addition, the rate of return on total
assets (or return on equity) decreases. Many firms prefer to report
leases as operating leases because of this impact on their financial
statements.

Off-Balance Sheet Financing

Many corporate executives act as though the off-balance sheet
recording of leases has value. Careful studies, however, have found
that the capitalization of leases has no significant impact on the
stock or bond prices of lessee firms.[4] From the point of view of cash
flow, the company is in the same position whether the lease is
accounted for as an operating or a capital lease, given that the *tax
treatment is the same.* If a lease is classified as operating, the debt
ratio will appear smaller and the rate of return higher, making the
lessee firm look stronger financially. Financial analysts, bank loan
officers, and analysts for bond rating agencies, among others, however, are trained to look for such off-balance sheet obligations as
leases, which are clearly reported in the footnotes as discussed
above. Therefore, despite such an accounting "deception," it is unlikely firms can really appear stronger to anyone except the most
naive investors.

---

[4] For example, see A. Rashad Abdel-khalik, "The Economic Effect on Lessees of
FASB Statement No. 13, Accounting for Leases," *Research Report* (Stamford, Conn.:
Financial Accounting Standards Board, 1981).

Standard & Poor's Example

One example of an analyst's adjustment for operating leases reported only in the footnotes to the financial statement is reported by Standard & Poor's *Creditstats*.[5] The adjustment process consists of six steps:

1. Annual payments for the first five years are stated in the footnotes.

2. The remaining years are computed by dividing the amount labeled "thereafter" by the year-five payment amount, rounding to the nearest year.

3. The remaining number of years calculated in step (2) is divided into the "thereafter" payments, which are assumed to be an annuity.

4. The present value of these annual lease payment amounts is discounted at the rate of 10 percent (S&P's assumption).

5. Implicit interest from operating leases is calculated by multiplying the average of the current and previous year's lease net present values by 10 percent.

6. Depreciation expense from operating leases is assumed to be the average of the first-year lease payment from the current and previous year less the implicit interest from step (4).

The present value of the operating leases is added to reported debt and assets to recalculate debt and capital ratios. The implicit interest and depreciation expenses are used to recompute interest coverage and EBIT (earnings before interest and taxes) figures. Finally, S&P reduces the selling, general, and administrative expense by the sum of the implicit interest and depreciation amounts so that there is no change in reported net income as a result of the operating lease adjustment process.

If we apply the S&P operating lease analytical model to the numbers reported by Ameritech for 1992 in Table 4.2 (and for 1991 not reported in Table 4.2), these calculations follow:

---

[5] Standard & Poor's, "Operating Lease Analytical Model," *Creditstats*, October 21, 1992.

S&P Lease Model Calculation

Year-End 1992   Year-End 1991

Year	Payment	Year	Payment
1993	$ 92.7	1992	$ 80.1
1994	78.6	1993	71.2
1995	54.8	1994	54.0
1996	46.0	1995	44.0
1997	37.3	1996	40.0
1998–2003	36.7	1997–2002	39.7
1992 NPV @ 10%	344.2	1991 NPV @ 10%	334.4

After computing the NPV of the operating leases, the implicit interest and depreciation are calculated as follows:

$$1992 \text{ Implicit interest} = \text{Average NPV} \times \text{Interest rate}$$
$$= [(344.2 + 334.4)/2)] \times 10\%$$
$$= 339.3 \times 0.10$$
$$= \$33.9$$

$$\text{Lease depreciation expense} = \text{Average 1st-year payment}$$
$$- \text{Implicit interest}$$
$$= [(92.7 + 80.1)/2] - 33.9$$
$$= 86.4 - 33.9$$
$$= \$52.5$$

Finally, selling, general, and administrative expenses are reduced by the sum of the implicit interest and depreciation, which total $86.4 million in this case.

Capitalization of the operating leases can have a large impact on various financial ratios. The direction of the impact, positive or negative, depends on several factors. Debt ratios tend to increase, interest coverage ratios tend to decrease, and profitability ratios can go up or down. The reason for the indeterminacy is that capitalization of the operating leases and the implicit interest and depreciation will influence both the numerator and denominator of the financial ratios.

Table 4.4 shows the impact of the capitalization of the operating leases for the 1992 Ameritech example and for a sample taken from Standard & Poor's. The numbers in Table 4.4 show that the impact on the financial ratios can be very different. The impact from capital-

Table 4.4: Examples of Ratios with and without Capitalization

Ratios	Without Capital	With Capital	Without Capital	With Capital
Pretax interest coverage (times)	4.7	4.3	3.9	2.3
EBITDA interest coverage (times)	8.7	8.2	5.1	3.4
Pretax return on capital (%)	11.5	11.2	23.5	17.8
Operating income to sales (%)	39.2	40.0	14.7	22.4
Free operating cash flow to total debt (%)	10.7	10.9	36.1	19.9
Funds flow to total debt (%)	34.4	33.7	43.3	27.7
Total debt to capital (%)	58.4	59.3	43.4	66.4

Note: Definition of ratios is found in Exhibit 4.1.

ization of the operating leases is minimal for Ameritech. The sample firm from S&P, however, shows a very large impact from capitalization of operating leases. For example, the debt ratio rises from 43 percent to 66 percent, and the ratio of free cash flow to total debt falls from 36 percent to 20 percent.

There may be a valid economic reason for off-balance sheet financing if the firm has a bond or loan covenant that restricts additional borrowing but does not restrict leasing. Leasing may be one way to circumvent restrictive bond covenants. It is simple, however, to correct this loophole in the bond or loan contract, and many bond indentures now place limits on leasing as well as borrowing. Finally, managers might prefer to report operating rather than capital leases because compensation or bonuses tied to accounting earnings can affect the amount of compensation received.

Special Accounting Issues

There are many special accounting issues that add to the complexity of lease accounting. Here is a list of problems that frequently confront lessee firms:

1. Residual values.
   a. Guaranteed residual value.
   b. Unguaranteed residual value.
   c. Residual value guaranteed by a third party.
2. Bargain purchase options.

Exhibit 4.1:   Definition of Key Financial Ratios

FORMULAS FOR KEY RATIOS

$$\text{Pretax interest coverage} = \frac{\text{Balances for pretax returns and coverage}}{\text{Gross interest}}$$

$$\begin{array}{l}\text{Pretax interest} \\ \text{coverage including rents}\end{array} = \frac{\text{Balances for pretax returns and coverages + Gross rents}}{\text{Gross interest + Gross rents}}$$

$$\text{EBITDA interest coverage} = \frac{\begin{array}{c}\text{Balances for pretax returns and coverages +}\\ \text{Depreciation and amortization}\end{array}}{\text{Gross interest}}$$

$$\begin{array}{l}\text{Funds from operations} \\ \text{as a \% of total debt}\end{array} = \frac{\text{Funds from operations}}{\text{Total debt}} \times 100$$

$$\begin{array}{l}\text{Free operating cash} \\ \text{flow as a \% of total debt}\end{array} = \frac{\text{Free operating cash flow}}{\text{Total debt}} \times 100$$

$$\text{Pretax return on permanent capital} = \frac{\begin{array}{c}\text{Balances for pretax}\\ \text{returns and averages}\end{array}}{\text{Permanent capital}} \times 100$$

$$\text{Operating income as a \% of sales} = \frac{\text{Operating income}}{\text{Sales}} \times 100$$

$$\begin{array}{l}\text{Long-term debt as a} \\ \text{\% of capitalization}\end{array} = \frac{\text{Long-term debt}}{\text{Long-term debt + Equity}} \times 100$$

$$\begin{array}{l}\text{Total debt as a \% of capitalization +} \\ \text{short-term debt}\end{array} = \frac{\text{Total debt}}{\text{Total debt + Equity}} \times 100$$

$$\begin{array}{l}\text{Total debt + 8 times rents} \\ \text{as a \% of capitalization +} \\ \text{short-term debt + 8 times rents}\end{array} = \frac{\begin{array}{c}\text{Total debt + 8 times}\\ \text{Gross rentals paid}\end{array}}{\begin{array}{c}\text{Total debt}\\ \text{+ 8 times}\\ \text{Gross rentals paid}\end{array}} \times 100$$

Definition of Terms:

Balances for pretax returns and coverages. Net income from continuing operations before (1) special items, (2) minority interest, and (3) gains on reacquisition of debt, plus income taxes plus interest expense.

Eight times rents. Gross rents paid multiplied by capitalization factor of eight.

Equity. Shareholders' equity (including preferred stock) plus minority interest.

Free operating cash flow. Funds from operations minus capital expenditures and minus (plus) the increase (decrease) in working capital (excluding changes in cash, marketable securities, and short-term debt).

Funds from operations. Net income from continuing operations plus depreciation, amortization, deferred income taxes, and other noncash items.

Gross interest. Gross interest incurred before subtracting (1) capitalized interest, and (2) interest income.

Gross rents. Gross operating rents paid before sublease income.

Interest expense. Interest incurred minus capitalized interest.

Long-term debt. As reported, including capitalized lease obligations on the balance sheet.

Operating income. Sales minus cost of goods manufactured (before depreciation and amortization), selling, general, and administrative, and research and development costs.

Permanent capital. Sum of (1) the average of the beginning of year and end of year current maturities, long-term debt, non-current deferred taxes, minority interest and shareholders' equity, and (2) average short-term borrowings during year per footnotes to financial statements.

Total debt. Long-term debt plus current maturities, commercial paper, and other short-term borrowings.

Source: Standard & Poor's *Creditstats,* October 21, 1992.

3. Bargain renewal options.

4. Discount rate of interest.

5. Executory costs.

6. Sale-and-leaseback.

7. Real estate leases.

8. Lease disclosure requirements.

9. Comparison of accounting and tax rules for leasing.

Residual Values

Aside from tax considerations, the main economic difference between leasing and purchase is the residual or salvage value. At the end of the lease, the asset is usually "owned" by the lessor. In economic terms, this means that the lessor can dispose of the asset as he or she sees fit. Sometimes, the lease allows the lessee to acquire the asset at maturity of the lease. The acquisition by the lessee can be "required" by a guarantee, or it can be an option held by the lessee. The accounting for residual value depends on the lease contract and its provision for residual value.

Guaranteed Residual Value

If the lessee guarantees to make up any deficiency below a stated amount in the lease contract for realization of the residual value at the end of the lease term, the stated amount is the guaranteed residual value. The guaranteed residual value affects the lessee's minimum lease payments and the amount that must be capitalized.

Again we can use the ABC Warehouse Stores example to illustrate residual value accounting. Suppose that the forklift on the five-year lease has a guaranteed residual value of $5,000. The lease payments will be adjusted to reflect the *present value* of the residual value guaranteed. The present value of the $5,000 residual value at the interest rate of 10 percent is $3,104.60.[6] The new lease payments are based on the present value, at 10 percent, of the previous lease payments less the present value of the residual value guaranteed, $37,907.87 − $3,104.60. Table 4.5 shows the new lease payment amortization schedule with the guaranteed residual value.

The new lease payments with the guaranteed residual value are $9,181.01, over $800 lower than the lease without the residual value guarantee. This reduction in payments reflects the lower risk that the lessor assumes. In return, the lessee assumes the obligation of $5,000 at the end of the lease as shown in Table 4.5.

The journal entries for this lease are the same as those for ABC's capital lease, with the new payments and interest amounts as shown in Table 4.5. The straight-line depreciation amounts for the lease are now $6,581.57 per year, based on the $5,000 residual value of the forklift.

Suppose that ABC Warehouse Stores decides to purchase the forklift at the maturity of the lease for the guaranteed residual value amount of $5,000. The journal entries will show the following:

December 31, 1998 (to record purchase of leased equipment and removal of lease liability)

Equipment	37,907.87
Accumulated Depreciation—Capital	32,907.87
Leases (6,581.57 × 5, + 0.02 for rounding)	

---

[6] This calculation is the present value of $1 in five years at 10 percent interest times the $5,000 residual value (0.6209213 × $5,000 = $3,104.60). The Appendix describes present value calculations.

Table 4.5: ABC Warehouse Stores Lease Amortization Schedule Lessee Guaranteed Residual Value of $5,000

Date	Lease Payment and Residual	Interest (10%) on Unpaid Balance	Reduction of Lease Obligation	Lease Obligation
1/1/94				$37,907.87
12/31/94	$ 9,181.01	$ 3,790.79	$ 5,390.23	$32,517.64
12/31/95	9,181.01	3,251.76	5,929.25	26,588.39
12/31/96	9,181.01	2,658.84	6,522.17	20,266.22
12/31/97	9,181.01	2,006.62	7,174.39	12,891.83
12/31/98	9,181.01	1,289.18	7,891.83	5,000.00
12/31/98	5,000.00	0.00	5,000.00	0.00
	$50,905.05	$12,997.19	$37,907.87	

Lease Liability (guaranteed residual value)	5,000.00	
Leased Asset		37,907.87
Accumulated Depreciation—Equipment		32,907.87
Cash		5,000.00

Now suppose the lessee returns the asset to the lessor, but the asset has a fair market value of $3,000 at the maturity date of the lease. ABC must report a loss of $2,000 for this transaction. The journal entries would appear as follows:

December 31, 1998 (to record removal of lease liability)

Accumulated Depreciation—Capital Leases (6,581.57 × 5, + 0.02 for rounding)	32,907.87	
Lease Liability (guaranteed residual value)	5,000.00	
Loss on Lease Contract	2,000.00	
Leased Asset		37,907.87
Cash		2,000.00

If the fair market value at maturity exceeds the guaranteed residual value, the lessor is under no obligation to make a refund to the lessee unless the contract specifies an agreement to share in such a gain.

Unguaranteed Residual Value

If the lease contract does not specify any rights to the residual value for the lessee, any residual value is retained by the lessor. The accounting entries for the lessee will be the same as for the basic capital lease. Assume the same information as the previous example, except that the $5,000 residual value is unguaranteed by the lessee. The lease payments, however, will *not* be the same ($9,181) if the economics of the situation are not ignored. In other words, although the expected residual value of $5,000 is the same, the *risk* of realizing the residual value is not the same, depending on whether the residual value is guaranteed. If it is guaranteed, it is reasonable to assume that the risk of realizing the residual value is the same as the risk of all the lease payments, and the same discount rate can be used as above (10 percent in this example). If the residual value is not guaranteed, the risk of realization is different. And this risk must be priced, in the form of higher lease payments charged to the lessee.

To illustrate the pricing of residual value risk, suppose the lessor determines 15 percent to be the proper discount rate to use on the residual value component of the lease. The present value of the residual value under this assumption is $2,485.88.[7] The new lease payments of $9,344.23 are determined by the present value, at 10 percent, of the original ($10,000) lease payments, less the present value, at 15 percent, of the (risky) residual value, $37,907.87 − $2,485.88 = $35,421.99.

Table 4.6 shows the amortization of the lease under these new assumptions. The lease payments with the residual value assumption are lower than the original $10,000 lease payments, where no residual value is assumed. Of more interest, the lease payment with the unguaranteed residual value is approximately $163 higher than the lease payment with the guaranteed residual value. But this makes sense. A rational lessor will charge for the increased residual value risk in the form of higher lease payments.

The journal entries to record the leased asset and liability, depreciation, interest, and payments are all recorded in the same way as for a capital lease, as illustrated earlier. The amounts will change

---

[7] This calculation is the present value of $1 in five years at 15 percent interest times the $5,000 residual value (0.4971767 × $5,000 = $2,485.88). Present value calculations are shown in the Appendix. The economics of residual values and determination of the proper discount rate are the topic of Chapter 8.

as reflected in Table 4.6. In addition, straight-line depreciation will be computed on the basis of a capitalized lease value of $35,421.99. The amount of depreciation is $7,084.40 per year. At the end of the lease, the lessee returns the asset to the lessor. Regardless of the fair market value of the asset, the final journal entries for the lessee to remove the asset from the books are:

December 31, 1998 (to record removal of capital lease)
Accumulated Depreciation—Capital   35,421.99
Leases (7,084.40 × 5, less 0.01 for
rounding)
    Leased Asset   35,421.99

At the end of the lease term the lease liability is zero.

Residual Value Partially Guaranteed by the Lessee

When the lessee guarantees only a part of the estimated residual value of the lease asset, the lessor must compute the periodic lease payments on both the guaranteed and unguaranteed portions of the residual value. This means that the present value of the residual value must reflect both components of risk, which may require two different discount rates. To compute the amount capitalized, the lessee must add the present value of the partially guaranteed residual value to the present value of the lease payments. (The amounts recorded by the lessee and lessor would not be the same.)

Table 4.6: ABC Warehouse Stores Lease Amortization Schedule Unguaranteed (Risky) Residual Value of $5,000

Date	Annual Lease Payment	Interest (10%) on Unpaid Balance	Reduction of Lease Obligation	Lease Obligation
1/1/94				$35,421.99
12/31/94	$ 9,344.23	$ 3,542.20	$ 5,802.03	$29,619.95
12/31/95	9,344.23	2,962.00	6,382.24	23,237.72
12/31/96	9,344.23	2,323.77	7,020.46	16,217.26
12/31/97	9,344.23	1,621.73	7,722.50	8,494.76
12/31/98	9,344.23	849.48	8,494.76	0.00
	$46,721.15	$11,299.17	$35,421.99	

Residual Value Guaranteed by a Third Party

An interesting business transaction has arisen, in part, to circumvent the accounting rules described in this chapter. The transaction involves a third-party guarantor, who guarantees the whole or part of the residual value of the leased asset for a fee, similar to an insurance premium. The lessee does not include the present value of the guaranteed residual value in the cost of the leased asset because the residual value is guaranteed by a third party. This may let the lessee classify the lease as an operating lease, something the lessee finds valuable. At the same time, the lessor can classify the same lease as a capital lease, something the lessor finds valuable. "Unwittingly, the FASB, in publishing *SFAS No. 13*, must take credit for spawning a new submarket of third-party guarantor companies whose sole function is, for a fee, to guarantee the residual values of business leases."[8]

Bargain Purchase Options

A bargain purchase option permits a lessee to purchase the leased asset at a price below the fair market value at that time, usually at the maturity of the lease, although some leases provide a schedule of purchase options for different specified dates during the life of the contract. The fixed or exercise price of the purchase option is substantially lower than the fair market value at the lease's inception so that it is reasonably assured the lessee will take advantage of the bargain. If a bargain purchase option exists, the lessee must increase the present value of the minimum lease payments by the present value of the option.

For example, the guaranteed residual value of $5,000 in the ABC Warehouse Stores example could also represent an option to buy the equipment for $5,000. To qualify as a bargain purchase option, however, the fair market value must be expected to be much larger than the fixed price. In our example, the expected future fair market might be $10,000, an amount substantially greater than the $5,000 option exercise price. If this is the case, the accounting for the bargain purchase option is the same as that for the guaranteed residual value.

---

[8] Thomas Dyckman, Roland Dukes, and Charles Davis, *Intermediate Accounting* (Homewood, IL: Irwin, 1992), p. 978.

The only difference between the accounting treatment given a bargain purchase option and a guaranteed residual value is in computation of the amount of depreciation. When there is a bargain purchase option, the lessee depreciates the leased asset over its total expected useful life rather than the lease term. For our example, suppose the economic life of the asset is seven years rather than five years. The amount of depreciation changes from $6,581.57 to $5,415.41. It is assumed that the bargain purchase option will be exercised.

If the purchase option is not exercised, the accounting entries must reflect the loss. Suppose that the lease shown in Table 4.5 reflects a bargain purchase option of $5,000. The fair market value of the asset at maturity of the lease, however, is only $3,000. The journal entries made to reflect this outcome are:

December 31, 1998 (to record the removal of a bargain purchase option not exercised)

Lease Liability	5,000.00	
Accumulated Depreciation—Capital Leases (5,415.41 × 5)	27,077.05	
Loss on Lapse of Lease Purchase Option	5,830.82	
Leased Asset		37,907.87

Bargain Renewal Options

Most leases stipulate a fixed maturity date. Some leases allow for the extension of the term of the lease and some contracts specify the amount of the payments for extending the lease. A bargain renewal option allows the lessee to renew the lease for a lease payment that is less than the expected fair market rental at the time the option is exercisable.

If the lease payments under the bargain renewal option are sufficiently discounted so that renewal is highly likely, the lease term is extended to cover the additional period. This provision applies to the capital lease accounting rules to determine whether the lease is an operating or capital lease, and to determine the term for capitalization, amortization, and depreciation. Finally, if the lease contains both a bargain renewal option and a bargain purchase option, the lease term never extends beyond the exercise date of the purchase option.

Discount Rate of Interest

I have used the ABC Warehouse Stores example to show that the choice of the discount rate to compute the present value of the lease payments or residual value is extremely important in lease accounting. As pointed out earlier, *SFAS No. 13* states that the lessee is required to compute the present value of the minimum lease payments using the lower of the lessee's incremental borrowing rate or the discount rate used by the lessor (also known as the implicit rate computed by the lessor) if known or determinable by the lessee. The lessee's incremental borrowing rate is defined by *SFAS No. 13* as "the rate that, at the inception of the lease, the lessee would have incurred to borrow the funds necessary to buy the leased asset on a secured loan with repayment terms similar to the payment schedule called for in the lease."

The lessee should use the lessor's interest rate implicit in the lease "if known or determinable by the lessee." In many instances, the "lease rate" is known by the lessee as part of the lease negotiation process. The residual value component of the lease (if *not* a guaranteed residual value by the lessee), however, depends on differing conditions for lessee and lessor.

Differing interest rate assumptions are important to lessees who want to treat a lease as an operating lease rather than a capital lease. A higher interest rate used to compute the present value of the minimum lease payments will result in a lower capitalization amount. In particular, if the capitalized lease can be kept below 90 percent of the asset cost, the lessee can treat the transaction as an operating lease, substituting rental expense for capital expenditures.

In the ABC Warehouse Stores example, suppose that the marginal borrowing rate assumed by the lessee is 13 percent rather than the previous 10 percent. The present value of the five annual lease payments of $10,000 changes significantly.

Discount Rate of Interest	Five-Year Annuity Factor	Present Value of Lease Payments	Percentage of Asset Cost ($40,000)	Type of Lease
10%	3.790787	$37,907.87	94.8%	Capital
13%	3.517231	$35,172.31	87.9%	Operating

If it assumes a discount rate of interest of 13 percent rather than 10 percent, ABC's lease changes from a capital lease to an operating lease according to criterion number 4 for capital leases (see Figure 4.1). At the same time, if the lessor uses 10 percent as the discount rate, the same lease that ABC classifies as an operating lease becomes a capital lease for the lessor.

This example helps illustrate the effects of discount rates on lease classification. Earlier I showed that lease classification can also be manipulated with assumptions about the residual value or with third-party guarantees of the residual value.

Executory Costs

Leased assets require certain expenses such as insurance, maintenance, and taxes, which are called "executory costs." If the lessor retains responsibility for the payment of these costs, a portion of each lease payment that represents executory costs should be excluded in computing the present value of the minimum lease payments. Instead, they should be reported as an expense when incurred. If executory costs are not known, they should be estimated. Many lease contracts specify that all executory costs are to be paid by the lessee. In these cases, the lease payment requires no adjustment for present value computation.

Sale-and-Leaseback

The same four criteria in Figure 4.1 apply to the treatment of the leaseback as a capital lease or as an operating lease. The accounting methodology is essentially the same as has been illustrated. There is, however, a difference because of the initial sale of the asset by the lessee to the lessor. Accounting for the sale makes the sale-and-leaseback different.

If the criteria for a capital lease are met, the gain or loss on the sale of the asset must be deferred and amortized over the term of the lease, and at the same rate as the lease asset itself is amortized. If the sale-and-leaseback is classified as an operating lease, the gain or loss is also deferred, but different terms and accounts apply. The deferred gain or loss is amortized over the lease term in proportion to the rental payments.

There are two exceptions for this gain/loss reporting. First, if the fair market value of the asset is less than the book value, a loss is recognized immediately and not deferred. The amount of the loss immediately recognized is up to the difference between the book value and the fair market value. For example, if the lessee firm has a book value for an asset of $450,000 but a fair market value of $300,000, the difference of $150,000 is accounted for as an immediate loss. For the second exception, if the sale-and-leaseback results in a present value of lease payments that are 10 percent or less than the fair market value of the asset, the transaction is called a "minor leaseback." A minor leaseback essentially is a sale, and any gain or loss is reported immediately.

To illustrate the accounting treatment for a sale-and-leaseback transaction, assume that ABC Warehouse Stores sells a warehouse to Pacific Leasing Company for $80,000. Here are some of the necessary conditions to complete the reporting of this transaction.

1. The sale-and-leaseback transaction is completed on January 1, 1994. The annual lease payments are $20,000 per year for five years, beginning on January 1, 1994 (the periodic payments are an annuity due).

2. The warehouse is carried on the lessee's books at $75,000 and has an estimated remaining economic life of ten years and no residual value. The fair market value of the warehouse is $90,000.

3. Depreciation expense is computed using the straight-line method over five years.

4. There is no transfer of ownership back to the lessee in the lease agreement, nor is there a bargain purchase option.

5. The lessor will earn 12.6 percent on the lease, which is the incremental borrowing rate of ABC Warehouse Stores.

The information as given qualifies this lease as an operating lease because none of the four criteria for capital leases is met. Alternatively, if the remaining economic life of the asset is six years, criterion number 3 for capital leases is met, so the lease qualifies as a capital lease. The journal entries are as follows, first as an operating lease and then as a capital lease:

I. Accounting for Sale-and-Leaseback as an Operating Lease
   January 1, 1994 (sale of warehouse)

Cash	80,000	
Warehouse		75,000

Unearned Gain on Sale-and-Leaseback		5,000

January 1, 1994 (to record first lease payment)

Rent Expense	20,000	
Cash		20,000

December 31, 1994 (to record amortization of gain)

Unearned Gain on Sale-and-Leaseback	1,000	
Rent Expense ($5,000 ÷ 5 years)		1,000

II. Accounting for Sale-and-Leaseback as a Capital Lease

January 1, 1994 (sale of warehouse)

Cash	80,000	
Warehouse		75,000
Unearned Gain on Sale-and-Leaseback		5,000

January 1, 1994 (to record capital lease)

Leased Asset	80,000	
Lease Liability		80,000

January 1, 1994 (to record first lease payment)

Lease Liability	20,000	
Cash		20,000

December 31, 1994 (to record amortization of gain)

Unearned Gain on Sale-and-Leaseback	1,000	
Rent Expense ($5,000 ÷ 5 years)		1,000

December 31, 1994 (to record accrued interest on lease liability)

Interest Expense (from amortization schedule)	7,560	
Lease Liability		7,560

December 31, 1994 (to record depreciation expense)

Depreciation Expense—Capital Leases	16,000	
Accumulated Depreciation—Capital Leases ($80,000 ÷ 5 years)		16,000

Real Estate Leases

Special accounting rules apply to leases that involve real estate. There are three categories for such leases: (1) leases for land only,

(2) leases that include both land and building, and (3) leases that involve real estate and equipment.

Land.

A lease involving only land is classified as an operating lease unless criterion 1, transfer of ownership, or criterion 2, a bargain purchase option, exists. If criterion 1 or 2 is met, the lessee classifies the lease as a capital lease. No depreciation, however, is taken on land because land normally does not depreciate.

Land and Building.

If a lease involves both land and building, and criterion 1 or 2 is satisfied, the land and the building should be classified separately as operating or capital by the lessee. The present value of the minimum lease payments is allocated between the land and buildings according to their fair market values at the inception of the lease.

If both land and building are involved and criterion 3 (75 percent of economic life) or criterion 4 (90 percent of the asset's value) is met, the accounting treatment depends on the proportion of the lease represented by the land. If the land is less than 25 percent of the total fair market value of the property, the land and building are considered a single unit.[9] In this case, the lease is a capital lease, and the land and the building are amortized together. If the land represents 25 percent or more of the total fair market value, the lessee accounts for the land as an operating lease and the building as a capital lease. If none of the four criteria is met, the lessee uses the operating method for the total lease.

Equipment and Real Estate.

Some real estate leases include equipment along with buildings and land. In these cases, the fair market value of the equipment should be estimated and separated from the rest of the lease. Criterion 4 should be used to classify the equipment. The real estate should be subject to the rules outlined above.

---

[9] The 25 percent criterion is an arbitrary rule adopted by the FASB because separating land and building can be very difficult.

Lease Disclosure Requirements

SFAS No. 13 requires specific disclosure for both capital and operating leases in the financial statements or the accompanying notes. The disclosures required by the lessee are:

1. For capital leases:
   a. The gross amount of assets recorded under capital leases presented by nature or function.
   b. Future minimum lease payments in the aggregate and for each of the five succeeding fiscal years. Separate deductions for executory costs included in the minimum lease payments and the amount of the imputed interest necessary to reduce the net minimum lease payments to present value.
   c. Total non-cancelable minimum sublease rentals to be received in the future.
   d. Total contingent rentals.
   e. Assets recorded under capital leases and the accumulated amortization, obligations under capital leases, and depreciation on capitalized leased assets should all be identified separately in the lessee's balance sheet or footnotes.

2. For operating leases having initial or remaining non-cancelable lease terms in excess of one year:
   a. Future minimum rental payments required in the aggregate and for each of the five succeeding fiscal years.
   b. Total minimum rentals to be received in the future under non-cancelable subleases.

3. For all operating leases, rental expense for each period with separate amounts for minimum rentals, contingent rentals, and sublease rentals.

4. A general description of the lessee's arrangements including, but not limited to:
   a. The basis on which contingent rental payments are determined.
   b. The existence and terms of renewal or purchase options and escalation clauses.
   c. Restriction imposed by lease agreements, such as those concerning dividends, additional debt, and further leasing.

Comparison of Accounting and Tax Rules for Leasing

There is an interesting comparison to be made between the accounting rules for capital leases and the tax rules or guidelines covered in Chapter 3. The four criteria that define a capital lease in most cases will *not* qualify the lease as a *true lease* for tax purposes. Consider the four accounting criteria for a capital lease as discussed at the beginning of the chapter:

1. **Transfer of Ownership.** Any transfer of ownership prior to the maturity of the lease will not qualify as a *true lease* for tax purposes. This violates guideline 1 for minimum at-risk requirement on the part of the lessor (see Chapter 3).

2. **Bargain Purchase Option.** There can be no bargain purchase option for a lease to qualify as a *true lease,* which is guideline 4 from Chapter 3.

3. **Seventy-five Percent of Economic Life.** For the economic life criterion, there is a slight difference between the accounting rule and the tax rule. The tax rule requires a remaining economic life for the asset at the end of the lease of at least one year or 20 percent of the originally estimated life, guideline 3. The accounting rule is slightly more liberal than the tax rule. Nevertheless, the concept of "economic life" leaves a great deal of room for subjective assumptions.

4. **Ninety Percent of Asset's Value.** Guideline 2 for tax-deductible lease payments requires that the lessor maintain a minimum of 20 percent of the asset's cost throughout the life of the lease. Therefore, if a lease qualifies as a capital lease under criterion 4, it would not qualify as a *true lease.*

Most capital leases would not qualify as tax-deductible under IRS law and guidelines. It is common practice, however, for a firm to keep separate financial statements for financial reporting and tax reporting. Therefore, it is possible that a capital lease qualifies as a *true lease* if different assumptions are applied under financial accounting as opposed to tax accounting. As this chapter shows, it is fairly easy to make different assumptions about the economic life of the asset, the discount rate of interest, and residual value and residual value guarantees. Finally, lessees may want a lease to qualify as an operating lease, because the case before the IRS is stronger. That is, an operating lease is closer to a *true lease* for tax purposes than a capital lease.

Summary

This chapter describes the basic accounting rules for leasing that businesses are required to follow. I first establish the rules for categorizing leases as capital or operating leases. Next, I demonstrate the impact on key accounting ratios from lease classification. To show the adjustments that financial analysts make to financial statements in order to account for operating leases, I discuss Standard & Poor's operating lease analytical model.

Several special problems and qualifications for lease accounting are considered. Special cases include the accounting for residual values, bargain purchase options, bargain renewal options, executory costs, sale-and-leaseback transactions, and real estate leases. Special problems or opportunities, depending on your point of view, concern the discount rate assumptions to compute the present value of lease payments, residual value assumptions, and the economic life of the asset assumptions. These factors can swing the qualification of a lease from capital to operating. This chapter also describes the lease disclosure requirements according to generally accepted accounting principles (GAAP) and compares the requirements under accounting rules and tax rules.

Chapter 5

The Concept of the Equivalent Loan

*T*here is, without question, great similarity between debt and lease contracts. Lease contracts, especially financial leases, commit the lessee to a series of fixed payments as does a loan contract. In the case of default, the lessor can repossess the asset, sell or release it, and sue the lessee for any deficiencies—like any other creditor. So the real question is not whether a lease is equivalent to debt, but rather, "How much debt is equivalent to leasing?" Another way to state the question is, "Is leasing really 100 percent financing?" as advertised by leasing companies.

The Equivalent Loan

The fundamental difference between leasing and borrowing to purchase an asset, excluding the tax aspects, concerns the residual value. If all payments are made on a loan contract, the asset belongs to the borrower. If all payments are made on a typical lease contract, the asset belongs to the lessor. This fundamental difference between borrowing and leasing makes the comparison between the two complex. In order to make the comparison more direct and to make life simpler, we avoid the salvage value question altogether. In fact, almost all the literature in this area makes the same assumption. (I return to the salvage value issue in greater detail in Chapter 8.) I also assume the lease is a *net lease* and does not include maintenance of the asset. Adding maintenance expense is more complicated and does not add anything to our understanding of leasing and borrowing.

The comparison of leasing to borrowing is the foundation of the popular leasing model by Myers, Dill, and Bautista (MDB).[1] The presentation here is based on their model.

The question that needs to be answered concerns the amount of debt that is equivalent to the lease. There are many ways one can address this question. One approach is to base the analysis on borrowing the total cost of the asset. Another good approach is to use the same debt-to-equity ratio that the firm uses to finance its existing assets. Perhaps the best approach is to determine a schedule of loan payments that exactly match the set of cash flows from the lease. This is the approach that I take.

The answer to the question "How much debt is equivalent to the lease?" prompts yet another question: "What are the costs that result from the lease?" The answer to this question is fairly straightforward. The periodic costs resulting from leasing are the lease payments. But don't forget taxes! So the periodic cash flows from leasing are the *after-tax* lease payments. There is, however, a significant opportunity cost that must be taken into account. If an asset is leased, the depreciation tax shield is relinquished. To summarize, the periodic costs resulting from leasing (the cost of leasing) are both the after-tax lease payments and the loss of the depreciation tax shield.

Single Lease Payment

For a single lease payment, the concept can be represented using the following notation:

COL = *Cost of leasing*
L = *Lease payment*
T = *Tax rate*
D = *Depreciation*

$$COL = L - L \times T + D \times T = L - L(T) + D(T)$$
$$= L(1 - T) + D(T)$$

Notice that the term $(1 - T)$ acts to reduce the lease payment by subtracting the tax deduction of the lease payment or $L(1 - T) = L - L(T)$. Similarly, the term $D(T)$ represents the tax shield from depreciation. Remember that a one-dollar increase in

---

[1] Stewart C. Myers, David A. Dill, and Alberto J. Bautista, "Valuation of Financial Lease Contracts," *Journal of Finance*, v. 31 (3), 1976, pp. 799–819.

an expense item reduces your taxable income by one dollar. If the tax rate, T, is 34 percent, a one-dollar decrease in taxable income reduces your taxes by $0.34. Because depreciation expense does not represent any cash flow (no check is written for depreciation), the additional one dollar of depreciation creates a $0.34 tax shield, or the amount of depreciation times the tax rate.

As a simple example, consider a lease payment of $1,000, depreciation of $900, and a tax rate of 35 percent. Then the (after-tax) cost of leasing is $965 or:

$$COL = \$1,000(1 - 0.35) + \$900(0.35)$$
$$= \$965$$

What is the cost of borrowing? It is the amount of the loan, repaid, plus interest. Again, don't forget taxes! Because the interest payment is tax-deductible, there is the tax shield of interest to consider. In symbols, we have the following:

$COB = $ *Cost of borrowing*
$B = $ *Amount borrowed*
$I = $ *Amount of interest*
$T = $ *Tax rate*
$r_B = $ *Interest rate on loan*

$$COB = B + I - I \times T$$
$$= B + I(1 - T)$$
$$= B + r_B B(1 - T)$$
$$= B[1 + r_B(1 - T)]$$

The cost of borrowing is the repayment of the loan amount and the *after-tax* interest expense. Note that the amount of interest is simply the interest rate times the amount borrowed, $I = r_B \times B$.

We can now define the equivalent loan. **The equivalent loan is the amount of borrowing that equates the cost of borrowing to the cost of leasing.** In other words, set the cost of borrowing equal to the cost of leasing and solve for the amount of borrowing. In symbols:

$$COL = L(1 - T) + D(T)$$
$$COB = B[1 + r_B(1 - T)]$$

Then:

$$COB = COL$$
$$B[1 + r_B(1 - T)] = L(1 - T) + D(T)$$
$$B = \frac{L(1 - T) + D(T)}{[1 + r_B(1 - T)]}$$

B is the amount of the equivalent loan.

In the simple example of a $1,000 lease payment and $900 depreciation, the equivalent loan is $906 if the interest rate is 10 percent and the tax rate is 35 percent:

$$B = \frac{\$1,000(1 - 0.35) + \$900(0.35)}{[1 + 0.10(1 - 0.35)]}$$
$$= \$906.10$$

Multiple Lease Payments

Now that we have examined the case of a single lease payment, we consider a more complicated case of several lease payments. Suppose the lease payments are $10,000 per year for five years. The cost of the asset is $40,000. The depreciation schedule is assumed to be a three-year recovery period, modified accelerated cost recovery system, producing the calculation:

	Year 0	Year 1	Year 2	Year 3	Year 4	Year 5
Percentage		33.33	44.45	14.81	7.41	0.00
Depreciation		$13,332	$17,780	$5,924	$2,964	$0

Table 5.1 shows the computation of the cost of leasing for this example. The lease payments and the tax deduction for the lease payment are shown in the first two rows of the table. The tax shield for depreciation is shown in the third row. This is computed as the amount of depreciation, as shown in the depreciation schedule, times the tax rate, assumed to be 35 percent. So for example, the first year of the depreciation tax shield is computed as follows:

Year 1 Depreciation $= \$13,332(0.35) = \$4,666.20$
(tax shield)

The cost of leasing is illustrated in the fourth row of Table 5.1. Now we undertake the task of computing the equivalent loan amount and loan amortization table. To derive the equivalent loan schedule, we "begin" at the end. At the end of five years, the remaining loan balance is zero. Stepping back one period to the end of the fourth year, we employ the simple equivalent loan calculation for the one-payment lease and add the end-of-year balance or:

$$B_4 = \frac{L(1 - T) + D(T) + B_5}{[1 + r_B(1 - T)]}$$

$$= \frac{\$6,500.00}{[1 + 0.10(1 - 0.35)]}$$

$$= \frac{\$6,500.00}{1.065} = \$6,103.29$$

Because $B_5 = 0$, $B_4 = \$6,103.29$ is the amount of the equivalent loan or the balance remaining at the end of the fourth year. Stepping back in time to the end of the third year, the equivalent loan balance is:

$$B_3 = \frac{L(1 - T) + D(T) + B_4}{[1 + r_B(1 - T)]}$$

$$= \frac{\$7,537.40 + \$6,103.29}{[1 + 0.01(1 - 0.35)]}$$

$$= \frac{\$13,640.69}{1.065} = \$12,808.16$$

In a similar fashion, we can compute B_2 and B_1. Finally, at the present time or year 0, the total equivalent loan is:

$$B_0 = \frac{L(1 - T) + D(T) + B_1}{[1 + r_B(1 - T)]}$$

$$= \frac{\$11,166.20 + \$30,797.73}{[1 + 0.10(1 - 0.35)]}$$

$$= \frac{\$41,963.93}{1.065} = \$39,402.75$$

Table 5.1: Five-Year Lease Example and Equivalent Loan

Item	Year 0	Year 1	Year 2	Year 3	Year 4	Year 5
Lease Payment		$10,000.00	$10,000.00	$10,000.00	$10,000.00	$10,000.00
Tax Deduction		(3,500.00)	(3,500.00)	(3,500.00)	(3,500.00)	(3,500.00)
Depreciation (tax shield)		4,666.20	6,223.00	2,073.40	1,037.40	0.00
Cost of Leasing		$11,166.20	$12,723.00	$8,573.40	$7,537.40	$6,500.00
Equivalent Loan	$39,402.75			Amortization Schedule		
Payment		$11,166.20	$12,723.00	$8,573.40	$7,537.40	$6,500.00
Interest		3,940.27	3,079.77	2,007.66	1,280.82	610.33
Tax Deduction		(1,379.10)	(1,077.92)	(702.68)	(448.29)	(213.62)
Principal		8,605.02	10,721.15	7,268.42	6,704.87	6,103.29
Loan Balance	$39,402.75	$30,797.73	$20,076.58	$12,808.16	$6,103.29	$0.00

This means that the total equivalent loan has a value of approximately $39,403 at year 0. That is, the present value of the equivalent loan is $39,403. We can also describe this number as the *exact* amount of borrowing that is equivalent to the lease.

The presentation of the equivalent loan is the heart of the Myers, Dill, and Bautista model. The only requirements for calculation of the equivalent loan are a schedule of lease payments and depreciation, a tax rate, and a cost of borrowing. All these numbers are easy to obtain, although the actual calculation of the equivalent loan amortization schedule is somewhat complicated. The amortization schedule, however, is not necessary to obtain the exact same solution. That is, the cost of leasing row in Table 5.1, discounted at the after-tax cost of debt interest rate, results in the same equivalent loan balance as the amortization schedule. This result is used in the NPV model to be presented in Chapter 6.

Debt and Leases as Substitutes

It is worth noting some important assumptions inherent in the MDB model. First and foremost, "the firm regards lease payments as contractual obligations, equivalent to interest and principal payments on the firm's debt."[2] This is the first point I made in this chapter. The MDB model also assumes that the firm has a certain "debt capacity." Because interest payments are tax-deductible, borrowing is valuable up to the "debt capacity." While the MDB model does not specify the limits of debt, most financial managers would agree that the firm reaches its debt limitation or "debt capacity" when the potential costs of financial distress and bankruptcy outweigh the tax benefits of debt. The MDB model also assumes that the firm borrows "100 percent of the value of the tax shields generated by interest, depreciation and lease payments."[3]

The complete MDB model, which is developed in Chapter 6, is used to compare leasing and borrowing by determining whether debt or leasing "uses up" less debt capacity. If leasing uses up less debt capacity than borrowing, leasing is the preferred financing alternative. Alternatively, if borrowing is cheaper and uses up less

---

[2] *Ibid.*, p. 804.

[3] *Ibid.* MDB also allow for the possibility that the firm borrows less than 100 percent of the lease payments and the various tax shields created by leasing. This extension of the model has produced few practical applications and has helped create much controversy about the substitution of debt and leases.

debt capacity, borrowing is preferred to leasing. The important point of this analysis is that leasing and debt are substitutes. This means that the firm chooses one financing method or the other. More leasing means less debt and more debt means less leasing.

Are Debt and Leases Substitutes?

The notion that leasing is a substitute for debt financing is widely accepted in academic finance. The MDB model assumes that lease payments, which are fixed obligations like other loans, displace debt and reduce debt capacity. The intuition is straightforward. If one assumes that firms have an optimal debt-equity ratio, to the extent that leasing represents off-balance sheet financing, it reduces debt capacity. This logic has become ingrained in the finance literature. For example, Ross, Westerfield, and Jaffe state: "If a firm leases, it will not use as much debt as it would otherwise. The benefits of debt capacity will be lost, particularly the lower taxes associated with interest expense."[4] For another example, Brigham and Gapenski state: "Therefore, leasing is not likely to permit a firm to use more financial leverage than could be obtained with conventional debt."[5] A drawback of these models is that they fail to consider the interaction between leasing and the firm's choice of an optimal capital structure.

The Lewis and Schallheim (LS) model provides new insights into the debt and leasing choice.[6] First, because the optimal leasing and capital structure decision is determined endogenously, the model does *not assume* that debt and leases are substitutes. This is important because the theory demonstrates that the relation between debt and leases can be complementary. That is, a lessee firm optimally uses more debt with leasing than it would if it restricted itself to debt alone. Second, even though the marginal tax rate is assumed to be the same for the lessor and the lessee, the lessee firm can derive a benefit from leasing.[7] This result contrasts with most existing models, including

---

[4] See Stephen A. Ross, Randolph W. Westerfield, and Jeffrey F. Jaffee, *Corporate Finance* (Homewood, IL: Irwin, 1990), p. 632.

[5] See Eugene F. Brigham and Louis C. Gapenski, *Financial Management Theory and Practice* (Chicago: The Dryden Press, 1991).

[6] Craig Lewis and James Schallheim, "Are Debt and Leases Substitutes?" *Journal of Financial and Quantitative Analysis*, December 1992, pp. 497–511.

[7] These statements are a little misleading. The LS model does not assume a single marginal tax rate for the lessee/lessor. Because the model assumes *uncertainty* about future earnings, the lessee/lessor may be in a zero tax position if earnings are low.

the MDB model, where the only time leasing provides an advantage is when the marginal tax rates differ for the lessor and lessee.

A Theory of Optimal Capital Structure

The MDB model assumes that the firm has a certain undefined debt capacity. Usually, we imagine that the potential costs of financial distress and bankruptcy help determine the limits of borrowing. Debt capacity, then, is the maximum amount that lenders are willing to lend to the firm. The MDB model would be more complete if debt capacity were defined in the model. Unfortunately, the literature has not definitively determined optimal amounts of debt.

Franco Modigliani and Merton Miller (MM), two Nobel Prize laureates in economics, developed a path-breaking theory in the 1950s that revolutionized modern finance. Their theory, now called the "MM Theory," demonstrates that the amount of debt or the capital structure of the firm is *irrelevant* to the total value of the firm.[8] The MM Theory is developed under the assumption of perfect capital markets.[9] In order for financing to matter, the perfect capital market assumptions must be violated.

Taxes are the obvious violation of perfect capital market assumptions. The corporate tax code provides a strong preference for debt financing because interest payments are tax-deductible, while payments to equity are not. As Merton Miller points out in subsequent work, however, the tax code for individuals penalizes interest income over equity income. (While dividends and capital gains have not carried a tax preference since the 1986 TRA, *unrealized* capital gains are not taxed at all.) Miller argues that the tax disadvantage of interest income to the investor is just enough to offset the tax advantage of debt to the firm.[10]

It is interesting to note that Miller's theory of debt and taxes originated from his work on leasing. In his examination of lease contracts, Miller suggested that lease payments must be "grossed

---

[8] Franco Modigliani and Merton H. Miller, "The Cost of Capital, Corporation Finance, and the Theory of Investment," *American Economic Review*, 48 (1958), pp. 261–297.

[9] In Chapter 1, I defined perfect capital markets as satisfying the idealized conditions: (1) no taxes; (2) no transaction costs, flotation costs, contracting costs, or brokerage fees; and (3) no single investor or firm can affect the market price of a security by trading in that security.

[10] Merton Miller and Robert Merton, "Debt and Taxes," *Journal of Finance*, 32 (1977), pp. 261–275.

up" (raised) in order to cover the taxes that the lessor owes on rental income. This insight carries over to the debt market. Investors (lenders) in the debt market must pay taxes on interest income. Thus, interest payments must be grossed up to compensate investors for their tax liabilities.

DeAngelo and Masulis add yet another ingredient to the tax-based capital structure story.[11] They suggest that non-debt tax shields, namely, depreciation, mitigate the tax advantage of debt at the firm level. Non-debt tax shields can substitute for debt tax shields so that the firm will borrow less in the presence of these non-debt tax shields.

Simple Numerical Examples

The DeAngelo and Masulis theory can be explained using a simple example. The approach hinges on the potential loss of tax shields when the earnings of the firm are low. Therefore, we must consider *uncertainty* of future earnings to explain the model. We assume that there are two future outcomes or states for the economy, boom or bust, with uncertainty about which state will occur. Our firm will earn $100 if the boom occurs and $50 if the bust does. The probability that the economy will boom or bust is 50 percent for each state. The corporate tax rate is the usual 35 percent. The individual tax rate is 28 percent on interest income. The individual tax rate on equity income is zero because no gain need be realized (if funds are needed, capital gains can be pledged for borrowing). We also assume that the firm has depreciation deductions worth $40. The net income and cash flow calculations for both states of the world are:

Example 1

	Boom	Bust
Earnings	$100	$50
Depreciation	(40)	(40)
Earnings before Tax	60	10
Taxes	(21)	(3.5)
Net Income	$ 39	$ 6.5
Add: Depreciation	40	40
Cash Flow	$ 79	$46.5

---

[11] Harry DeAngelo and Ronald Masulis, "Optimal Capital Structure Under Corporate and Personal Taxation," *Journal of Financial Economics*, 8 (March 1980), pp. 3–30.

According to these calculations, the total value of the firm is 50 percent of the cash flows if the boom occurs, plus 50 percent of the cash flows if the bust occurs, or:

$$Total\ value\ =\ 0.5 \times \$79 + 0.5 \times \$46.5$$

$$=\ \$62.75$$

This is an all-equity financing policy that leads to a total firm value of \$62.75.[12] Let's see what happens to total firm value if we add some debt to the capital structure of the firm. Suppose the firm makes a tax-deductible debt payment of \$10. The income and cash flow calculations now appear as:

Example 2

	Boom	Bust
Earnings	$100	$50
Depreciation	(40)	(40)
Debt	(10)	(10)
Earnings before Tax	50	0
Taxes	17.5	0
Net Income	$ 32.5	$ 0
Add: Depreciation	40	40
Cash Flow	$ 72.5	$40

Now the total value of the firm is the combination of the cash flows to equity and to debt. The cash flows to equity are shown above. The cash flow to debt is \$10 (in both boom and bust). Unlike equity, however, the debt is taxed at the *individual* level. Since the individual tax rate is 28 percent, the value of the debt will be \$10 less the tax on debt, \$10 − 0.28 × \$10 = \$10(1 − 0.28) = \$7.20. According to these calculations, the total value of the firm with the \$10 debt is:

$$Total\ value\ =\ Equity\ value + Debt\ value$$

$$=\ (0.5 \times \$72.5 + 0.5 \times \$40)$$

$$+\ [0.5 \times \$10(1 - 0.28)$$

---

[12] The simple valuation technique used in this state-of-the-world example assumes a zero interest rate and risk neutrality (no risk premium). Also, the firm pays no dividends, so personal taxes on equity income can be ignored.

$$+ 0.5 \times \$10(1 - 0.28)]$$

$$= \$56.25 + \$7.2$$

$$= \$63.45$$

The addition of $10 of debt now leads to a total firm value of $63.45, which is greater than the all-equity financed firm value of $62.75.

For a third example, suppose the firm wishes to finance with more debt, say, $20. The cash flow calculation is now:

Example 3

	Boom	Bust
Earnings	$100	$50
Depreciation	(40)	(40)
Debt	(20)	(20)
Earnings before Tax	40	(10)
Taxes	(14)	0
Net Income	$ 26	($10)
Add: Depreciation	40	40
Cash Flow	$ 66	$30

The total firm value with $20 of debt is:

$$Total\ value\ =\ Equity\ value\ +\ Debt\ value$$

$$= (0.5 \times \$66 + 0.5 \times \$30)$$

$$+ [0.5 \times \$20(1 - 0.28)$$

$$+ 0.5 \times \$20(1 - 0.28)]$$

$$= \$48 + \$14.4$$

$$= \$62.40$$

The use of $20 of debt now leads to a total firm value of $62.40, which is *lower* than the firm value with $10 of debt ($63.45) and, in fact, lower than the firm value with all-equity financing ($62.75).

These examples illustrate the DeAngelo and Masulis theory of optimal capital structure. Debt has a tax advantage to the firm, but a tax disadvantage to the investors. Depreciation also creates a tax shield for the firm. When earnings are low and debt is high, however, the debt and depreciation tax shields become *redundant*. Because the debt is paid first (no payment is made for depreciation), the investors are paying taxes on debt but the firm is not gaining any tax advantage from the debt. In example 3, the firm has income of only $50 in a bust state of the economy, but $60 worth of tax shields ($40 for depreciation and $20 for debt). So $10 worth of tax shields is lost.[13] The optimal level of debt for the firm as illustrated in examples 1, 2, and 3 is $10, which maximizes the firm value at $63.70.

The DeAngelo and Masulis theory of optimal capital structure depends only on the market imperfection of taxes, both corporate and personal, and on the existence of non-debt tax shields such as depreciation. The theory does not depend on the costs of financial distress or bankruptcy. The existence of financial distress costs, however, causes the firm to borrow even less.

The Lewis and Schallheim Model

While existing leasing models assume that debt and leases are substitutes, the LS model assumes the substitution is between debt and non-debt tax shields, as does the capital structure model of DeAngelo and Masulis.[14] This implies that a firm makes an optimal capital structure choice by trading off the tax benefits of debt financing against the costs associated with its potential redundancy relative to other tax shields (e.g., depreciation expense).

The LS model also assumes that leasing offers the opportunity to transfer or "sell" non-debt tax shields. If the lessee firm can locate a buyer (the lessor) that has a higher probability of using these tax deductions, this buyer will pay more for them than they are worth to the lessee. The lessor "buys" these tax shields by reducing the lease payment. This second assumption, which is consistent with the IRS's tax treatment of financial leases, motivates firms to lease.

The sale of non-debt tax deductions is the key observation for our argument that debt and leases can be complements. As non-debt tax deductions are sold, their potential redundancy with debt deductions is reduced, and the marginal value of debt becomes positive. The lessee responds to this incentive by issuing additional debt. Thus, there is a positive relation between debt and leases.

---

[13] One could argue that tax shields can be carried back or carried forward as allowed by the tax code. Yet many firms cannot carry back tax shields for an instant refund. Carry forwards have the disadvantage of waiting until the future for the tax credit.

[14] Lewis and Schallheim, "Are Debt and Leases Substitutes?"

Simple Numerical Examples of the Model

The simple numerical example used to illustrate the DeAngelo and Masulis model results in an optimal debt level of $10 and an optimal firm value of $63.45. Now we introduce leasing. Leases have a priority claim to cash flows relative to debt, which, in turn, has a priority claim to cash flows relative to equity. However, in order to show the firm's cash flow with leasing, an optimal lease payment is required. Given a competitive leasing market, the optimal lease payment is defined as the lease payment that results in a zero net present value for the lessor. The lease payments illustrated below are derived from this leasing market equilibrium, assuming perfectly competitive markets.

Suppose the firm decides to lease 50 percent of the assets and purchase the remainder. The lease payment is $27. The firm will retain one-half of the depreciation, or $20. The optimal amount of debt is $3 (explained below). Then the cash flow calculation is:

Example 4

	Boom	Bust
Earnings	$100	$50
Depreciation	(20)	(20)
Debt	(3)	(3)
Lease	(27)	(27)
Earnings before Tax	50	0
Taxes	17.5	0
Net Income	$32.5	0
Add: Depreciation	20	20
Cash Flow	$52.5	$20

The total firm value with 50 percent leasing is:

$$
\begin{aligned}
Total\ value\ &=\ Equity\ value + Debt\ value + Lease\ value \\
&=\ (0.5 \times \$52.5 + 0.5 \times \$20) + \$3(1 - 0.28) + \$25 \\
&=\ \$36.25 + \$2.2 + \$25 \\
&=\ \$63.45
\end{aligned}
$$

The value of the lease payment is $25. This value is determined by noting that the lessor company will have income of $27 in both boom and bust. After subtracting the $20 depreciation deduction, this leaves $7. The lessor will optimally shelter the $7 from taxes by borrowing. But the lender will pay personal taxes on the $7 of debt that equals $2. This personal tax from the lenders to the leasing company reduces the value of the lease payment from $27 to $25. Finally, the limit of borrowing for the lessee firm is $3 because that amount drives the tax bill to zero if a bust occurs.

The total value of the firm with the 50 percent leasing alternative is $63.45, which is exactly the same value under the DeAngelo and Masulis theory. Leasing neither helps nor hurts the firm in this case. Leasing is a zero net present value transaction.

What happens if the firm leases all of the assets? The lease payment is now $58.50. But the optimal amount of debt for the lessee firm is now $41.50. The cash flow calculation is:

Example 5

	Boom	Bust
Earnings	$100	$50
Depreciation	(0)	(0)
Debt	(41.5)	(41.5)
Lease	(58.5)	(58.5)
Earnings before Tax	0	(50)
Taxes	0	0
Net Income	$ 0	(50)
Add: Depreciation	0	0
Cash Flow	$ 0	$ 0

The cash flow to equity is zero (what this means will become clear below). However, consider the total firm value with 100 percent leasing:

$$Total\ value\ =\ Equity\ value\ +\ Debt\ value\ +\ Lease\ value$$
$$=\ \$0\ +\ [0.5 \times \$41.5(1 - 0.28) + 0.5 \times \$0]$$
$$+\ [0.5 \times (\$58.5 - \$8.5(0.35) - \$10(0.28))$$
$$+\ 0.5 \times (\$50 - \$10(0.28))]$$
$$=\ \$0 + \$14.9 + \$49.96$$
$$=\ \$64.86$$

The total value of the firm in example 5 has increased to $64.86, the highest value possible under the tax regime presented here. This has been accomplished by 100 percent leasing of the assets and borrowing the remainder of the value of the firm. The equilibrium lease payment of $58.50 cannot be fully paid if there is a bust. This does not present a problem if we assume no bankruptcy costs, which is one of our perfect capital market assumptions.

Furthermore, the lease payment of $58.50 in boom, but only $50.00 in bust, will be properly valued in the leasing market. The value is $49.96, which assumes the lessor borrows an optimal amount of $10 to reduce the tax bill to zero if a bust occurs ($50 less $40 depreciation less $10 debt). If boom occurs, the lessor will pay a tax of 35 percent on $8.50 ($58.50 − $40 − $10). The lenders to the leasing company will pay $2.80 in personal taxes. Thus the value of the lease is $52.725 ($58.50 − $8.50(0.35) − $10(.28)) in boom and $47.20 ($50 − $10(0.28)) in bust for a combined value of $49.96 when each is weighted by a 50 percent chance of occurrence [$52.725(0.5) + $47.20(0.5)].

The firm will borrow $41.50 in order to drive the tax rate to zero in boom. Of course, the firm will be unable to pay any of the debt and only part of the lease payment in bust. In other words, the firm is bankrupt if the economy is in bust. Given the assumption of no costs of financial distress or bankruptcy, the fact that the lender receives nothing in bust is not a problem. The debt is priced so that there is a 50 percent chance of receiving $41.50 less the personal taxes that the lender must pay. The debt value is $14.90 (0.5 × $41.50(1 − 0.28)). In other words, a lender is willing to pay $14.90 today in order to receive a 50 percent chance of receiving $41.50 in the future.

Finally, given these values of debt and leases, why is the value of equity zero? Rest assured, the holders of equity are not slighted. Recall from example 1 that the all-equity financed firm is worth $62.75. The equity holders can turn around and sell the firm to the lessor and lender for $49.96 and $14.90, respectively, or a total of $64.86 as just derived. This transaction results in an immediate profit of $2.11 (64.86 − 62.75), which belongs to the equity holders (not a bad deal!).

A summary of the results of the numerical examples is presented in Table 5.2.

A firm that is totally financed by debt and leasing cannot exist. The costs of financial distress and bankruptcy, as well as the Internal

Table 5.2: Summary of the Numerical Examples

Proportion of Asset Leased	Lease Payment	Amount of Debt	Value of Firm	The Ratio of Debt and Leases to Value of Firm
0%	$ 0	$10	$63.45	0.16
50	27	3	63.45	0.47
100	58.5	41.5	64.86	1.00

Revenue Service, do not allow this limit to be reached, although the recent developments in leveraged buyouts (LBOs) have caused some firms to push toward the 100 percent debt limit. The point of this exercise is not to encourage firms to use as much debt and lease financing as possible, but rather, to demonstrate three main points:

1. Firm value can be maximized with a combination of debt and lease financing.

2. Leasing can be advantageous in perfectly competitive markets when both lessee and lessor have identical marginal tax rates.

3. The interaction of debt and leasing can induce the lessee firm to increase the optimal amount of debt relative to the no leasing option.

That is, debt and leases can be complements.

Empirical Evidence

The theoretical results of the LS model are particularly important when viewed in the context of empirical evidence that demonstrates a positive association between leasing and debt. Ang and Peterson argue that debt and leases appear to be complements.[15] Evidence by Bowman also demonstrates a positive correlation between relative

---

[15] James Ang and Pamela P. Peterson, "The Leasing Puzzle," *Journal of Finance*, v. 39 (4), 1984, pp. 1055–1065.

levels of debt and leases.[16] A drawback of these studies is that they document only a cross-sectional relationship, and thus, the findings may merely demonstrate that firms with high external financing requirements use debt and leasing interchangeably. Hence, the observed relationship cannot be used to reject the hypothesis that debt and leases are substitutes. Nonetheless, the results of these studies raise the possibility that debt and leases are used as complements.

Other empirical studies support the model of debt and leasing as substitutes. Marston and Harris use a time series analysis of changes in debt and leasing ratios.[17] For the period 1976–1982, Marston and Harris find that leasing and debt are substitutes, although less than dollar-for-dollar substitutes. Bayless and Diltz find similar results using a survey technique in which they ask banks to indicate the maximum amount of lending they would provide to a hypothetical firm.[18] From this data, Bayless and Diltz measure the unused debt capacity of the firm and the percentage of debt displacement from leasing. Their results also lead to the conclusion that leasing and debt are substitutes. It is not clear, however, if the substitution is more or less than dollar for dollar. Finally, Mukherjee surveyed *Fortune* 500 firms to ask about their leasing activities and form of analysis.[19] About 47 percent (38 firms in the sample) of the firms responding view leasing as a substitute for debt, and 22 percent view leasing as a complement to debt, while 31 percent believe that debt and leases are independent decisions. Nevertheless, almost all of the respondents use models that are based on the assumption that debt and leases are substitutes, such as the MDB model presented in this chapter.

This brief survey of the empirical literature demonstrates the disagreement over the assumption that debt and leases are substitutes, although the assumption is used in all the leasing models. As a working assumption, it is probably not a bad place to start. After making model calculations, one can include other factors in the decision process.

---

[16] Robert G. Bowman, "The Debt Equivalence Of Leases: An Empirical Investigation," *The Accounting Review*, v. 55 (2), 1980, 237–253.

[17] Felicia Marston and Robert S. Harris, "Substitutability of Leases and Debt in Corporate Capital Structures," *Journal of Accounting, Auditing and Finance*, New Series, v. 3 (2), 1988, pp. 147–170.

[18] Mark E. Bayless and J. David Diltz, "An Empirical Study of the Debt Displacement Effects of Leasing," *Financial Management*, v. 15 (4), 1986, pp. 53–60.

[19] Tarun K. Mukherjee, "A Survey of Corporate Leasing Analysis," *Financial Management*, v. 20 (2), 1991, pp. 96–107.

Summary

This chapter examines the question of lease and debt equivalence. In the beginning, I argue that the payments on financial leases and the payments on debt are almost equivalent. I then showed the *exact* amount of debt payment that is equivalent to the leasing cash flow. This led me to the derivation of the equivalent loan. After that, I advance the argument that leasing may allow the firm to borrow *more!* The evidence on this subject is mixed. Therefore, the question of whether debt and leases are substitutes or complements has not yet been answered satisfactorily. For decision-making purposes, the appropriate discount rate for the fixed payment component of leases is the after-tax equivalent debt or loan rate of interest.

Chapter **6**

Net Present Value Analysis

The basis of lease versus purchase decision making is net present value (NPV) analysis. The intuition behind this analysis is quite simple. The lessee is saving the cost of purchasing the asset. In return, the lessee commits to a series of lease payments that are generally tax-deductible. The lessee thereby gives up the depreciation tax shields and any other tax credit associated with ownership, forgoes the interest tax shields that come from any debt financing, and loses the salvage or residual value of the asset. NPV analysis compares the *present value* of all these cash flows in terms of today's dollars. (A review of present value analysis as applied to leasing is in the Appendix.)

If the NPV is positive, the present value of leasing is superior to purchasing; if the NPV is negative, the present value of purchasing is superior to leasing. The answer for sound decision making is clear!

General NPV Analysis

The state of the art in lease versus purchase analysis in the early 1970s (models that are still in use) is best presented in an article by Bower.[1] This comprehensive review identifies seven different approaches by nine different authors. While Bower identifies the differences among the approaches, his first concern is to find points of agreement.

---

[1] Richard S. Bower, "Issues in Lease Financing," *Financial Management*, v. 2(4), 1973, pp. 25–34.

Almost all analyses of lease versus purchase decision are derived from a general NPV equation, also known as the "net advantage of leasing" (NAL) equation. Equation 6.1 presents the general NPV or NAL formula (the Appendix reviews present value mathematics, a necessary tool for lease analysis):

$$NPV = A_0 - \sum_{t=0}^{N-1} \frac{L_t}{(1 + r_1)^t} + \sum_{t=0}^{N-1} \frac{L_t(T)}{(1 + r_2)^t}$$

$$- \sum_{t=1}^{N} \frac{D_t(T)}{(1 + r_3)^t} - \sum_{t=1}^{N} \frac{I_t(T)}{(1 + r_4)^t} \qquad (6.1)$$

$$+ \sum_{t=1}^{N} \frac{O_t(1 - T)}{(1 + r_5)^t} - \frac{S_N}{(1 + r_6)^N} - TC$$

where:

NPV = net present value of leasing or the net advantage of leasing to the *lessee firm*

A_0 = price of the asset at present time ($t = 0$)

L_t = lease payment at time t

D_t = depreciation charge at time t

I_t = interest charge on the "equivalent loan" at time t

O_t = operating expenses that are higher if the asset is purchased but not if the asset is leased

S_N = expected after-tax salvage or residual value of the asset at time N

r = appropriate discount rate for each of the cash flows above: r_1, r_2, r_3, r_4, r_5, and r_6

T = marginal corporate tax rate of the lessee

N = number of time periods covered by the lease

TC = tax credits applicable to the asset that are taken by the lessor and not the lessee

The first of the eight terms in equation 6.1 represents the savings to the lessee of the cost of the asset. The second represents the present value of the series of lease payments that the lessee has committed to pay. The third symbolizes the present value of the tax deductions applicable to the lease payments. The fourth shows the present value of the opportunity loss of the tax deductions allowed for depreciation. The fifth also shows the present value of the opportunity loss of the tax deductions for interest, assuming that some amount of the asset cost would be borrowed if the asset is purchased. The sixth represents the present value of savings from after-tax operating expenses that may be higher if the asset is purchased rather than leased. (This is applicable only if the lease includes some provision for asset maintenance.) The seventh stands for the present value of the after-tax salvage value of the asset, another opportunity loss if the asset is leased. Finally, the eighth term in equation 6.1 represents any tax credits that apply to the asset and are taken by the lessor. If no tax credit applies or if the tax credit is taken by the lessee, this term is zero.

When Bower reviewed the leasing literature prior to 1973, the authors generally agreed on the elements of the NPV equation 6.1. They disagreed, however, on the discount rates, r_1 to r_6, and on the interest payments for the equivalent loan. Disagreement over the choice of these terms persists. Some experts argue that the discount rate should be the (after-tax) cost of debt; others argue that the discount rate should be the weighted-average cost of capital.[2] Higher discounts rates will favor leasing over purchase, so leasing companies have a natural bias to argue for the use of the higher cost of capital rather than the cost of debt. The Myers, Dill, and Bautista model provides theoretical support for the choice of the after-tax cost of debt as the appropriate discount rate to use in the NPV analysis.

One controversy that Bower helps resolve concerns inclusion of A_0 in equation 6.1. Other approaches delete the asset cost from equation 6.1, and introduce the principal and interest payments on the equivalent loan instead. In fact, these two approaches—asset cost versus loan payments—are equivalent *if* the total cost of the asset is borrowed (100 percent financing) and the discount rate is the after-tax cost of debt. This basic fact seems to get overlooked by some presenters of lease versus purchase models.

Numerical Example of One-Period Loan

To demonstrate the equivalence of the two approaches, suppose an asset costs $100,000, a loan to purchase the asset carries an interest rate of 10 percent, and the tax rate is 35 percent. For a one-year loan, the principal payment is $100,000, interest payment is $10,000, and the tax shield created by the interest payment is $3,500 (10,000 × 0.35). If the loan is discounted to the present, it is relatively

---

[2] Elements of this controversy are discussed in H. Martin Weingartner, "Leasing, Asset Lives and Uncertainty: Guides to Decision Making," *Financial Management*, v. 16(2), 1987, pp. 5–12.

simple to see that the present value of the loan is the amount borrowed, or $100,000:

$$Present\ Value\ of\ Loan = \frac{\$100,000 + \$10,000 - \$3,500}{[1 + 0.10(1 - 0.35)]}$$
$$= \$100,000$$

The discount rate is the after-tax cost of debt, in this case:

$$r_B(1 - T) = 0.10(1 - 0.35) = 0.065$$

The simple one-period example illustrates that discounting the loan at the after-tax cost of borrowing will always result in the amount borrowed.[3]

Numerical Example of Multiperiod Loan

To illustrate this principle for a multiperiod loan, consider a five-payment term loan to repay $100,000 at 10 percent and a 35 percent tax rate. Table 6.1 shows the amortization of the loan, principal and interest payments, and after-tax loan payments. The final step in the analysis is to discount the after-tax loan payments, the last row of Table 6.1, at the after-tax cost of debt, which is 6.5 percent as in the one-period example.

The calculation is:

$$Present\ Value = \frac{\$22,880}{1.065} + \frac{\$23,453}{1.065^2} + \frac{\$24,084}{1.065^3} + \frac{\$24,776}{1.065^4}$$
$$+ \frac{\$25,541}{1.065^5}$$
$$= \$100,000$$

---

[3] The before-tax loan payment discounted at the before-tax interest rate also results in the amount borrowed, for example:

$$Present\ Value\ of\ Loan = \frac{\$100,000 - \$10,000}{(1 + 0.10)}$$
$$= \$100,000$$

where 10 percent is the before-tax cost of debt.

Table 6.1: Loan Amortization and After-Tax Payment Calculation

Item	Year 0	Year 1	Year 2	Year 3	Year 4	Year 5
Payment		$26,380	$26,380	$26,380	$26,380	$26,380
Interest		10,000	8,362	6,560	4,582	2,398
(Tax deduction)		(3,500)	(2,927)	(2,296)	(1,604)	(839)
Principal		16,380	18,018	19,820	21,802	23,982
Loan balance	$100,000	83,620	65,602	45,782	23,980	0
After-tax payment		$22,880	$23,453	$24,084	$24,776	$25,541

Therefore, you have a choice. You can amortize the loan and calculate after-tax loan payments, or you can use the asset cost. In most cases, using the asset cost results in the same answer and saves a lot of time and effort.

Competitive Equilibrium in Leasing Markets

In order to use a leasing model like the one in equation 6.1, the lease payments must be specified, or, in the language of economics, the lease payments are determined exogenously. When lease payments are assumed to be determined in competitive markets, however, a powerful conclusion follows. Assuming competitive leasing, perfect capital markets, and a corporate tax rate that is common to all firms, the decision to lease or purchase will be immaterial, i.e., NPV = 0. Two articles that make this point effectively are by Miller and Upton and Lewellen, Long, and McConnell.[4]

One way to approach the competitive equilibrium in leasing markets is to argue that, in equilibrium, the NPV will be zero. Then, the lease payments in equation 6.1 will adjust so that the NPV will be zero, given all the other terms in the equation. This approach is taken by Lewellen, Long, and McConnell. Miller and Upton use the Capital Asset Pricing Model to drive the same conclusion.

The reason that NPV equals zero in an equilibrium rests on a basic economic argument. Equation 6.1 shows the NPV of leasing

---

[4] Merton H. Miller and Charles W. Upton, "Leasing, Buying, and the Cost of Capital Services," *Journal of Finance*, v. 31(3), 1976, pp. 761–786; and Wilbur G. Lewellen, Michael S. Long, and John J. McConnell, "Asset Leasing in Competitive Capital Markets," *Journal of Finance*, v. 31(3), 1976, pp. 787–798.

from the lessee's point of view. Suppose that the NPV of leasing is more than zero because the lease payments are "low." Two results will follow. First, demand for leases will increase if there are favorable (low) lease payments. Second, leasing companies will exit the market because, again, lease payments are low. Also, owners of assets will be unwilling to enter into lease contracts because the assets could be sold and the funds invested at a rate of return to yield dollar returns in excess of the lease payments. These effects will drive up lease payments.

Suppose the NPV of leasing is less than zero because the lease payments are "high." Again, two results will follow. First, demand for leases will drop because of the high lease payments. Second, more leasing companies will be willing to enter the market because lease payments are high. However, more leasing companies means more competition. Both of these effects will drive down lease payments. Therefore, in equilibrium, supply equals demand, and the equilibrium lease payments will result in a zero NPV.

The equilibrium indifference position holds under perfect capital markets and equal corporate tax rate assumptions. There can be conditions, however, when the NPV can be positive to the lessee; there are gains for the lessor too. Lewellen, Long, and McConnell describe the requisite conditions as follows.

> In particular, if the lessor (a) can acquire the assets at a price below A_0, (b) can realize a salvage proceeds greater than S_N, (c) can depreciate the assets more rapidly or more reliably than the lessee, or (d) levers the transaction to a greater extent than B_0, the market price associated with the lessor's equivalent of [equation 6.1] will indeed be positive.[5]

Interestingly, the tax benefits can cause leasing to be more or less favorable than purchasing. In equation 6.1, you can see that the tax rate is considered explicitly on the right-hand side of the equation in the third, fourth, fifth, and sixth terms. But, the signs for two of the terms are positive and two are negative, so the net effect of the corporate tax rate will depend on the specific asset life (lease term), the depreciation schedule, the discount rates, and the leverage or equivalent loan possibilities.

---

[5] Lewellen, Long, and McConnell, "Asset Leasing in Competitive Capital Markets," p. 795. The notation has been changed to be consistent with the notation used here, and B_0 is the dollar amount of the equivalent loan to the lessee.

When corporate tax rates differ among firms, it is not necessarily the case that the high-tax-rate firm should become the lessor and the low-tax-rate firm should be the lessee, as is commonly believed. Each lease must be evaluated on the merits of the individual case.

The Myers, Dill, and Bautista Model

The Myers, Dill, and Bautista model, introduced in Chapter 5, is perhaps the most popular of the existing models. The MDB model simultaneously solves the problem of the proper discount rate for the cash flows and the equivalent amount of borrowing. This remarkable solution is achieved through the derivation of the equivalent loan, which was shown in Chapter 5. The result of this derivation for one lease payment is:

$$B = \frac{L(1 - T) + D(T)}{[1 + r_B(1 - T)]}$$

and B is the amount of the equivalent loan. For multiperiods, the amount of the equivalent loan is:

$$B = \sum_{t=1}^{N} \frac{L_t(1 - T) + D_t(T)}{[1 + r_B(1 - T)]} \tag{6.2}$$

We learn from the equivalent loan approach of the MDB model that the amount of borrowing equivalent to the lease is the present value of the after-tax lease payments and depreciation tax shields, all discounted at the after-tax cost of debt. The after-tax cost of debt is represented in equation 6.2 as r^*, where $r^* = r_B(1 - T)$.

The MDB model can be represented as follows:

$$NPV = A_0 - \sum_{t=1}^{N} \frac{L_t(1 - T) + D_t(T)}{(1 + r^*)^t} \tag{6.3}$$

where NPV is the net present value of leasing (to the lessee), A_0 is the cost of the asset net of any lease payments at time 0, L_t is the lease payment at time t, T is the corporate tax rate, D_t is the amount of depreciation at time t, N is the number of periods for the lease, and r^* is the after-tax cost of debt, $r^* = r_B(1 - T)$.

The first term on the right-hand side of equation 6.3 represents the value of leasing. The second term on the right-hand side of the equation represents the present value of the equivalent loan. The NPV of leasing according to the MDB model is simply the asset cost less the value of the equivalent loan, $NPV = A_0 - B$.

Recall that the equivalent loan is endogenously determined in the MDB model in such a way that the after-tax cash flows from leasing exactly equal the after-tax cash flows of the equivalent loan. In the MDB model, debt and leases are very much substitute financial securities.

The MDB model is very practical. All that is needed to perform the lease versus purchase analysis are five inputs: (1) cost of the asset; (2) schedule of lease payments; (3) depreciation schedule; (4) the firm's borrowing rate; and (5) the firm's marginal tax rate. It is important, however, to note that the MDB model does not include the salvage value of the leased asset, differences in operating costs, or tax credits other than depreciation. After presenting examples for the application of the MDB model, we will show how to modify the model for inclusion of the salvage value, operating costs, and tax credits.

Examples of Simple Lease Versus Purchase Analysis

Basic Example

The basic example of ABC Warehouse Stores and Pacific Leasing Company used in Chapter 4 is used here to illustrate the lease versus purchase NPV calculation. On January 1, 1994, ABC Warehouse Stores and Pacific Leasing Company sign a lease agreement calling for annual payments of $10,000 per year for five years, with payments due at the end of the year. If purchased, the forklift equipment would cost $40,000, has an estimated economic life of five years, and has no residual value. ABC's marginal borrowing rate is 10 percent.

The after-tax cash flows are in Table 6.2. Applying these numbers to the MDB model equation results in the following:

$$NPV = \$40,000 - \frac{\$11,166.20}{(1.065)^1} - \frac{\$12,723.00}{(1.065)^2} - \frac{\$8,573.40}{(1.065)^3}$$

$$- \frac{\$7,537.40}{(1.065)^4} - \frac{\$6,500.00}{(1.065)^5} \qquad (6.4)$$

Table 6.2: ABC Warehouse Stores After-Tax Leasing Cash Flows

Item	Year 1	Year 2	Year 3	Year 4	Year 5
Depreciation schedule	$13,332.00	$17,780.00	$ 5,924.00	$ 2,964.00	$ 0.00
Lease payment	$10,000.00	$10,000.00	$10,000.00	$10,000.00	$10,000.00
Tax deduction	(3,500.00)	(3,500.00)	(3,500.00)	(3,500.00)	(3,500.00)
Depreciation (tax shield)	4,666.20	6,223.00	2,073.40	1,037.40	0.00
Cost of leasing	$11,166.20	$12,723.00	$ 8,573.40	$ 7,537.40	$ 6,500.00

$$= \$40,000 - \$39,402.75$$
$$= \$597.25$$

Equation 6.4 demonstrates a positive NPV or NAL of almost $600. Also shown in equation 6.4, on the third line, is the amount of the equivalent loan of $39,402.75 (this is, of course, the same number from the basic example of Chapter 4). Again, the point is that the MDB model compares the cost of the asset (the cost of purchasing) to the cost of leasing (or the amount of the equivalent loan). In this case, leasing is cheaper.

The NPV of leasing is sensitive, of course, to the variables that enter the equation. One variable that the lessee "controls" is the discount rate, the after-tax cost of debt. Figure 6.1 illustrates the sensitivity of the NPV of leasing for the basic example to changes in the discount rate. The NPV is an increasing function of the discount rate. In this example, leasing is preferred to purchase for after-tax discount rates above 6 percent.

Another factor over which the lessee has some control, or at least the power to negotiate, is the lease payment. Figure 6.2 shows the sensitivity of the NPV of leasing to the amount of the annual lease payment. The NPV is a decreasing function of the annual lease payments. Leasing is preferred to purchase for lease payments that are less than about $10,500 for this basic example.

Example 2

Suppose you are considering an asset that costs $100,000 for purchase or lease. The lease payments are $25,000 per year, *paid at*

Figure 6.1: NVP of Leasing: Sensitivity to Changing Discount Rates

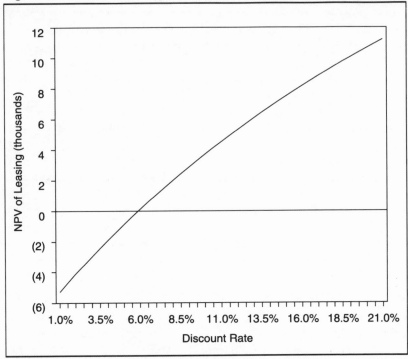

the beginning of the year, for five years. Note that the prepayment of the rental fee makes these lease payments an *annuity due.* If you borrow to purchase the asset, your cost of borrowing is 12 percent per year. Depreciation of the asset is simply straight-line for five years to a zero salvage value, or $20,000 per year for depreciation. The marginal tax rate of your firm is 35 percent. The five inputs for equation 6.3 are satisfied, and we can now use the MDB model.

A schedule for this lease appears in Table 6.3. In this example, equation 6.3 is also simple to apply:

$$NAL = \$100,000 - \sum_{t=0}^{4} \frac{\$25,000\ (1 - 0.35)}{[1 + 0.12\ (1 - 0.35)]^t}$$

$$- \sum_{t=1}^{5} \frac{\$20,000\ (0.35)}{(1 + 0.078)^t}$$

$$= \$100,000 - \$70,312.54 - \$28,096.92$$

$$= \$1,590.54$$

Figure 6.2: NVP of Leasing: Sensitivity to Changing Lease Payments

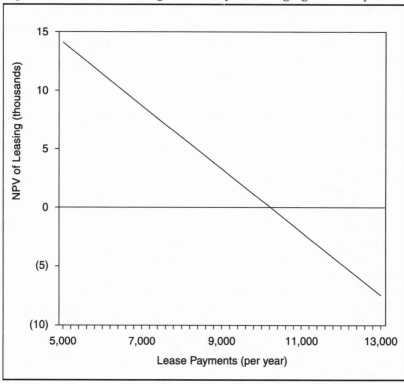

Table 6.3: Example 2 Lease Cash Flows

Item	Year 0	Year 1	Year 2	Year 3	Year 4	Year 5
Depreciation schedule		$20,000	$20,000	$20,000	$20,000	$20,000
Lease payment	$25,000	$25,000	$25,000	$25,000	$25,000	
Tax deduction	(8,750)	(8,750)	(8,750)	(8,750)	(8,750)	
Depreciation (tax shield)		7,000	7,000	7,000	7,000	7,000
Cost of leasing	$16,250	$23,250	$23,250	$23,250	$23,250	$7,000

The answer tells us that the lease is immediately cheaper than purchasing (and borrowing) by $1,590. We should take the lease.

An interesting but subtle point comes up in Example 2. Because the lease payments are an annuity due, the $25,000 before-tax lease payment ($16,250 after-tax) is due immediately. Therefore, the equivalent loan using the MDB method, which matches the cash flows from the lease, is an after-tax present-value amount of $82,159.46 plus a $16,250 after-tax down payment.

Example 3

Now consider the same problem with some modifications that are often found in real-world leases, namely, monthly payment schedules. The lease payments are $2,000 per month, prepaid, for six years (72 months). Depreciation is computed from the schedule for a five-year recovery period class according to the 1986 Tax Reform Act:

Item	Year 1	Year 2	Year 3	Year 4	Year 5	Year 6
Percentage (%)	20.00	32.00	19.20	11.52	11.52	5.76
Depreciation	$20,000	$32,000	$19,200	$11,520	$11,520	$5,760

The borrowing rate remains at 12 percent and the marginal tax rate at 35 percent.

For this example, a schedule is desirable, but such a presentation here would be quite cumbersome, so the formula is an easier format. The MDB model will, however, need to be adjusted to satisfy the *monthly* lease payments with the *annual* depreciation amounts. Equation 6.3 can be rewritten in the form:

$$NAL = A_0 - \sum_{t=1}^{M} \frac{L_t(1 - T)}{\left(1 + \frac{r^*}{12}\right)^t} + \sum_{t=1}^{N} \frac{D_t(T)}{(1 + r^*)^t} \tag{6.5}$$

In equation 6.5, M represents the number of monthly lease payments, while N represents the number of annual depreciation charges. Using the numbers for example 3, we get the calculation:

$$NPV = \$100,000 - \sum_{t=0}^{71} \frac{\$2,000\,(1 - 0.35)}{\left(1 + \dfrac{0.078}{12}\right)^t} - \frac{\$20,000\,(0.35)}{(1.078)^1}$$

$$- \frac{\$32,000\,(0.35)}{(1.078)^2} - \frac{\$19,200\,(0.35)}{(1.078)^3}$$

$$- \frac{\$11,520\,(0.35)}{(1.078)^4} - \frac{\$11,520\,(0.35)}{(1.078)^5} - \frac{\$5,760\,(0.35)}{(1.078)^6}$$

$$= \$100,000 - \$75,044.10 - \$28,535.65$$

$$= -\$3,579.75$$

Under the terms for this example, the NPV of leasing is a negative $3,590.60.[6] The cost of leasing is higher than the cost of purchase by more than $3,500, so purchasing and borrowing is the preferred financing alternative.

If you are faced with the results calculated above, are there other alternatives to purchasing? The answer is a definite yes. If you can negotiate with the lessor for sufficiently lower lease payments, the leasing alternative is preferred. In the example above, if you can lower the lease payments by $100 per month, leasing is the cheaper alternative. At a lease payment of $1,900 per month for 72 months (prepaid), the NPV of leasing, computed in the same manner as above, is a positive $172.

Operating Costs and Salvage Value

The basic MDB model assumes that the lease or purchase alternatives require identical operating expenditures. It also assumes no salvage value. But in fact, many leases do offer maintenance and other operating costs as part of the lease contract. Almost all true leases include a salvage or residual value component. What happens to the model if these additional components are included?

A Modified MDB Model

The modified MDB model that includes operating expenses and salvage value can be represented as follows:

---

[6] For monthly compounding, I use the annual rate divided by 12. A 12 percent annual rate becomes a 1 percent monthly rate. This procedure is the most common. An alternative methodology is to compute the geometric monthly compounded rate: $[(1 + 0.12)^{1/12} - 1.0] = 0.0095$ or 0.95 percent per month.

$$NPV = A_0 - \sum_{t=1}^{N} \frac{L_t \, (1 - T) + D_t(T)}{(1 + r^*)^t} + \sum_{t=1}^{N} \frac{O_t \, (1 - T)}{(1 + r_1)^t} \quad (6.6)$$
$$- \frac{S_N}{(1 + r_2)^N}$$

where NPV is the net present value of leasing (to the lessee), A_0 is the cost of the asset net of any lease payments at time 0, L_t is the lease payment at time t, T is the corporate tax rate, D_t is the amount of depreciation at time t, N is the number of periods for the lease, and r^* is the after-tax cost of debt, $r^* = r_B (1 - T)$. In addition, O_t represents any operating cost savings offered by the lease contract, and S_N represents the expected salvage or residual value at the end of the lease (time period N). Finally, r_1 and r_2 are used to represent the discount rates appropriate for the operating expenses and salvage value, respectively.

Unresolved Issues Concerning Discount Rates

While there is general agreement about the use of the after-tax cost of debt as the discount rate for the after-tax lease payments and depreciation tax shields, there is disagreement about the discount rates to use for the added factors in the modified MDB model. In other words, what are the appropriate rates for r_1 and r_2 in equation 6.6?

There have been several answers to this question. Some argue that r_1 and r_2 should be the after-tax cost of debt. Others suggest that r_1 and r_2 are the weighted-average cost of capital (WACC). Perhaps the best answer to the question of the appropriate discount rate is a general one: *Use the discount rate that appropriately reflects the riskiness of the cash flows.* For the cash flows represented by the operating cost savings, a case can be made for using the after-tax cost of debt or the weighted-average cost of capital.

The appropriate discount rate for the residual value is not an easy question to answer. (Chapter 8 is partly devoted to addressing this very question.) Nevertheless, the general answer given above applies: Use the discount rate of interest that reflects the riskiness of the residual value. Unquestionably there are situations where the riskiness of the leased asset is different from the riskiness of other cash flows of the lessee firm. A common example is the leasing of computers by firms whose business has nothing to do with computers.

Basic Example

For illustrative purposes, let's modify the basic lease example for ABC Warehouse Stores to include operating cost savings and residual value. Suppose that the $10,000 lease payment includes maintenance of the equipment. An independent maintenance contract is worth $1,000 per year. Assume that the residual value is estimated to be 20 percent or $8,000. The modified MDB model is now:

$$NPV = \$40,000 - \frac{\$11,166.20}{(1.065)^1} - \frac{\$12,723.00}{(1.065)^2}$$

$$- \frac{\$8,573.40}{(1.065)^3} - \frac{\$7,537.40}{(1.065)^4}$$

$$- \frac{\$6,500.00}{(1.065)^5} + \sum_{t=1}^{5} \frac{\$1,000\,(1 - .35)}{(1.065)^t} \qquad (6.7)$$

$$- \frac{\$8,000\,(1 - .35)}{(1.065)^5}$$

$$= \$40,000 - \$39,402.75 + \$2,701.19 - \$3,795.38$$

$$= -\$496.94$$

Notice that the new terms on the third line of equation 6.7 capture the present values of the after-tax operating cost savings (positive) and the after-tax residual value lost (negative). Because the asset is fully depreciated to a zero book value, the entire $8,000 residual value is a gain that is fully taxed. The resulting NPV or NAL is a negative $497. In this example, I use the same discount rate, the after-tax cost of debt, for all the cash flows. It is simple, however, to change the discount rate for the separate cash flows.

Again for the purposes of illustration, assume that the appropriate after-tax discount rate for the operating cost savings is 11 percent, ABC's cost of capital. For the residual value, assume that the appropriate after-tax discount rate, given the riskiness of this particular asset, is 15 percent. The other cash flows remain the same (i.e., the equivalent loan portion remains the same), so the new calculation appears as follows:

$$NPV = \$40,000 - \$39,402.75$$

$$+ \sum_{t=1}^{5} \frac{\$1,000\,(1 - 0.35)}{(1 + 0.11)^t} - \frac{\$8,000\,(1 - 0.35)}{(1 + 0.15)^5}$$

$$= \$597.25 + \$2,402.33 - \$2,585.32$$

$$= \$414.26$$

These new assumptions about the discount rate cause the NPV of leasing to be a positive $414. It is clear from this example that the assumption about the discount rate for each of the cash flows is an important determinant in deciding whether a lease is preferable to purchasing.

How sensitive is the NPV of leasing to changes in the residual value? Figure 6.3 shows the sensitivity of the NPV of leasing for the basic example, without the operating cost savings and assuming a discount rate of 6.6 percent, to changes in the amount of the residual value. The NPV is a decreasing function of the residual value because this is an opportunity cost to the lessee. The lessee gives up the right to the residual value under typical lease contracts. In this example, for residual values above about $1,500, the lessee is better off purchasing the asset in order to obtain the rights to the residual value.

Figure 6.3: NVP of Leasing: Sensitivity to Changing Residual Value

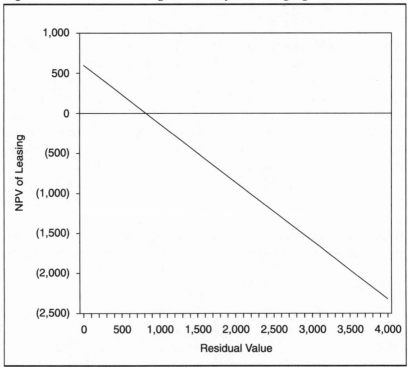

The Differences Between Before-Tax and After-Tax Discount Rates

At the beginning of the chapter, I show that the appropriate discount rate to use in lease versus purchase analysis is the after-tax cost of debt. In the case of operating cost savings and residual value, however, the appropriate discount rate may be the firm's cost of capital or another rate that is specifically related to the leased equipment. Nevertheless, all of these discount rates should be after-tax rates.

Are there any exceptions to the rule that after-tax cash flows are discounted at after-tax interest rates? The answer is a qualified yes. The following equation for the calculation of the NPV of leasing uses the before-tax cost of debt as the discount rate:

$$NPV = A_0 - \sum_{t=1}^{N} \frac{L_t (1 - T) + D_t(T) + I_t(T)}{(1 + r_B)^t} \qquad (6.8)$$

This NPV equation differs from the MDB model by inclusion of the tax shield of interest, $I_t(T)$, and use of the before-tax cost of debt, r_B, rather than the after-tax cost of debt as the discount rate. Nevertheless, equation 6.8 leads to the same answer as the one given by the MDB model if the interest deduction is based on the amortization of the equivalent loan.

Basic Example

To illustrate the equivalence of equations 6.8 and 6.3, I again turn to the basic example of ABC Warehouse Stores. First, from Table 5.1, the amortization schedule for the basic example is presented in Table 6.4. This amortization table is needed in order to obtain the amounts listed in the row marked "Tax deduction." If we add these

Table 6.4: Equivalent Loan Amortization Schedule

Item	Year 1	Year 2	Year 3	Year 4	Year 5
Payment	$11,116.20	$12,723.00	$ 8,573.40	$7,537.40	$6,500.00
Interest	3,940.27	3,079.77	2,007.66	1,280.82	610.33
Tax deduction	(1,379.10)	(1,077.92)	(702.68)	(448.29)	(213.62)
Principal	8,605.02	10,721.15	7,268.42	6,704.87	6,103.29
Loan balance	$30,797.73	$20,076.58	$12,808.16	$6,103.29	$ 0.00

interest tax shield amounts to the after-tax lease payments and depreciation tax shields, we obtain the schedule in Table 6.5.

These revised cash flow numbers are discounted at the before-tax cost of debt as follows:

$$NPV = \$40,000 - \frac{\$12,545.30}{(1.10)^1} - \frac{\$13,800.92}{(1.10)^2}$$

$$- \frac{\$9,276.08}{(1.10)^3} - \frac{\$7,985.69}{(1.10)^4}$$

$$- \frac{\$6,713.62}{(1.10)^5}$$

$$= \$40,000 - \$39,402.76$$

$$= \$597.24$$

The bottom line, $597, is the same as before, which is what I set out to demonstrate. To make this work, however, the payments for the equivalent loan are computed from the lease cash flows that include only the after-tax lease payments and depreciation tax shield. Again, this method is more tedious to apply than the MDB model and results in the same answer. Therefore, I recommend using the simpler MDB model.

Alternative Minimum Tax

As explained in Chapter 3, the alternative minimum tax (AMT) was introduced as part of the Tax Reform Act of 1986 and later

Table 6.5: Lease Cash Flow Schedule (includes interest tax shield)

Item	Year 1	Year 2	Year 3	Year 4	Year 5
Lease payment	$10,000.00	$10,000.00	$10,000.00	$10,000.00	$10,000.00
Tax deduction	(3,500.00)	(3,500.00)	(3,500.00)	(3,500.00)	(3,500.00)
Depreciation (tax shield)	4,666.20	6,223.00	2,073.40	1,037.40	0.00
Interest (tax shield)	1,379.10	1,077.92	702.68	448.29	213.62
Cost of leasing (with interest)	$12,545.30	$13,800.92	$ 9,276.08	$ 7,985.69	$ 6,713.62

modified by the Tax Reform Act of 1993. Tax adjustments and tax preferences are used to modify the regular taxable income into what is known as the alternative minimum tax income (AMTI). That AMTI is multiplied by 20 percent to compute the AMT. The AMT is paid if the amount exceeds the regular tax amount, based on the current 35 percent tax rate. The AMTI always will be larger than regular taxable income.

Bierman shows how to modify the lease versus purchase analysis to include the AMT, and his methodology is applied here.[7] An example will help explain the AMT application.

Basic Example

Once again consider the ABC Warehouse Stores example as the starting point for application of the AMT to lease versus purchase analysis. Under the assumptions of the basic lease example, leasing is desirable because the net advantage to leasing is valued at $597. Suppose that ABC Warehouse Stores, because of a relatively small amount of taxable income, is subject to the AMT. The analysis is now more complex. In addition, and this is not unusual, there is a difference between the tax rules for 1993 and later years. Therefore, we first look at the tax rules for 1993 and then for the years after 1993.

The depreciation schedule used in the basic example is a three-year depreciable life using MACRS (modified accelerated cost recovery system), with the half-year convention. This results in a tax preference amount, one-half the difference between MACRS and 150 percent declining balance. Therefore, in the first year, MACRS depreciation is $13,332, and 150% declining-balance depreciation, four-year ADR midpoint using half-year convention, is $7,500. The difference, $5,832, is the tax preference amount that is added to AMTI. For financial reporting (book income), straight-line depreciation is $8,000 per year (assuming a five-year life). The difference between 150% declining-balance, $7,500, and straight-line depreciation, $8,000, is $500. The tax adjustment, or ACE, is three-fourths of the difference or $375.

Table 6.6 shows the lease versus purchase analysis for ABC Warehouse Stores subject to the AMT and a tax rate of 20 percent on the (higher) AMTI.

[7] Harold Bierman, Jr., "Buy Versus Lease With An Alternative Minimum Tax," *Financial Management*, v. 17(4), 1988, pp. 87–91.

Table 6.6: ABC Warehouse Stores (with the AMT-1993 Rules)

Item	Year 1	Year 2	Year 3	Year 4	Year 5
Depreciation Schedule MACRS	$13,332.00	$17,780.00	$ 5,924.00	$ 2,964.00	$ 0.00
Lease payment	$10,000.00	$10,000.00	$10,000.00	$10,000.00	$10,000.00
Tax deduction (20%)	(2,000.00)	(2,000.00)	(2,000.00)	(2,000.00)	(2,000.00)
Depreciation (tax shield)	2,666.40	3,556.00	1,184.00	592.80	0.00
Tax-preference					
150% D.-B.	7,500.00	12,188.00	8,124.00	8,124.00	4,064.00
less MACRS	(13,332.00)	(17,780.00)	(5,924.00)	(2,964.00)	(0.00)
Tax Preferences (× 0.2)	(1,166.40)	(1,118.40)	440.00	1,032.00	812.80
Tax adjustment					
Straight-Line Depreciation	8,000.00	8,000.00	8,000.00	8,000.00	8,000.00
less 150% D.-B.	(7,500.00)	(12,188.00)	(8,124.00)	(8,124.00)	(4,064.00)
Tax Adjustment (ACE) (× 0.2 × 0.75)	75.00	(628.20)	(18.60)	(18.60)	590.40
Cost of leasing	$ 9,575.00	$ 9,809.40	$ 9,606.20	$ 9,606.20	$ 9,403.20

The last step in the analysis is to apply the MDB formula to the cash flows listed across the bottom row. The after-tax cost of debt for ABC is 10 percent times $(1 - 0.2)$, or 8 percent. The calculation of the NPV of leasing is:

$$NPV = \$40,000 - \frac{\$9,575.00}{(1.08)^1}$$

$$- \frac{\$9,809.40}{(1.08)^2} - \frac{\$9,606.20}{(1.08)^3}$$

$$- \frac{\$9,606.20}{(1.08)^4} - \frac{\$9,403.20}{(1.08)^5}$$

$$= \$40,000 - \$38,361.94$$

$$= \$1,638.06$$

The result is an NPV of leasing of $1,638 that is more than $1,000 higher than the basic example without the AMT.

Under the Tax Reform Act of 1993, the ACE adjustment reported in the ninth row of Table 6.6 has been eliminated. The resulting after-tax cash flows reported in the last row of Table 6.6 change, and the NPV calculation appears as:

$$NPV = \$40,000 - \frac{\$9,000.00}{(1.08)^1}$$

$$- \frac{\$10,437.60}{(1.08)^2} - \frac{\$9,624.80}{(1.08)^3}$$

$$- \frac{\$9,624.80}{(1.08)^4} - \frac{\$8,812.80}{(1.08)^5}$$

$$= \$40,000 - \$38,457.69$$

$$= \$1,542.31$$

Suppose that ABC would not pay an AMT if the lease is taken, but ABC would pay the tax if the asset is purchased. Under this scenario, a 35 percent tax rate applies to the tax-deductible lease payment, but a 20 percent tax rate applies to the depreciation tax shield, tax preference, and tax adjustment. Also, the appropriate after-tax cost of debt returns to 6.5 percent, 10 percent times $(1 - 0.35)$. The cash flow changes, and the resulting NPV calculation is shown in equation 6.9.

$$NPV = \$40,000 - \frac{\$8,000.00}{(1.065)^1}$$

$$- \frac{\$8,937.60}{(1.065)^4} - \frac{\$8,124.80}{(1.065)^3}$$

$$- \frac{\$8,124.80}{(1.065)^4} - \frac{\$7,312.80}{(1.065)^5} \tag{6.9}$$

$$= \$40,000 - \$33,770.83$$

$$= \$6,229.17$$

The NPV of leasing is over $6,000 on the asset that costs $40,000. This example conclusively illustrates the value of leasing to a company that would be subject to the alternative minimum tax (for the next five years) if the asset is purchased, but is not subject to the AMT if the asset is leased. An overwhelming advantage to leasing exists in this case!

Several words of caution are necessary. The calculation shown in this section assumes that the lease payments remain at $10,000 per year. This assumes that the lessor, Pacific Leasing Company, is not subject to the AMT. If the lessor is, the lease payments would surely be higher to compensate for the lessor's increased taxes. Alternatively, depending on the competitiveness of the tax-oriented leasing market, the lessor may demand some of the tax savings illustrated in these examples as part of the "gains-to-trade." In other words, lease payments will adjust in complex ways as the leasing market reaches an equilibrium, given the scarce resource of taxable income and tax shields.

A second caution involves the fact that there is a tax credit generated when a firm that pays the AMT begins to pay regular taxes. This further complicates the decision, and reduces the NPV numbers as illustrated in the examples. A third caution is that the decision maker cannot know with certainty when or for how long the firm will be subject to the AMT, which has a major impact on the NPV of leasing.

Summary

In this chapter the nuts and bolts of NPV analysis of the lease or purchase decision have been presented and illustrated with several examples. The MDB model is very practical and simple to use. The model can be modified to include operating cost savings and residual value. The complex question concerning the appropriate discount rate to use for these added cash flows remains to be addressed.

The MDB model and several modifications are illustrated with many examples. At the end of the chapter the complexity of the tax code regarding the alternative minimum tax is shown. Firms subject to the AMT may find the leasing alternative highly cost-effective. Decision makers need to use NPV analysis to reach conclusions about lease or buy alternatives.

Chapter 7

Yields on Leasing Contracts

Chapter 6 describes net present value analysis of the lease versus purchase decision. This chapter describes an alternative approach, the internal rate of return (IRR) or yield methodology. A word of caution, however: Yields have certain inherent problems, and because of them, many decision makers prefer NPV analysis. An analyst who is aware of these problems, however, can use yields to arrive at the "correct" answer. Just be very cautious about the use of yields for lease versus purchase decisions.

How to Calculate Yields

One of the major issues of disagreement in the NPV approach is the choice of discount rate. One way to solve this problem is actually to calculate *the discount rate* in the NPV equation. The solution to the problem is then the *internal rate of return* or *yield* on the lease.

To calculate the yield on a lease, the NPV is set equal to zero. Then the discount rate is determined by a method of trial and error. The trial-and-error, or iterative, technique is available in computer spreadsheet software and many financial calculators. The after-tax yield, y, is determined by applying this technique to equation 6.1 from Chapter 6.

$$NPV = 0 = A_0 - \sum_{t=0}^{N-1} \frac{L_t(1-T)}{(1+y)^t} - \sum_{t=1}^{N} \frac{D_t(T)}{(1+y)^t} \tag{7.1}$$

$$- \sum_{t=1}^{N} \frac{I_t(T)}{(1+y)^t} + \sum_{t=1}^{N} \frac{O_t(1-T)}{(1+y)^t} - \frac{S_N}{(1+y)^N} - TC$$

where:

NPV = net present value of leasing or the net advantage of leasing to the *lessee firm*

A_0 = price of the asset at present time (t = 0)

N = number of time periods covered by the lease

L_t = lease payment at time t

T = marginal corporate tax rate of the lessee

y = yield (after-tax) on the lease

D_t = depreciation charge at time t

I_t = interest charge of the "equivalent loan" at time t

O_t = operating expenses that are greater if the asset is purchased but not if the asset is leased

S_N = expected after-tax salvage or residual value of the asset at time N

TC = Tax credits applicable to the asset that are taken by the lessor and not the lessee

A before-tax yield can be calculated from this equation by simply setting the tax rate equal to zero, T = 0, and then solving iteratively for the yield, y.

The modified MDB equation can also be solved for the yield, which is represented as follows:

$$NPV = 0 = A_0 - \sum_{t=1}^{N} \frac{L_t(1 - T) + D_t(T)}{(1 + y)^t} + \sum_{t=1}^{N} \frac{O_t(1 - T)}{(1 + y)^t} \quad (7.2)$$
$$- \frac{S_N}{(1 + y)^N}$$

Two serious problems arise with the yield calculation for lease versus purchase decisions.[1] The first is what to do with the yield once it is calculated. Usually the yield would be compared to the cost of debt or the yield on the equivalent loan.

A second and more serious problem concerns the element of *risk*. In Chapter 6, I raised the question about the proper discount rate to use for the operating expense and residual value cash flows. A powerful case can be made that the riskiness of the residual value is different from the risk of the other cash flows in leasing. But the

---

[1] There is a third serious problem with IRR or yield calculation that could arise. The problem is *multiple* rates of return when cash flows have multiple changes in sign-over time. This problem arises very infrequently for lessees, but much more frequently for lessors using leverage lease financing.

yield calculation cannot differentiate the riskiness of the cash flows. One and only one yield is required or desired, and sometimes this can be problematic. The yield on leases is often a complicated mixture reflecting different cash flow risks.

Examples of Yields

Consider our basic example of ABC Warehouse Stores. Table 7.1 shows the after-tax leasing cash flows. If we want the before-tax yield, the tax rate is assumed to be zero, the tax deductions for the lease payments and depreciation are zero, and the lease yield is simply:

$$\$40,000 = \sum_{t=1}^{5} \frac{\$10,000}{(1 + y)^t} \tag{7.3}$$

$$y = 7.93\%$$

For an after-tax yield, the cash flows from the table are inserted into the MDB model, equation 7.2, for a yield calculation that looks like this:

$$\$40,000 = \frac{\$11,166.20}{(1 + y)^1} + \frac{\$12,723.00}{(1 + y)^2}$$

$$+ \frac{\$8,573.40}{(1 + y)^3} + \frac{\$7,537.40}{(1 + y)^4} \tag{7.4}$$

Table 7.1: ABC Warehouse Stores After-Tax Leasing Cash Flows

Item	Year 1	Year 2	Year 3	Year 4	Year 5
Depreciation schedule	$13,332.00	$17,780.00	$5,924.00	$2,964.00	$ 0.00
Lease payment Tax deduction Depreciation (tax shield)	$10,000.00 (3,500.00) 4,666.20	$10,000.00 (3,500.00) 6,223.00	$10,000.00 (3,500.00) 2,073.40	$10,000.00 (3,500.00) 1,037.40	$10,000.00 (3,500.00) 0.00
Cost of leasing	$11,166.20	$12,723.00	$8,573.40	$7,537.40	$6,500.00

$$+ \frac{\$6,500.00}{(1 + y)^5}$$

$$y = 5.88\%$$

For the basic lease example, the before-tax yield is approximately 8 percent, and the after-tax yield is approximately 6 percent. These numbers can be compared to the cost of debt, which is 10 percent before tax and 6.6 percent after tax.

As shown in Chapter 6, the basic example is complicated with operating expense savings of $1,000 per year ($650 after tax) and a residual value of $8,000 ($5,200 after tax). The calculation of the after-tax yield is:

$$\$40,000 = \frac{\$11,166.20}{(1 + y)^1} + \frac{\$12,723.00}{(1 + y)^2} + \frac{\$8,573.40}{(1 + y)^3}$$

$$+ \frac{\$7,537.40}{(1 + y)^4} + \frac{\$6,500.00}{(1 + y)^5} \tag{7.5}$$

$$- \sum_{t=1}^{5} \frac{\$1,000(1 - 0.35)}{(1 + y)^t} + \frac{\$8,000(1 - 0.35)}{(1 + y)^5}$$

$$y = 6.97\%$$

In this case, the yield of 7 percent is greater than the after-tax cost of debt of 6.5 percent, so purchasing (and borrowing) is the preferred alternative. For the NPV analysis, leasing had a negative NPV of $497 *if the discount rate is 6.5 percent.* If the discount rate on the residual value differs because of its riskiness, however, the NPV could be positive, as illustrated in Chapter 6. The yield cannot be adjusted to handle this kind of problem, which represents a serious shortcoming for yield analysis.

Next, consider the *before-tax* yield for this example:

$$\$40,000 = \sum_{t=1}^{5} \frac{\$10,000 - \$1,000}{(1 + y)^t}$$

$$+ \frac{\$8,000}{(1 + y)^5} \tag{7.6}$$

$$y = 9.18\%$$

The before-tax yield is about 9 percent, compared to the before-tax cost of debt of 10 percent. According to this criterion, leasing is preferred. This example shows another problem with yield and NPV analysis—whether to use a before- or after-tax analysis. The correct answer to this question is to perform after-tax analysis!

FASB 13 *Yields*

The accounting rules for capital or operating leases are explained in Chapter 4. In order to capitalize a lease, to place a capital lease on the balance sheet for the lessee, or to record an operating lease for the lessor, a discount rate is required. One way to compute the discount rate is to back out a yield from the contracted (minimum) lease payments and the present value of the residual value (if known).

Examples

Apex Leasing agrees to lease a $100,000 bulldozer to Coles Construction for five years at equal annual payments of $23,981.62 at the beginning of each year. Assuming no salvage value, the yield calculation is:

$$\$100,000 = \sum_{t=0}^{4} \frac{\$23,981.62}{(1 + y)^t} \qquad (7.7)$$

$$y = 10.0\%$$

The 10 percent yield can be used as the appropriate discount rate for capitalizing the lease as per *FASB 13*.

Next, assume that the same lease has an expected residual value of 20 percent or $20,000. What happens to the yield in this case? The answer depends on the discount rate used to compute the *present value* of the residual value. First, assume a discount rate of 10 percent for the residual value, which leads to a present value of $12,418.43 [$20,000/(1.1)^5]. The new yield changes substantially and is calculated as:

$$\$100,000 - \$12,418.43 = \sum_{t=1}^{5} \frac{\$23,981.62}{(1 + y)^t} \qquad (7.8)$$

$$y = 18.7\%$$

If the appropriate discount rate for the residual value is 20 percent, the present value of the residual is $8,037.55 [$20,000/(1.1)^5], and the yield calculation is:

$$\$100,000 - \$8,037.55 = \sum_{t=1}^{5} \frac{\$23,981.62}{(1 + y)^t} \qquad (7.9)$$

$$y = 15.4\%$$

For a third and final example, suppose that the lessor requires a return of 10 percent on the lease payments and the expected residual value. The lease payments will be $21,003.45 in this case, and the yield will be, naturally, 10 percent as shown in equation 7.10. Also, note that the present value of the residual value, $12,418.43, is the same as the case presented in equation 7.8.

$$\$100,000 - \$12,418.43 = \sum_{t=1}^{5} \frac{\$21,003.45}{(1 + y)^t} \qquad (7.10)$$

$$y = 10.0\%$$

FASB 13 requires capitalization of capital leases and thus necessitates using a discount rate. The simple examples in this section demonstrate that the discount rate can vary enormously depending on assumptions about the present value of the residual value. These examples also illustrate the great flexibility that decision makers have in computing lease discount rates. This flexibility extends into the classification of a lease as capital or operating, as described in Chapter 4.

What Determines Yields on Financial Leasing Contracts?

Schallheim, Johnson, Lease, and McConnell (SJLM) explored the economic determinants of leasing yields by studying a large sample of leases from a national sample of contracts written over the period 1972 through 1982 and covering a wide variety of asset types.[2] This study is one of the most comprehensive investigations

---

[2] James S. Schallheim, Ramon E. Johnson, Ronald C. Lease, and John J. McConnell, "The Determinants of Yields on Financial Leasing Contracts," *Journal of Financial Economics*, v. 19(1), 1987, pp. 45–68.

of financial leases by independent researchers. The analysis uses the literature of academic finance as well as the practical insights gleaned from members of the leasing community.

There are obvious factors that influence the lease yield such as the contract terms, timing of the lease payments, and maturity of the contract, as well as tax considerations such as the amount of depreciation tax shield available for the leased asset. In Chapter 2, I described eight factors that determine the pricing (lease payment) of a lease: (1) the lessor's cost of funds; (2) the risk of default by the lessee; (3) the service and processing costs; (4) the type of leased asset as well as the economic depreciation and obsolescence risk associated with that asset; (5) the value of the tax benefits to the lessor; (6) the options offered in the contract; (7) maintenance and service provisions; and (8) the degree of competition in the market. The study by SJLM concentrates on four of the factors.

Previous Literature

Only a handful of published articles have examined the yields on lease contracts. In perhaps the first empirical study, Sorensen and Johnson examined 520 retail financial lease contracts originated in the western United States from 1970 to 1975.[3] An internal rate of return, yield, is computed for each lease. The authors conclude that the implied yields were quite high, with an average annual before-tax yield of 24.98 percent. The after-tax yield calculations (assuming a flat tax rate of 50 percent) produced an average the authors still characterized as high—18.69 percent per year.

A later study by Crawford, Harper, and McConnell examined the yields on a sample of 50 financial leases originated from 1973 through 1980. They report an average before-tax yield of 20.7%— significantly higher than returns on government securities and BBB bonds during the same period. The authors characterize their results as a "puzzle," and suggest that lease contracts must differ in "some systematic but as yet not widely recognized way from approximately comparable debt contracts."[4]

These last two articles provide excellent documentation of lease yields and the description of the leases in their samples. Finance

---

[3] Ivar W. Sorensen and Ramon E. Johnson, "Equipment Financial Leasing Practices and Costs: An Empirical Study," *Financial Management,* Spring 1977, pp. 33–40.

[4] Peggy J. Crawford, Charles P. Harper, and John J. McConnell, "Further Evidence on the Terms of Financial Leases," *Financial Management,* Autumn 1981, pp. 7–14.

theory suggests that fundamental economic factors drive yields in any market, including the leasing market. The four economic determinants driving leasing yields are: (1) prevailing interest rates, (2) transaction and information costs, (3) default risk, and (4) asset risk.

Prevailing Interest Rates

The yield on the lease must exceed the lessor's cost of funds. The exact cost of funds for each lessor in the SJLM sample cannot be determined, but theory argues that the cost of funds exceeds the rate on a Treasury bond with the same maturity as the lease contract. Furthermore, changes in the lessor's cost of funds should be highly correlated with movements in Treasury bond rates. Therefore, the Treasury bond rate is a rough estimate of the lessor's cost of funds.

Transaction and Information Costs

In a lease contract, transaction costs are the per-unit costs of writing the contract, specifying the security agreement, identifying the asset, negotiating the terms of the lease, and so forth. Many of these costs are fixed and independent of the characteristics of the lessor, lessee, or the leased asset. Therefore, transaction expenses are expected to decline proportionately as the cost of the asset increases. These expenses are recaptured over time by the lessor through periodic lease payments.

For example, suppose the transaction costs are $200 per lease. If so, the transaction cost as a percentage of the cost of a $1,000 asset is 20 percent. But the same $200 is only two-tenths of 1 percent of an asset that costs $100,000. Therefore, for leases on higher-priced assets, transaction costs are a less significant component of the yield, and for leases on lower-priced assets, transaction costs are a more significant component of the yield.

Information about the lessee firm is extremely relevant when default potential is considered. Finance theory suggests that when lessors have adequate information about the financial condition of lessees, lease yields accurately reflect default potential. Lease yields will be lower for financially strong lessees, all other factors equal. In the absence of adequate and reliable financial information, the lessor will assume the worst, and the lease yield will be commensurately high.

In the empirical analysis, a precise measure of information quality or reliability is difficult to obtain. The size of the lessee, however, is a reasonable approximation for the amount of information about the firm. Thus, the book value of the lessee's assets is used as an indication of the availability of reliable information. The hypothesis is that lease yields are inversely related to the book value of the lessee's assets. Theory proposes that lease yields will be related positively to the relative level of transaction costs and negatively to the quality of information about the lessee.

Default Risk of the Lessee

Because financial statements are not always an accurate reflection of a firm's financial situation, a precise measure of the lessee's financial strength is difficult to ascertain. Several measures of default risk, based on traditional financial ratios, are used as approximations. Lenders use these ratios to evaluate default risk because research has shown them to be reliable in predicting corporate bankruptcies.

Research on corporate failures suggests that four primary variables are useful in predicting corporate bankruptcies: (1) firm size, (2) leverage ratio, (3) profitability, and (4) liquidity. Firm size is already used to represent the quality of information about the lessee firm. Using financial research as a guide, *leverage* is measured as (total debt/total assets), *profitability* as (net income/total assets), and *liquidity* as (current assets/current liabilities).

A Measure of Salvage Value Risk

Finance theory has developed a measure of an asset's individual risk that is called its "beta." The intuition behind beta is simple. Because an investor (or a lessor) holds a portfolio of assets (or a portfolio of leasing contracts), not just a single asset at a time, the proper measure of the risk of an individual asset is its contribution to the risk of the total portfolio. Therefore, beta is the measure of the asset's contribution to portfolio risk. For this purpose, the beta of the leased asset is used as a measure of the asset's salvage or residual value risk.[5]

One more step is used to capture the beta risk of an individual lease. Because salvage value risk does not occur until the expected

---

[5] Beta is discussed further in Chapter 8.

termination date of the lease, lease terms reflect the time-adjusted value of beta. In the analysis, asset betas are discounted using the yield of a Treasury bond that matches the maturity of the lease contract.[6]

Each leased asset is classified by its general type, for example, computers or machine tools. Then betas are estimated for each asset category by calculating the betas of a sample of firms whose primary business is the manufacture of that asset.[7] For example, for leases covering construction equipment, the representative sample includes American Hoist, Caterpillar Tractor, Clark Equipment, and Harnischfeger. The use of stock market data for firms manufacturing the asset to estimate the beta of the asset assumes that the risk of the asset producer is closely linked with the risk of the asset being produced. Both theoretical and practical evidence support this relationship.[8]

Using firm betas to proxy for individual asset risk may introduce additional error into the procedure for estimating asset betas. By picking firms whose primary business is manufacturing the asset under lease, and by averaging over several firms in an industry, an analyst should "wash out" many of the firm-specific errors or idiosyncracies. Thus this procedure uses the best information available to measure the residual value risk.

To review, finance theory suggests that yields depend on: (1) prevailing interest rates, (2) transaction and information costs, (3) lessee default risk, and (4) asset salvage value risk. (Of course, the actual yield calculation also depends on such contract terms as maturity of the lease and timing of the lease payments.) Four categories of variables capture these factors: (1) government bond yields of the same maturity, (2) size (as measured by both cost of asset

---

[6] For a theoretical justification of this procedure, see John J. McConnell and James S. Schallheim, "Valuation of Asset Leasing Contracts," *Journal of Financial Economics*, August 1983, pp. 237–261.

[7] Studies have established, both theoretically and empirically, that betas are affected by financial risk or leverage. To capture only the pure business risk of the asset, each beta is "purged" of financial leverage. (The details of this adjustment were developed by Robert Hamada and are to be found in most textbooks in corporate finance.)

[8] The theory behind our beta technique is developed more precisely in Schallheim, Johnson, Lease, and McConnell, "The Determinants of Yields on Financial Leasing Contracts" on which this discussion is based. Another body of literature in finance discusses the so-called pure play technique for estimating divisional (or asset) betas. One example is R. Fuller and H. Kerr, "Estimating the Divisional Cost of Capital: An Analysis of the Pure Play Technique," *Journal of Finance*, December 1981, pp. 997–1009.

and total assets of lessee firm), (3) financial ratios, and (4) the beta of the leased asset.

Empirical Analysis of Lease Yields

Schallheim, Johnson, Lease, and McConnell collected data from the files of seven non-bank leasing companies and one bank-owned leasing company. Four companies were headquartered in the Rocky Mountains, two in the Midwest, and one each in the Southwest and on the West Coast. These firms allowed inspection of their files on the condition that their customers not be identified or contacted. The lessors allowed access to both currently active contracts and completed contracts.

A sample of 453 contracts was drawn randomly for evaluation. Because of certain data requirements, only 363 contracts were usable. Of these, 223 were active contracts, and 140 had been completed as of September 1982. The 363 contracts were all non-cancelable financial leases.

Data Description

The information recorded for each lease includes:

- origination date of the contract
- geographic location of the lessee
- type and cost of the leased asset
- type and maturity of the lease
- date the lessor paid for the asset
- date and amount of any lease prepayments
- due dates and amounts of the periodic rental payments
- amount of any broker commissions paid to originate the lease
- residual value of the asset (as estimated by the lessor)
- an indication as to whether the investment tax credit (ITC) was taken by the lessor or passed on to the lessee
- various accounting data from the lessee's application

Data describing the sample are shown in Table 7.2. The average size of the lease as measured by the cost of the asset is $636,690. The sample is, however, dominated by smaller-size leases, because the median, or the midpoint in size, is closer to $20,000. The average maturity for the sample is about five years. The average size of the lessee firm, as measured by the book value of total assets, is $136 million, but the median-size lessee is $845,000. The oldest lease was written in January 1973, and the most recent one in the sample was written in June 1982. The lessees are located in at least 43 different states.

Both the before- and after-tax yields are reported for two reasons. First, the before-tax yield is more accurate because several assumptions must be made in order to calculate the after-tax yield. Second, most of the leasing firms reported before-tax yields in the files that were examined. In all cases, however, yield calculations are made by a computer program with careful consideration of such factors as the timing of the payments, prepayment amounts (if any), commissions paid to third-party brokers (if any), security deposits (if any), and the residual value as estimated by the lessor. The average before-tax yield on the sample of leases is 18.6 percent, and the average after-tax yield is 13.4 percent. The after-tax yields are calculated on the basis of the most favorable depreciation method available at the time the lease was originated, adjusting for ITC and assuming maximum corporate tax rates.

As discussed above, to measure the salvage value risk of the leased assets using betas, each of 363 leases is classified into one of 18 asset categories (sample size in parentheses): aircraft (10

Table 7.2: Description of the Sample of 363 Financial Leasing Contracts

Category	Minimum	Maximum	Average	Median
Cost of asset	$1,000	$63,000,000	$636,690	$19,396
Maturity (months)	11	300	61.3	60
Size of lessee (book value in $1,000's)	$5	$8,972,000	$135,800	$845
Before-tax yield (annual percent)	4.4	45.3	18.6	19.6
After-tax yield (annual percent)	3.5	29.0	13.4	13.9

leases), auto repair equipment (12), computers and processors (43), construction equipment (35), copy machines (30), farm equipment (17), food preparation equipment (16), industrial laundry machines (8), machine tools (28), marine equipment (4), medical equipment (19), miscellaneous electronic equipment (21), motel and hotel furnishings (6), office equipment (15), office furniture (23), railroad rolling stock (6), telephone systems (20), and trucks and trailers (50). The betas of asset-manufacturing firms are available for each category.

Empirical Results

A statistical technique, multiple regression analysis, is used to examine the consistency between leasing theory and actual lease yields. This technique seeks to determine which variables are important in explaining lease yields. In general, the data from this sample of leases are consistent with finance theory.

The variables used to explain lease yields are: (1) the yield-to-maturity of the Treasury bond with the same maturity as the lease; (2) the book value of the assets of the lessee firm; (3) the purchase price of the leased asset; (4) the asset's beta, adjusted for maturity; and (5) three lessee financial ratios—return on assets, liquidity, and leverage. All but the lessee's return on assets and leverage ratio have the predicted relationship with the yield and are significant in explaining lease yields.[9]

As expected, the results indicate that lessors are sensitive to the frequently changing cost of funds when determining the terms of a lease. In addition, adjustments are made to capture the impact of transaction costs, information quality, and the asset salvage value risk. The one puzzling result is that, with the exception of the liquidity ratio, the other two financial ratios used to capture default risk do not show up as significant. At first blush, this evidence might suggest that lessors are not sensitive to default potential when writing leases. Yet perhaps the lessees' size and liquidity ratios capture the default potential in the sample to such a degree that the other two ratios do not help explain lease yields.

---

[9] The regression equations are all reported in Schallheim, Johnson, Lease, and McConnell, "The Determinants of Yields on Financial Leasing Contracts." The t-statistics for the individual variables are highly significant, and the total equations explain more than 60 percent of the variability of the yields.

The data send another important message. The descriptive statistics in Table 7.2 illustrate that the average before-tax lease yield of 18.63 percent is substantially above the yields of AAA corporate bonds over the period covered by the study (from 7.15 percent to 15.49 percent). A natural question is: Why would lessees raise capital leasing when borrowing appears to be a much less expensive form of financing?

One answer to this question is that only the largest corporate borrowers are able to issue publicly traded debt at AAA corporate bond rates. This argument suggests that the appropriate lease comparisons to AAA bond rates are the yields on the largest leases issued by the largest lessees. Evidence on this point is presented in Table 7.3.

Table 7.3 is a cross-tabulation of the average lease yields by lessee size and asset size after subtracting out the AAA corporate bond returns of maturity matching the lease at the time the lease contract was originated. The AAA corporate bond yield is chosen in this case because it captures interest rate risk (as does the Treasury bond yield) *and* a premium for default risk. This calculation is performed on both a before- and an after-tax basis. Row categories are the purchase prices of the leased asset by four size categories, from the smallest to the largest lease. Column categories are the book values of the lessee's assets, again in four size classifications. Each cell contains average spreads (lease yield minus AAA yield) for the before- and after-tax yields, with the after-tax yield reported in parentheses.[10]

The largest yield spread occurs in the figures at the upper left-hand corner, which corresponds to the smallest assets leased by the smallest lessees. The yield spread shown at the lower right-hand corner is nearly the smallest one in the table. This cell corresponds to the largest assets leased by the largest lessees.[11] Moreover, the row averages decline uniformly as the book value of the lessees' assets increases, and the column averages decline uniformly as the purchase price of the leased assets increases. In short, these results indicate that the cost of leasing approaches the cost of issuing debt for large corporations that lease large assets. If small corporations

[10] In computing the after-tax yield spreads, the AAA bond yield is multiplied by one minus the maximum statutory corporate tax rate applicable at the origination of the corresponding lease.

[11] The smallest spread occurs at the lower left-hand corner, but this cell contains only one lease.

Table 7.3: Average Before-Tax (and After-Tax) Yield Spreads by
Purchase Price and Lessee Size[a]

		Quartile of Book Value of Lessee's Assets[b]				Row Average
		1	2	3	4	
Quartile of purchase price of leased asset[c]	1	12.3 (10.9) [33]	11.6 (9.7) [22]	10.4 (10.7) [6]	6.2 (6.2) [4]	11.5 (10.2) [65]
	2	11.6 (9.6) [21]	10.1 (8.6) [24]	9.0 (9.2) [13]	10.2 (7.4) [6]	10.4 (9.0) [64]
	3	10.6 (9.0) [9]	9.0 (7.9) [16]	4.0 (4.4) [19]	1.0 (3.1) [21]	5.2 (5.5) [65]
	4	−3.8 (2.3) [1]	0.1 (3.4) [3]	−1.1 (2.7) [25]	−1.3 (2.8) [35]	−1.2 (2.8) [64]
Column Average		11.6 (10.1) [64]	9.9 (8.6) [65]	3.6 (5.3) [63]	0.9 (3.5) [66]	

Note: Numbers in brackets are the number of observations in each cell.

[a]Each cell contains the average of the lease before-tax yield (after-tax yield in parentheses) *less* the yield of a AAA corporate bond index (after-tax yield in parentheses) with the same maturity and on the origination date of the lease. Rows present the purchase price quartile, and columns give the book value of the lessee's assets quartile.

[b]Book value of lessee asset quartiles:
  Quartile 1 = less than $250,000
  Quartile 2 = greater than $250,000 and less than $1,000,000
  Quartile 3 = greater than $1,000,000 and less than $5,000,000
  Quartile 4 = greater than $5,000,000

[c]Purchase price of leased asset quartiles:
  Quartile 1 = less than $10,000
  Quartile 2 = greater than $10,000 and less than $50,000
  Quartile 3 = greater than $50,000 and less than $100,000
  Quartile 4 = greater than $100,000

that lease small assets also face significant fixed costs in borrowing to finance their assets, leasing is no more costly than borrowing, once the cost of each is adjusted for transaction and information costs.

This observation on lease versus AAA borrowing costs is important, and suggests that the academic literature on leasing has not made the proper adjustments for transaction and information costs when concluding that leasing is an expensive alternative to borrowing.

The Schallheim, Johnson, Lease, and McConnell study points out, once again, the problem decision makers face with yield analysis. Comparing lease yields to the appropriate borrowing rate is difficult. In my opinion, this difficulty points to the superiority of NPV analysis.

One curious observation from Table 7.3 is the negative sign of the before-tax yield spreads on the largest assets (category 4) leased. The lease yields are lower than the AAA corporate bond yields, on average. Yet the after-tax yields on these same leases, which include ITC and depreciation tax shields, are uniformly positive. This observation indicates that taxes are an important consideration in determining the terms of lease contracts for big ticket items.

Lease Comparison with High-Yield Bonds

As I argue in Chapter 5, leasing can be considered a substitute for borrowing. The question is what type of borrowing is equivalent to leasing. For high-risk firms, an appropriate benchmark is high-yield bonds. Altman and Asquith, Mullins, and Wolff have conducted comprehensive analyses of default frequencies of high-yield ("junk") bonds.[12] Both studies report that cumulative default rates for such bonds are about 30 percent over the life of the bonds. On bond issues that default, the recovery rate is roughly 40 percent of the face value of the debt.

Lease, McConnell, and Schallheim studied the performance of a sample of 137 lease contracts over the period 1973–1982.[13] These leases experienced a default rate of approximately 20 percent and a recovery rate of about 38 percent relative to the original cost of the asset, or 64 percent relative to the present value of the remaining lease payments, plus estimated salvage value. The numbers related to this sample of leases and the experience of the junk bonds are similar.

---

[12] Edward I. Altman, "Measuring Corporate Bond Mortality and Performance," *Journal of Finance*, v. 44(4), 1989, pp. 909–922; Paul Asquith, David W. Mullins, Jr., and Eric D. Wolff, "Original Issue High-Yield Bonds: Aging Analyses of Defaults, Exchanges, and Calls," *Journal of Finance*, v. 44(4), 1989, pp. 923–952.

[13] Ronald C. Lease, John J. McConnell, and James S. Schallheim, "Realized Returns and the Default and Prepayment Experience of Financial Leasing Contracts," *Financial Management*, v. 19(2), 1990, pp. 11–20.

Other similarities between junk bonds and leases exist regarding the call of the bonds or the prepayment of leases. As one might expect, the early payoffs depend on the interest rate environment. For example, between 26 percent and 47 percent of the bonds issued between 1977 and 1982 had been called by the end of 1988. This call frequency reflects the sharp interest rate decline that began in 1982. In contrast, for bonds issued between 1983 and 1986, only 3 percent to 14 percent had been called by the end of 1988. For the leasing sample, roughly 30 percent of the leases were prepaid prior to maturity. These numbers are somewhat difficult to compare because the time periods for the bonds and leases are not matched. Nevertheless, similarities exist.

Finally, Blume and Keim report that for lower-grade bonds issued during 1977–1978, the annual promised yield of 11.2 percent exceeded the realized return of 8.5 percent by 2.61 percentage points.[14] For our sample of leases, the contract yield exceeds the realized return by 2.62 percentage points. Therefore, while the evidence is far from complete, there are a number of similarities between the outcomes associated with leases and high-yield debt. This comparison is consistent with the hypothesis that leases and lower-grade debt are comparable sources of funds for high-risk firms.

Summary

This chapter has presented the procedures for the mechanical calculation of lease yields and demonstrated the application of yields to basic leasing examples. I also showed the impact on yields from operating cost savings and residual value.

The chapter also discusses the determinants of yields on asset leasing contracts. The relationship between leasing yields and various economic determinants that finance theory suggests are important in determining returns earned by lessors is explored. Theory suggests that there are four general factors that determine the yield on a lease contract: prevailing interest rates, transaction and information costs, the default risk of the lessee, and the salvage value risk of the leased asset. Specifically, a positive relationship among

---

[14] Marshall E. Blume and Donald B. Keim, "Realized Returns and Defaults on Low-Grade Bonds: The Cohort of 1977 and 1978," *Financial Analysts Journal*, v. 47(2), 1991, pp. 63–72.

lease yields and interest rates, lessee default risk, and the salvage value risk of the leased asset is substantiated; there is a negative relationship among lease yields and the size of the lessee, and the cost of the asset being leased. These findings provide evidence that lease yields are set in a rational and competitive market.

The claim that lease rates are high relative to borrowing costs is not supported. Studies that have made that claim fail to account for variables such as transaction costs, information quality, and default risk that are important in the rate setting process.

Chapter *8*

Residual Value Analysis: The Wild Card

One of the major differences between leasing and borrowing is the salvage or residual value component of leasing. When a debt contract is paid in full, the asset, along with the ownership rights to the residual value, belongs entirely to the borrower. When a lease contract is paid in full, the asset usually belongs to the lessor. This fundamental property of leasing dictates that the residual value is priced in some way in the lease payments. The pricing—evaluation of the risk and return—of the residual value component of leasing is the subject of this chapter. In turn, the risk and return properties of the residual value allow the decision maker to determine the appropriate discount rate to use with the residual value.

Residual value is the wild card of leasing because huge profits or losses are occasioned on realization of the salvage value. For example, leases of transportation vehicles sometimes have led to large gains at the end of the lease for the *lessor*. Toward the end of the 1970s, railroad rolling stock provided large residual value gains because of a shortage of such equipment in the United States. And while the lessor gains, the lessee correspondingly loses with such an unexpected shortage. Airlines provided similar gains to lessors for similar reasons at the end of the 1980s. In the early 1990s, however, the opposite happened: A worldwide recession in the airline industry depressed the prices for used aircraft. And there are frequently losses in residual values for computer equipment. In fact, the leasing of computers has resulted in so many losses in residual values that many lessors assume a zero salvage value for computers. The risks in the uncertain residual values—both the potential gain and the possible loss—are extremely important.

Residual Value Risk

At the time a lease contract is signed, the residual value at maturity is uncertain. This is the risk that differentiates the lease from a loan. The participants to the lease will derive an *expected* residual value. Of course, each participant could derive a different expected value. Suppose that the expected residual value can be represented through time as a straight line, as shown in Figure 8.1. Then the actual residual value will deviate from the expected value, sometimes above and sometimes below the line as the figure illustrates. At any particular time, the actual residual value likely will differ from the expected value. This deviation is most important at the end of the lease, when the parties to the lease must deal with the disposal of the asset. Figure 8.1 shows the case where the actual or realized residual value is higher than the expected or anticipated level.

Figure 8.1: Expected and Actual Residual Value

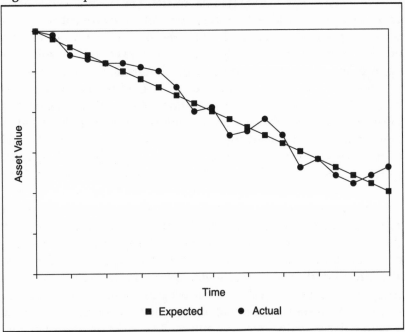

At maturity of the lease, the disposal of the asset depends on the type of lease. For a tax-deductible *true lease*, the ownership rights to the residual value must belong to the lessor. For a *true* lease, the risk of the residual value must be borne by the lessor. Some leases have a fixed-purchase option (the lease may or may not be tax-deductible). In the case of a fixed-purchase option, the lessee gains if the actual market value of the asset is greater than the fixed-purchase price. The lessee's "gain" is partially offset by the value of "purchasing" the fixed-purchase option. If the actual asset value is less than the fixed-purchase price, the lessee probably will not exercise the option. The lessor's "loss" will be offset by the value of "selling" the fixed-purchase option. If the lease is a conditional sales contract, the lessee bears the risk of the residual value because the ownership rights to the asset belong to the lessee at maturity of the contract. Thus the risk of residual value may be totally borne by the lessor or the lessee, or the risk may be shared through purchase options.

What factors contribute to residual value risk? First, there is periodic fluctuation in the market value of an asset. Basically, the economic forces of supply and demand contribute to price fluctuations as does economic depreciation. Economic depreciation encompasses the physical wear and tear on equipment and the decrease in value as new and improved products are introduced into the marketplace, or because of technological obsolescence. Technological obsolescence is an unpredictable source of risk that can have devastating impact on the value of an existing asset. Computers, for example, are most susceptible to technological obsolescence. When IBM computers ruled the mainframe marketplace, an announcement by IBM of a new generation of computers caused an immediate and sharp decline in prices of existing computers. In the rapidly changing markets of today, most technical equipment is susceptible to this risk.

It is possible that certain leasing companies have an advantage when it comes to the technological obsolescence problem. For example, GPA Group Ltd. is a lessor, reconditioner, and specialist in the airline industry. This specialization offers GPA the opportunity to write favorable aircraft leases. If a particular airplane becomes obsolete to one user, it may be satisfactory for other users. Given its global operations, GPA is well-suited for locating another user.

Figure 8.2 shows the impact of a sudden technological innovation on the actual residual value of an asset. At approximately the middle of the life of the lease, the actual value of the asset takes a sudden plunge in value because a new and improved asset has been introduced into the market. Thus the anticipated residual value is not realized. In this case, the actual residual value is far below the expected level of residual value at the end of the lease.

The most important problem with residual value risk is how to measure the risk in order to price the lease contract fairly, from both lessor and lessee perspectives. Figures 8.1 and 8.2 provide clues for one method of possible risk measurement: the variations of the actual residual values from the expected values.[1] Although total variability of an asset price through time is a valid risk measure, other measures are used in practice.

Perhaps the most common method of risk assessment could be called the "subjective" risk measure. Subjective risk measures

Figure 8.2: Expected and Actual Residual Value with Technological Obsolescence

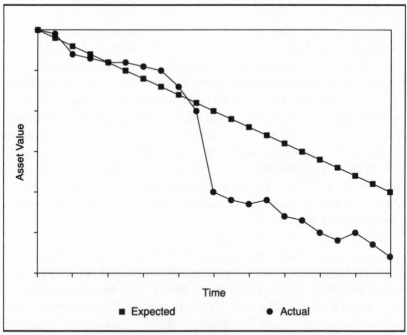

---

[1] In statistics, variability can be measured by the *variance* or the square root of variance, which is the *standard deviation*.

rely on the experiences and expertise of the evaluator; they are difficult to quantify. Some decision makers divide assets into risk categories and then translate these categories into residual value estimates. For example, one category would assume zero residual value, a second a 10 percent residual value, a third a 20 percent residual value, and so on. Another subjective risk assessment might measure risk on a subjective scale (for example, on a scale of one to ten). Finally, there is the risk measure based on modern portfolio theory.

The Portfolio Concept

A well-known concept in finance states that risk can be reduced through diversification. No one wants to put all their savings in one risky investment such as windmill farms in California or wildcat oil companies in Texas. A combination of many risky investments, along with some less risky securities such as corporate bonds and bank certificates of deposit, is a good investment strategy. This is diversification, which is as simple as "don't put all your eggs in one basket." The concept of diversification is more complex when statistical measurements of risk are used. Harry Markowitz was awarded the 1990 Nobel Prize in Economics for his statistical measures of the diversification effect.

The essence of Markowitz's contribution to modern portfolio theory is illustrated in Figure 8.3. The number of assets in a portfolio is measured on the horizontal axis against the risk of the portfolio measured along the vertical axis.[2] The point of this figure is that the risk of the portfolio can be decreased dramatically as the number of assets in the portfolio increases. At the same time, the risk of the portfolio cannot be eliminated completely, as shown by the horizontal line lying above zero in Figure 8.3. This line marks the minimum level of risk for a portfolio of risky assets and is called *market or systematic risk.* No matter how many assets in your portfolio, you cannot eliminate this type—market or systematic—of risk.

It is necessary to explain one more concept before discussing the applications of modern portfolio theory to residual value risk. The risk concept is called *beta,* a notion I briefly discussed in

---

[2] The total risk of the portfolio is measured statistically by the variance or the standard deviation.

Figure 8.3: The Diversification Effect

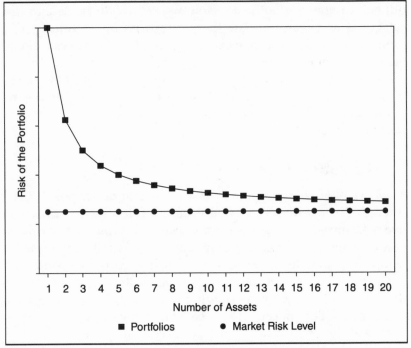

Chapter 7. Beta measures the market or systematic risk of *individual* assets. As I explained, the total amount of risk can be reduced by diversification so that only market risk remains. Therefore, beta measures the contribution of each individual asset to this total market risk. In the portfolio context, beta is the only relevant measure of risk.

Beta's Application to Residual Value

Modern portfolio theory has a simple and straightforward application to the evaluation of residual value risk. Leasing companies typically hold a portfolio of leases containing a well-diversified set of assets.[3] Because of the diversification effect, systematic risk is the only relevant risk for the residual values. Thus only systematic risk

---

[3] The opposite of the diversified leasing company is the specialized lessor, such as GPA for aircraft, IBM for computers, or Xerox for copy machines. Specialization, however, is the exception, rather than the rule. Most lessors, even those with some equipment specialization, hold diversified portfolios of assets.

as measured by beta is relevant for the pricing of the residual value risk in the lease contract.

These ideas from modern portfolio theory have led to a model known as the Capital Asset Pricing Model (CAPM). The model takes the form:

$$r = r_f + \beta \ (r_M - r_f) \qquad (8.1)$$

where
   r = expected return on the asset
   β = beta, the measure of systematic risk
   r_M = expected return on the market portfolio (usually a stock index)
   r_f = risk-free rate of return (a Treasury bill or bond rate)

Equation 8.1 or the CAPM is simple to use. For example, if the risk-free rate is 5 percent, the expected return on the market is 12 percent, and the beta is 1.4, the expected return on the asset is 14.8 percent:

$$r = r_f + \beta \ (r_M - r_f)$$
$$r = 0.05 + 1.4 \ (0.12 - 0.05) \qquad (8.2)$$
$$r = 0.148 \ or \ 14.8\%$$

How can beta be measured to capture the residual value risk of an asset? There are three possible ways:

1. Measure a time series of prices for used equipment, and then correlate the returns from this time series with the time series of returns from a marketwide index.

2. Measure the beta of a firm or group of firms that manufactures the leased asset. Remove the effect of leverage in order to obtain an asset beta.

3. Measure as in (2), except use the beta from a firm or firms that use the leased asset.

The first approach is very desirable because it measures the economic depreciation of an asset directly. It also provides information about the behavior of a used asset through time, which can be useful to the analyst trying to get a feel for the risk of the used asset. Unfortunately, obtaining the time series of used asset prices is often difficult. One exception is in the automobile industry where a *Blue Book* of used model prices is published monthly, so a time series of prices is readily available.

The second approach is possible to implement where a "pure play" firm or firms exist. A pure play firm is one whose earnings come mainly from a single asset or type of asset. Analysts using stock market data for firms manufacturing an asset to estimate the beta of the asset must be able to assume that the risk of the asset producer is closely linked with the risk of the asset being produced and the value of that asset over time. For example, economists at General Motors often look at the prices of used automobiles to help forecast the demand for new cars.

Boeing Corporation is an example of a pure play manufacturer. Boeing's beta can be measured from the correlation of its stock return with the return on a market index.[4] Boeing, however, has debt (leverage), contributing to financial risk, and increasing the equity beta. To remove this leverage effect, a formula developed by Hamada can be used:

$$\beta_U = \beta_L / \left(1 + \frac{DEBT}{EQUITY} \right) \qquad (8.3)$$

where
$$\beta_U = \text{unlevered or asset beta}$$
$$\beta_L = \text{levered or equity beta}$$
$$DEBT/EQUITY = \text{market value of debt divided by market value of equity}$$

With taxes, the formula changes to:

$$\beta_U = \beta_L / \left[1 + (1 - T) \frac{DEBT}{EQUITY} \right] \qquad (8.4)$$

where T is the corporate tax rate. To apply this equation, all you need are the equity beta, debt-to-equity ratio, and the tax rate. If

---

[4] Betas for many firms are published by investment advisory firms such as Value Line or Merrill Lynch.

the equity beta of Boeing Corporation is 1.15, the debt-to-equity ratio 0.49, and the tax rate 35 percent, the asset beta is calculated to be 0.87:

$$\beta_U = \beta_L \Big/ \left[1 + (1 - T)\frac{DEBT}{EQUITY} \right]$$

$$= 1.15/[1 + (1 - 0.35)0.49] \qquad (8.5)$$

$$= 0.87.$$

The procedure for estimating asset betas may introduce additional error because of the use of firm betas to proxy for individual asset risk. Selection of firms whose primary business is manufacturing the asset under lease and averaging over several firms in an industry should cancel out many of the firm-specific errors or idiosyncracies. Thus this procedure uses the diversification principle and the best information available to measure the residual value risk.

Approach three is also possible to implement in certain cases. Firms that use a single type of asset, for example, aircraft, are companies such as Delta or American Airlines. The beta of the airline company could be used as a proxy for the beta of the asset—aircraft. Interestingly, the study by Schallheim, Johnson, Lease, and McConnell finds that both manufacturing firms and user firms provide good proxies for asset betas.[5]

Table 8.1 shows the asset beta calculations for a selection of firms in different asset categories. The equity betas come from 1990 Value Line publications. The asset betas in the table illustrate the use of proxy betas from asset manufacturers and proxy betas from asset users. Proxy betas can be calculated using a single firm or a group of firms in the same asset category. For example, the asset beta for aircraft using Boeing as a single-firm producer is 0.92. For airline companies—American, Delta, and United—the average of the asset betas is 0.85. Table 8.1 also shows the wide variation in asset betas. The average automobile beta is 0.41. The average beta for medical equipment in 1990 is much higher, at 1.23. If the market risk premium is 8 percent, the expected discount rate for medical

---

[5] James S. Schallheim, Ramon E. Johnson, Ronald C. Lease, and John J. McConnell, "The Determinants of Yields on Financial Leasing Contracts," *Journal of Financial Economics*, v. 19(1), 1987, pp. 45–68.

Table 8.1: Asset Beta Calculations

Assets and Firms	Equity Beta	Debt-to-Equity Ratio	Asset Beta
Aircraft			
Boeing	0.95	0.04	0.92
Airlines			
AMR	1.40	0.69	0.96
Delta	1.05	0.35	0.85
UAL	1.15	0.82	0.75
Automobiles			
Chrysler	1.40	2.33	0.55
Ford	1.10	3.55	0.33
General Motors	0.95	2.57	0.35
Computers			
Control Data	1.20	0.82	0.78
IBM	0.90	0.28	0.76
Sun Microsystems	1.25	0.56	0.91
Construction			
Caterpillar	1.15	0.49	0.87
Harnischfeger	1.30	0.22	1.14
Ingersoll-Rand	1.30	0.19	1.15
Material Handling			
Clark Equipment	1.20	0.28	1.01
NACCO Industries	1.00	2.70	0.36
Medical			
Applied Biosystems	1.35	0.03	1.32
Bio-Medicus	1.30	0.00	1.30
Cobe Labs	1.20	0.20	1.06
Office Equipment			
Hunt Manufacturing	0.90	0.41	0.71
Pitney Bowes	1.10	0.82	0.71
Xerox Corp.	1.15	1.27	0.63
Telecommunications			
Andrew Corp.	0.95	0.08	0.91
DSC Communications	1.50	0.67	1.04
Mitel Corp.	1.00	0.02	0.99
Trucks			
Mack Trucks	1.00	1.38	0.52

equipment would be 6.6 percent higher than the expected discount rate for automobiles.[6] Clearly the measurement of asset betas and the resulting discount rates can have a major impact on the lease or buy decision.

Residual Value Experience

Lessor firms naturally have a great deal of experience with residual values. This experience is useful to lessee firms as well. Because the lessee gives up the right to the residual value, this opportunity loss is important. If the expected residual value is high, the lessee should negotiate lower lease payments or purchase the asset (finance through borrowing). In this section, I consider some of the actual experiences of leasing companies.

Lease, McConnell, and Schallheim examine the entire payment history of 137 leasing contracts.[7] Of the total, 68 leases are classified as "full-term," or, in other words, the leases were completed "more or less" as promised, with the asset sold at maturity. Table 8.2 summarizes the residual value experience with these 68 leases.

Actual residual values in the table average over 1.5 times the estimated residual values. This sample covers a number of years, 1973–1982; a wide range of asset costs, $1,000 to $1,500,000; a wide range of contract maturities, one year to eight years; and a wide

Table 8.2: Residual Value Data from LMS Study

Residual Values	Average	Median	Standard Development	Minimum	Maximum
Estimated	$3,789	$995	$9,686	$0	$74,154
Actual	$7,379	$1,075	$18,023	$0	$104,000
Actual divided by estimated	153.5%	100.0%			

---

[6] The 6.6 percent *higher* discount note is calculated using the CAPM equation. That is, the difference in expected returns is $(\beta_1 - \beta_2) \times (r_M - r_f) = (1.23 - 0.41) \times (.08) = .066$.

[7] Ronald C. Lease, John J. McConnell, and James S. Schallheim, "Realized Returns and the Default and Prepayment Experience of Financial Leasing Contracts," *Financial Management*, v. 19(2), 1990, pp. 11–20.

range of asset types. The residual value experiences of these leases are similar to more recent data discussed below.

Table 8.3 shows the estimated residual values as a percentage of the asset costs for leases classified as direct financing leases. Residual values for direct financing leases display a great deal of variation. Transportation equipment—aircraft, railroad rolling stock, trucks, and trailers—consistently displays the largest expected residual values as a percentage of the asset costs. Computer equipment has some of the lowest residual values. Figure 8.4 shows the time series percentage residual values from 1988 to 1992 for four equipment categories—aircraft, small computers, office machines, and railroad equipment. Notice that aircraft has showed a downward trend in the period 1990–1992, while office machines display a slightly upward trend over the same period. Railroad equipment shows large variations in residual values.

Table 8.3: Residual Values for Financial Leases (booked as a percentage of asset cost)

Assets	1988	1989	1990	1991	1992
Agricultural	10.5	11.8	9.9	11.6	9.5
Aircraft	18.3	20.5	26.9	20.8	17.9
Computers:					
Mainframes	8.7	11.6	11.9	10.7	8.8
Peripherals	8.1	9.2	11.3	6.0	7.0
Small systems	7.0	8.0	9.2	10.1	7.5
Software	—	—	7.3	6.4	6.1
Construction	11.6	13.1	13.8	13.9	16.0
Container	12.2	7.0	16.4	—	11.0
Furniture, etc.	8.0	8.6	11.4	9.0	6.3
Industrial	6.8	13.6	13.5	12.6	11.1
Manufacturing	8.7	9.2	12.5	11.7	11.0
Materials handling	13.8	10.4	17.8	16.4	14.5
Medical	7.4	7.0	11.5	9.3	4.6
Office machines	7.3	6.8	9.8	9.4	12.3
Railroad	20.4	25.9	17.5	35.3	22.6
Telecommunications	8.0	12.5	9.4	9.9	7.1
Trucks and trailers	14.8	15.5	21.4	15.7	18.2
Other	10.1	6.4	9.9	12.4	13.9
Simple average	10.7	11.6	13.6	13.1	11.5

Source: Equipment Leasing Association, *Survey of Industry Activity*, 1988, 1990, and 1992.

Figure 8.4: Residual Values for Selected Assets (estimated as a percentage of cost)

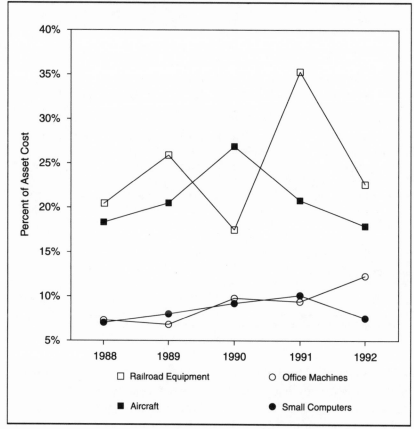

Actual residual values for some of these assets expressed as a percentage of the estimated values are reported in Table 8.4. These numbers are consistent with the results of the Lease, McConnell, and Schallheim study, which shows an average realized residual value of 150 percent of estimated value. These numbers confirm that lessors realize more than the estimated residual value with regularity. Figure 8.5 displays the numbers from Table 8.4 for four asset categories—agricultural, mainframe computers, industrial equipment, and trucks and trailers.

For the period 1988–1992, mainframe computers showed an increase in realized residual values relative to estimated values. Agricultural equipment generally decreased in actual value over the

Table 8.4: Residual Values for Financial Leases (residual value recovered as a percentage of original estimate)

Assets	1988	1989	1990	1991	1992
Agricultural	189.5	117.9	153.5	124.2	111.3
Computers:					
Mainframes	121.3	151.2	139.8	141.9	151.3
Peripherals	105.3	128.5	158.1	149.7	158.5
Small systems	105.4	148.2	157.4	154.0	123.3
Software	—	—	—	175.3	140.7
Construction	115.8	124.8	147.4	178.2	115.9
Furniture, etc.	130.8	118.8	134.9	156.2	132.9
Industrial	107.2	98.1	153.1	133.7	142.4
Manufacturing	140.1	138.8	151.9	148.7	145.3
Materials handling	133.9	153.8	141.4	159.8	112.8
Medical	149.2	127.4	147.2	144.4	153.7
Office machines	148.7	116.4	144.2	147.7	142.4
Telecommunications	116.6	113.6	135.4	157.2	143.8
Trucks and trailers	117.6	119.2	130.4	130.6	115.3
Other	131.3	110.9	131.1	160.4	144.1
Simple average	129.5	126.3	144.7	150.8	135.6

Source: Equipment Leasing Association, *Survey of Industry Activity,* 1988, 1990, and 1992.

same period, and also displayed significant variation. Nevertheless, every category of equipment, for every year from 1988 to 1992, showed an average actual residual value greater than expected with only one exception—industrial equipment in 1989.

What accounts for the higher actual residual values relative to estimated values? Two possible answers are:

1. Residual values are underestimated by lessors in order to obtain higher tax-deductible depreciation in earlier periods. Even though depreciation tax recapture is paid later, the time value of money makes this scheme profitable for lessees and lessors.

2. Residual values are systematically underestimated because actual inflation exceeds anticipated inflation in used asset prices.

The first answer implies that the IRS and the FASB accounting depreciation guidelines systematically exceed economic depreciation.

Figure 8.5: Residual Values for Selected Assets (actual as a percentage of estimated)

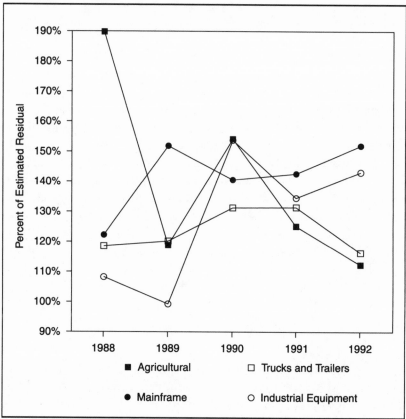

If unexpected inflation is the only cause of the deviation of realized salvage values from estimated residual values, the following relationship is expected:

$$ARV = ERV[(1 + u)^n] \qquad (8.6)$$

where ARV is the actual residual value, ERV is the estimated residual value, u is the unexpected inflation rate, and n is the time-to-maturity of the lease. Lease, McConnell, and Schallheim statistically estimated equation 8.6 and find a very strong fit between the data and the equation. They conclude that unexpected inflation appears to contribute significantly to the difference between estimated and actual residual value.

Specialization or Diversification?

The portfolio concept of risk measurement, beta, is based on the idea of diversification. Most leasing companies hold diversified portfolios of assets for lease because diversification helps reduce the residual value risk.

Some leasing firms choose not to diversify and specialize in a single asset. I mentioned the GPA Group, which specialized in aircraft leasing. This policy provided remarkable growth and profits for GPA in the 1980s, but led to financial distress and near collapse for the firm in the worldwide recession of the 1990s.

IFG Leasing, a division of Inter-Regional Financial Group, is a leasing company that tried to mix diversification and specialization, an approach that unfortunately did not work. IFG Leasing specialized in agricultural leases, but diversified across a wide range of asset categories in leases to small- and medium-sized businesses. IFG Leasing showed phenomenal growth and profits right up to the recession in the early 1980s. By 1983, Inter-Regional Financial Group discontinued the operations of IFG Leasing because of growing losses.

What do these experiences tell us? The main lesson is that the lessee has to shop carefully for a lease. If the lessee is looking for an operating lease that provides service as well as financing, the example of GPA must be kept in mind. Will the lessor remain in business for the duration of the lease? Another consideration is to shop around at both diversified leasing companies and specialized lessors, if the latter exists. Specialization, for both lessees and lessors, results in higher risk. As with all investments, the higher risk can result in large rewards or losses.

Options in Leases

As discussed in Chapters 1 and 2, lease contracts often include many different options. There are options to: (1) purchase the asset, (2) renew the lease, and/or (3) cancel the lease. These options can be very valuable, although they are difficult to price. An option pricing model can be used to value options contained in leasing contracts.

Black and Scholes Option Pricing Model

Fischer Black and Myron Scholes developed the Option Pricing Model (OPM) that helped revolutionize the options and futures industry.[8] Option traders are very familiar with the model, which is used extensively both for setting price guidelines and discovering arbitrage opportunities. The OPM is used to price *call options* (the option to *buy* a given stock at a fixed price) and *put options* (the option to *sell* a given stock at a fixed price) in the financial markets. The model can also be used to price *real* assets, such as the options contained in leasing contracts.[9] McConnell and Schallheim have developed a general model that can be used to price a multitude of options in leasing contracts.[10]

Option values are determined by the price of the underlying security. In the case of leasing, the price of the underlying security is directly or indirectly based on the price of the depreciating asset. As highlighted by the discussion of residual value risk earlier in the chapter, residual values will rise and fall depending on unpredictable information about asset values and unpredictable technological obsolescence. The difference between the *expected* asset value and the *actual* price is the source of the *uncertain* option value when the option is exercised. Figures 8.1 and 8.2 illustrate the difference between expected and actual residual values.

To begin the presentation of the OPM, let's review the pricing of the simple call option. The payoffs for a call option (the option to buy) at maturity are straightforward: If the stock price is greater than the exercise price, the call option payoff is the difference; but if the stock price is less than or equal to the exercise price, the payoff is zero. Call options are priced in the financial markets, where the value of a call option is dependent on the price of the underlying stock (another financial asset), the exercise price, the risk-free rate of interest, the time-to-maturity, and the variance or volatility of the underlying stock price.

The Black-Scholes OPM for Valuing a Call Option

The OPM is more accessible when illustrated with a numerical example. Equation 8.7 shows the formula and defines the notation:

---

[8] The seminal article presenting the Option Pricing Model is Fischer Black and Myron Scholes, "The Pricing of Options and Corporate Liabilities," *Journal of Political Economy*, v. 81(3), 1973, pp. 637–654.

[9] Real assets are distinguished from financial assets. Financial assets can be considered as "pieces of paper" that represent *claims* on real assets, including both tangible and intangible assets.

[10] John J. McConnell and James S. Schallheim, "Valuation of Asset Leasing Contracts," *Journal of Financial Economics*, v. 12(2), 1983, pp. 237–261.

$$C = SN(d_1) - Ee^{-rt}N(d_2)$$

$$d_1 = [\ln(S/E) + (r + \frac{\sigma^2}{2})\,t]/\sigma\sqrt{t} \qquad (8.7)$$

$$d_2 = d_1 - \sigma\sqrt{t}$$

The notation is:

C = call option value

N(d) = cumulative normal probability density function (i.e., the probability that a standardized, normally distributed, random variable will be less than or equal to d)

The five pricing parameters are:

S = current stock price

E = exercise price of the option

r = annual, continuously compounded, risk-free rate of interest

t = time-to-maturity or expiration date (in years)

σ^2 = variance (per year) of the continuously compounded, rate of return on the stock

Example

Apex Equipment Company has a stock price today of $50. A call option with an exercise price of $49 expires in exactly 199 days. The risk-free interest rate is 7 percent, and the stock has an annual variance of 0.09. Thus the five parameters are identified: (1) S = 50, (2) E = 49, (3) r = 0.07, (4) t = 0.545 (or 199/365), and (5) σ^2 = 0.09. The values of d_1 and d_2 are:

$$d_1 = [\ln(S/E) + (r + \frac{\sigma^2}{2})t]/\sigma\sqrt{t}$$

$$= [\ln(50/49) + (0.07 + \frac{0.09}{2})0.545]/\sqrt{(0.09)(0.545)}$$

$$= 0.3743 \qquad (8.8)$$

$$d_2 = d_1 - \sigma\sqrt{t}$$

$$= 0.3743 - \sqrt{(0.09)(0.545)}$$

$$= 0.1528$$

$N(d_1)$ = 0.6459 and $N(d_2)$ = 0.5607 are calculated from the stan-0dard normal cumulative density function (tables can be found in elementary statistics books, and formulas for the computation are programmed in many calculators on the market today).

Finally, the call value can be calculated:

$$C = SN(d_1) - Ee^{-rt}N(d_2)$$

$$= (\$50 \times 0.6459) - \$49 \times [e^{-0.07 \times 0.545}] \times 0.5607 \qquad (8.9)$$

$$= \$32.295 - \$26.447$$

$$= \$5.85$$

Although the valuation equation is complex, and its derivation is beyond the scope of this book, an intuitive presentation of the equation is possible. I mentioned that the payoff of the call option is the difference between the stock price at maturity and the exercise, if positive, and zero, if not. The Black-Scholes equation 8.7 can be restated as:

$$C = S \times (Probability\ Measure\ 1) - PV(E) \qquad (8.10)$$
$$\times (Probability\ Measure\ 2)$$

In words, the call price equals the current stock price times a probability less the present value of the exercise price times a second probability. Therefore, the Black-Scholes OPM, in one sense, derives precise probability measures to weigh the difference between the stock price and the exercise price.

Pricing Lease Options

There is one major problem in application of the Black–Scholes OPM to leasing: that the underlying asset for leasing is *depreciating* equipment. The underlying asset for a typical call option, by contrast, is an *appreciating* stock price. Therefore, an adjustment is necessary to the Black–Scholes formula that takes into account the asset's economic depreciation.[11] McConnell and Schallheim present such an adjustment in their general model for leasing options.[12]

---

[11] Economic depreciation represents the actual loss in *market value* of the asset over time. Economic, accounting, and tax depreciation can be very different from one another.

[12] McConnell and Schallheim, "Valuation of Asset Leasing Contracts." Also, see Thomas E. Copeland and J. Fred Weston, "A Note on the Evaluation of Cancellable

The adjustment to the present asset value that accounts for the economic depreciation is lambda, λ. The symbolic representation of lambda is:

$$\lambda = \left[\frac{(1 - d)}{(1 + r_f)}\right]e^{\sigma_{ly}} \tag{8.11}$$

where d represents the expected rate of economic depreciation and r_f is the risk-free rate of interest.

The last term in equation 8.11, the exponential term $\exp(\sigma_{ly})$, is an adjustment for the covariance of economic depreciation with the general market factor. This factor is very similar to the beta concept. What does the covariance term mean? The purpose is to adjust expected economic depreciation for *risk*.

Miller and Upton provide an interesting interpretation of this factor. If the depreciation is independent of the state of the economy, the covariance term is zero. "If, however, necessity is indeed the mother of invention and the pace of technological improvement steps up as the economy falls off," the covariance is negative. In this case, the adjustment term, λ, will be lower. "But if it is boom conditions in the economy that stimulate technological progress," the covariance term is positive, and the adjustment term will be higher.[13]

The best way to interpret the λ adjustment factor is using numerical examples. First, I examine the rate of economic depreciation. Table 8.5 gives the number of years until an asset reaches 50 percent or 20 percent of its original cost for rates of economic depreciation ranging from 5 percent to 25 percent. Obviously, the higher the rate of economic depreciation, the shorter the life of the asset. To reach a value of 20 percent of the original cost of an asset (i.e., a 20 percent residual value), it takes more than 31 years if the rate of depreciation is 5 percent, but it takes less than six years if the depreciation rate is 25 percent. Finally, it should be mentioned that all these examples represent *constant* rates of economic depreciation.

Operating Leases," *Financial Management*, v. 11(2), 1982, pp. 60–67; and Wayne Y. Lee, John D. Martin, and Andrew J. Senchack, "The Case for Using Options to Evaluate Salvage Values in Financial Leases," *Financial Management*, v. 11(3), 1982, pp. 33–41.

[13] Merton H. Miller and Charles W. Upton, "Leasing, Buying, and the Cost of Capital Services," *Journal of Finance*, v. 31(3), 1976, pp. 761–786.

Table 8.5: Effects of Economic Depreciation on the Life of Asset

Economic Depreciation (percentage)	Number of Years Until 50% of Cost (years)	Number of Years Until 20% of Cost (years)
5	13.5	31.4
10	6.6	15.3
15	4.3	9.9
20	3.1	7.2
25	2.4	5.6

The lambda factor that adjusts the asset for economic depreciation also contains the risk-free rate of interest. The purpose of the risk-free rate of interest is to adjust for the time value of money because the residual value comes at a future date. The lambda factor also contains the covariance term as described above. This last term adjusts the expected rate of economic depreciation for a market risk premium. The covariance term is difficult to estimate in a practical application.

Now I can illustrate the leasing option model for the purchase option. The pricing equation is:

$$C = \lambda^t \cdot A \cdot N(d_1) - E \cdot e^{-rt} \cdot N(d_2)$$

$$d_1 = [\ln(\lambda^t \cdot A/E)$$

$$+ (r + \frac{\sigma^2}{2})t]/\sigma\sqrt{t} \qquad (8.12)$$

$$d_2 = d_1 - \sigma\sqrt{t}$$

$$\lambda = [(1 - d)/(1 + r_f)]e^{\sigma_{ly}}$$

The equation is the same as for the call option described earlier, with the exception that the depreciating asset price, $\lambda^t A$, is substituted for the stock price in the typical call option.

Valuing a Lease Purchase Option

Suppose a $1 million equipment lease has a purchase option with an exercise price that is 20 percent of the asset cost. The purchase option can be exercised at the maturity of the lease, which is in five years. The rate of economic depreciation on the asset is 20 percent. The risk-free interest rate is 5 percent. The asset has an annual variance of 0.10. I assume that the covariance term is 0. Thus, the seven parameters for lease option valuation are identified:

$$A = 1,000,000,$$
$$E = 200,000,$$
$$r = 0.05,$$
$$t = 5,$$
$$\sigma^2 = 0.10,$$
$$d = 0.20,$$
$$\sigma_{ly} = 0.$$

The values of λ, d_1, and d_2 are:

$$\lambda = [(1 - d)/((1 + r)] \, e^{\sigma_{ly}}$$
$$= [(1 - 0.2)/(1 + 0.05)]e^0$$
$$= 0.7619$$

$$d_1 = [\ln(\lambda^t A/E) + (r + \frac{\sigma^2}{2})t]/\sigma\sqrt{t}$$
$$= [\ln(0.7619^5 \times 1,000,000/200,000) + (0.05 +$$
$$\frac{0.10}{2})5]/\sqrt{(0.10)\,(5)}$$
$$= 1.0603$$

$$d_2 = d_1 - \sigma\sqrt{t}$$
$$= 1.0603 - \sqrt{(0.10)\,(5)}$$
$$= 0.3532$$

From the standard normal cumulative density function:

$$N(d_1) = 0.8555$$
$$N(d_2) = 0.6380$$

Finally the lease purchase option can be calculated:

$$C = \lambda^t \cdot A \cdot N(d_1) - E \cdot e^{-rt} \cdot N(d_2)$$
$$= (0.7619^5 \times \$1,000,000 \times 0.8555) - \$200,000 \times [e^{-0.05 \times 5}]$$
$$\times 0.6380$$
$$= \$219,639 - \$99,375$$
$$= \$120,264$$

The value of the purchase option, over $120,000, is substantial enough that it could lead to a positive net advantage to leasing that otherwise might be negative.

The OPM can be used to price a multitude of options contained in leasing contracts. Besides the option to purchase the asset, these can include options to extend the lease (a call option), to cancel the lease (a put or call option as explained below), to guarantee the residual value (a put option), and various combinations of these options. The McConnell and Schallheim model provides a general framework to price all these options.

One interesting option problem concerns the option to cancel the lease. Copeland and Weston consider the cancelable operating lease to be a combination of a non-cancelable lease and a put option with an exercise price equal to the market value of the depreciating asset.[14] The cost of this option to the lessee is reflected in higher lease payments and hence a higher internal rate of return on the lease.

McConnell and Schallheim treat the cancelable lease as a compound option. The lease payment in any period of time buys both the use of the asset for one period plus a European call option to purchase the use of the asset for an additional period, exercisable at the end of the period. The last lease payment simply buys the use of the asset for one period. In this fashion, each call option (except the last) gives the lessee the right to purchase another call option. The value of this compound option depends on the value of all the subsequent call options, with the lease payment itself as the exercise price for these call options.

There is one critical problem with the way the put option is introduced in the Copeland and Weston model—the value of the put option is divided evenly over all the lease payments. In the event that the lease is canceled, the remaining lease payments are forfeited along with the remaining unpaid balance for the put option component. In other words, in the Copeland and Weston model, the put option to cancel the lease can be exercised before the option is paid for! The McConnell and Schallheim model overcomes this deficiency because it solves simultaneously for the lease payments and option values. The problem with the Copeland and Weston put model also could be resolved with a compound put option.

---

[14] Copeland and Weston, "A Note on the Evaluation of Cancellable Operating Leases."

Unfortunately, the computational effort makes this approach impractical.

Table 8.6 shows some simple examples of the cancellation option as illustrated by Copeland and Weston and McConnell and Schallheim. What these examples show is the huge impact that the lease cancellation option can have on the amount of the lease payments and on the lease's internal rate of return computation. The lease payments can increase by 25 percent or more. The internal rates of return or yields also can increase by substantial amounts. The amount of the lease payments and the internal rate of return for the Copeland and Weston example would increase even more if the compound option approach is used rather than the simple option approach.

Summary

This chapter considers the "wild card" of leasing, namely, the residual value. I demonstrate the large variations possible in residual values, implying large risks. Leasing companies deal with residual value risk in two general ways. They (1) diversify the risk by holding a portfolio of different types of assets, or (2) specialize in one type of asset in order to maximize the residual value through

Table 8.6: Simple Examples of the Cancellation Option

	Annual Rate of Economic Depreciation	Lease Payment without Cancellation Option	Lease Payment with Cancellation Option	IRR without Cancellation Option	IRR with Cancellation Option
Copeland and Weston ($10,000 asset)	>60%	$4619	$5392	10%	14%
McConnell and Schallheim ($1,000 asset)	15%	$197	$248	10%	19%
Same as above	25%	$250	$259	10%	21%

expertise in the resale market. Most lessors apply the portfolio concept.

One way to measure residual value risk, based on diversification and modern portfolio theory, is to use the Capital Asset Pricing Model. Equation 8.1 shows how the CAPM can be used to measure the discount rate if the beta of the asset can be measured or estimated. I show that the actual residual values exceed the estimated residual values, on average, for leasing companies over time and over all asset types. This result may be caused by (1) overdepreciating the asset for the present value of the tax savings, and/or (2) systematic underestimating unexpected inflation for used equipment. Options in leasing contracts almost always depend on the residual value of the asset. The Black–Scholes option pricing model, with proper modifications, can be used to price these options.

Chapter 9

Summary: Lease or Buy

We began with a lease or buy situation faced by Pat McDonald at AdTech. The first eight chapters of this book present all the details required to make such a lease or buy decision. In this chapter, I provide some answers to the questions posed in the preface. First, Exhibit 9.1 summarizes the five general rules for lease versus buy decisions. After a brief discussion of these rules, I analyze Pat McDonald's lease or buy decision, and I also illustrate all the general factors that can be analyzed by quantitative models.

Use Net Present Value (Net Advantage to Leasing) Analysis

Net present value analysis allows the decision maker to address all the components of the lease versus buy decision. You may use yield analysis, but the danger of making an incorrect decision is higher (as discussed in Chapter 7). Although the problem is stated as lease or buy, the NPV analysis really compares leasing to borrowing. The NPV analysis has an equivalent loan built in, and Chapter 5 discusses the principles behind this important assumption.

Exhibit 9.1: Rules for Lease or Buy Decision Making

1. Use net present value (net advantage to leasing) analysis
2. Do not ignore the residual value of the equipment
3. Consider all tax consequences of the lease
4. Follow the accounting rules for leases
5. Consider all the options in the lease

In order to use the basic NPV equation (the topic of Chapter 6), the following factors are required:

1. Cost of the equipment

2. The schedule of lease payments

3. The schedule of depreciation tax shields forgone

4. The marginal tax rate

5. The marginal borrowing rate

6. The residual value forgone, if any

Do Not Ignore the Residual Value of the Equipment

Almost by definition, when a lease contract is paid in full, the asset usually belongs to the lessor. Residual value is the "wild card" of leasing because huge profits or losses may occur from the realization of the salvage value. This fundamental property of leasing dictates that the residual value will be priced as the market determines the lease payments. The risk in the uncertain residual value is an extremely important consideration in the lease or buy decision. Residual value should be analyzed with great care as discussed in Chapter 8.

Consider All Tax Consequences of the Lease

Taxes play a very important role in many leases. Details of the tax laws are explained in Chapter 3. The loss or potential loss of depreciation tax shields can make leasing advantageous. In addition, a firm subject to the alternative minimum tax (ATM) could find leasing tax advantageous.

Follow the Accounting Rules for Leases

Accounting rules determine whether a lease is reported on the balance sheet or only in the footnotes to the statements. The question posed in Chapter 4 is whether the reporting of a lease on the balance sheet matters. There are two schools of thought. If you think off-balance sheet financing has value, the question that you must consider is "Why?" This point is discussed in Chapter 4.

Consider All the Options in the Lease

Lease contracts often include many different options (see Chapters 1 and 2). For example, there are options to purchase the asset at the end of the lease for a fixed price, renew the lease for a fixed period of time, or cancel the lease before the maturity date of the lease. These options can be very valuable, and, at the same time, difficult to price. The Option Pricing Model, which can be used to value options contained in leasing contracts, uses four easily obtainable inputs: the asset cost, the exercise price of the option, the time to maturity, and the risk-free rate of interest. Three other inputs to the model are more difficult to estimate: the variance of the return of the asset price over time, the rate of economic depreciation, and the covariance of economic depreciation with the general market factor. This last factor is very similar to the beta concept introduced in Chapters 7 and 8. If these inputs can be estimated, the analyst can actually compute the value of the options in the lease contract. Even if the model cannot be used, the idea that the lease options have value should not be ignored. The decision maker can implicitly factor the options into the lease or buy determination.

A Complex Example

Returning, finally, to the problem posed in the preface, recall that Pat McDonald at AdTech faces a difficult lease or buy decision. A duplicating machine costs $1.5 million. The borrowing rate for AdTech is 9 percent. If lease payments of $370,000 per year (end-of-year) for five years are offered, is the lease a better bargain than purchasing the machine?

Use NPV Analysis

In order to analyze this problem, let's turn to the Myers, Dill, and Bautista model, which can be represented as follows:

$$NPV = A_0 - \sum_{t=1}^{N} \frac{L_t(1 - T) + D_t(T)}{(1 + r^*)^t} \tag{9.1}$$

where NPV is the net present value of leasing (to the lessee), A_0 is the cost of the asset net of any lease payments at time 0, L_t is the lease payment at time t, T is the corporate tax rate, D_t is the amount of depreciation at time t, N is the number of periods for the lease, and r^* is the after-tax cost of debt, $r^* = r_B (1 - T)$.

To apply the model, a schedule of after-tax lease payments and the tax shield of lost depreciation are required. Assuming three-year MACRS depreciation, Table 9.1 displays the after-tax cash flows of leasing (also called the equivalent loan cash flows).

Applying AdTech's numbers to the MDB model equation 9.1 results in the following:

$$NPV = \$1,500,000 - \frac{\$415,482.5}{(1.0585)^1} - \frac{\$473,862.5}{(1.0585)^2}$$

$$- \frac{\$318,252.5}{(1.0585)^3} - \frac{\$279,402.5}{(1.0585)^4} - \frac{\$240,500}{(1.0585)^5} \quad (9.2)$$

$$= \$1,500,000 - \$1,487,363.37$$

$$= \$12,636.63$$

Equation 9.2 demonstrates a positive NPV or NAL of about \$12,637 for the AdTech lease. In other words, the lease saves the company more than \$12,000 in today's dollars. Pat McDonald should recommend leasing the duplicating machine.

Residual Value

In the AdTech lease example, any residual value for the duplicating machine is ignored. Suppose that the equipment is expected to have a value of \$275,000 at the end of five years. Also, assume that

Table 9.1: Leasing Cash Flows for AdTech Company

Item	Year 1	Year 2	Year 3	Year 4	Year 5
Depreciation schedule	\$499,950	\$666,750	\$222,150	\$111,150	\$0.0
Lease payment Tax deduction Depreciation (tax shield)	\$370,000 (129,500) 174,982.5	\$370,000 (129,500) 233,362.5	\$370,000 (129,500) 77,752.5	\$370,000 (129,500) 38,0902.5	\$370,000 (129,500) 0.0
Cost of leasing	\$415,482.5	\$473,862.5	\$318,252.5	\$279,402.5	\$240,500.0

the appropriate discount rate for this risky residual value is 18 percent. Modifying equation 9.2 to include the present value of the residual value results in the following calculation:

$$NPV = \$1,500,000 - \$1,487,363.37 - \frac{\$275,000}{(1.18)^5}$$

$$= \$12,636.63 - \$120,205.03 \qquad (9.3)$$

$$= -\$107,568.40$$

The present value of the residual value is more than $120,000. Now the net advantage to leasing is a *negative* $107,568. In other words, the residual value given up by leasing is too large, given this schedule of lease payments. Buying the asset (and the residual value) is now the better alternative.

Taxes

The AdTech example assumes that the firm is taxed at the corporate tax rate of 35 percent whether the asset is leased or purchased. Suppose that AdTech is subject to the alternative minimum tax because of low earnings or tax-loss carryforwards. In this case, the AdTech lease can be profitable, even with the opportunity loss of the large residual value. The outcome depends on the number of years that AdTech is subject to the AMT.

Figure 9.1 displays the net advantage of leasing given the number of years AdTech is in an AMT position. If AdTech remains subject to the AMT for more than one year, the advantage to leasing is positive.

Accounting Rules

The accounting rules allow the AdTech lease to be classified as either an operating lease or a capital lease. If there is no transfer of ownership or a bargain purchase option, the lease satisfies two rules for an *operating* lease. The other two rules refer to the economic life and the present value of the lease payments relative to the asset cost. If the economic life of the duplicating machine is greater than six years and eight months, the economic life rule is satisfied for an operating lease.

Finally, the present value of the lease payments is subject to assumptions about the appropriate discount rate. In the lease or

Figure 9.1: AdTech Corporation Equipment Lease (impact of AMT on NAL)

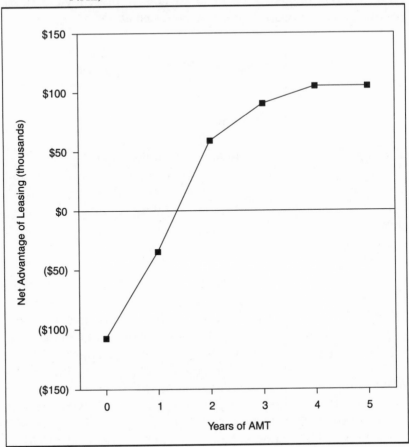

buy analysis, 9 percent is used as the borrowing rate for AdTech. At this rate, the present value of the lease payments is computed as follows:

$$PV \text{ of Lease Payments} = \sum_{t=1}^{5} \frac{\$370,000}{[1 + 0.09]} = \$1,439,170.97 \quad (9.4)$$

The present value of these lease payments is nearly 96 percent of the asset cost. The rule for a *capital* lease is satisfied, and the lease must be recorded on the balance sheet.

The calculation in equation 9.4 does not, however, consider the implicit rate of the lessor. This rate can be computed from the lease payments, asset cost, and assumed *residual value* as such:

$$\$1,500,000 = \sum_{t=1}^{5} \frac{\$370,000}{(1 + y)^t} + \frac{\$275,000}{(1 + y)^5} \tag{9.5}$$

$$y = 11.75\%$$

At the implicit rate of 11.75 percent, the present value of the lease payments is \$1,342,069.12, which is less than 90 percent of the asset cost. In order to assume that the discount rate is 11.75 percent, AdTech must argue that this rate is lower than the incremental borrowing rate. If this case can be made, the lease qualifies as an *operating* lease, and therefore is not reported on the balance sheet.

Options

The last point to consider in the AdTech lease are options. Does the lease contain any valuable options? Suppose the lease offers AdTech the option to purchase the duplicating machine for \$275,000 at the end of the lease. This is a *fixed*-purchase option but not a *bargain* purchase option because an expected residual value of \$275,000 is assumed. The option may still have value, however, which could be computed with the option pricing model presented in Chapter 8. The parameters of the option pricing model are the asset cost, the exercise price of the option, the time-to-maturity, the risk-free rate of interest, the variance of the return of asset price over time, the rate of economic depreciation, and the covariance of economic depreciation with the general market factor.

The AdTech lease has the following values for these inputs:

Asset cost (A) = \$1,500,000
Exercise price (E) = \$275,000
Time-to-maturity (t) = 5 years
Risk-free rate (r) = 6%
Variance (σ^2) = 4%
Rate of depreciation (d) = 28.77%
Covariance term (σ_{1y}) = 0

$$C = \lambda^{t} \cdot A \cdot N(d_1) - E \cdot e^{-rt} \cdot N(d_2)$$

$$d_1 = [\ln(\lambda^{t} \cdot A/E) + (r + \frac{\sigma^2}{2})\, t]/\sigma\sqrt{t} \qquad (9.6)$$

$$d_2 = d_1 - \sigma\sqrt{t}$$

$$\lambda = [(1 - d) / (1 + r_f)]\, e^{\sigma_{ly}}$$

Using the formula, one finds the value of the AdTech option to purchase the machine in five years is worth approximately $85,760 today. This makes up for much of the lost residual value, which had a present value of approximately $120,000.

Summary

We have reviewed the essential principles for the lease or buy decision with one comprehensive example. And although the example is comprehensive, it is not as complex as many leases in the marketplace. Nevertheless, the important factors for the lease or buy decision are illustrated.

To recapitulate, the checklist of important considerations contains:

1. Use net present value (net advantage to leasing) analysis
2. Do not ignore the residual value of the equipment
3. Consider all tax consequences of the lease
4. Follow the accounting rules for leases
5. Consider all the options in the lease

Now you have all the principles and all the factors required to analyze your own leases.

Appendix

Present Value Mathematics

In order to evaluate lease versus purchase analysis correctly, and in order to record capital lease liabilities correctly on the balance sheet, present value calculations are required. Present value and future value calculations do nothing more than take into account the *time value of money*. With leases, the concept of the annuity is important because many lease payments are annuities, or fixed periodic payments. Here I review present value mathematics.

Future Value

The best place to begin present value calculations is with *future value*. Suppose you borrow an amount at present, P, and promise to pay interest, I, at the end of the period. The future value, FV, is:

$$FV = P + I$$

If the interest rate is r, the amount of interest is r times P, and the future value can be written as

$$FV = P + r \times P = (1 + r)P$$

The number in the parentheses, $(1 + r)$, is called the one-period *future value factor*. To use this formula, suppose the interest rate is 10 percent, and the present amount is $1,000. The future value is:

$$FV = (1 + 0.10) \times \$1,000 = \$1,100$$

The interpretation can take two forms. First, if you borrow $1,000 at an interest rate of 10 percent, you must pay back $1,100 at the end of the period. Second, if you save $1,000 at an interest rate of 10 percent, you will have $1,100 at the end of the period.

Next, consider future values for two periods. Beginning with the last or second period, the future value is computed the same way as before, $FV = (1 + r) P$. Now subscript the values to represent the time period; FV_t, for example, represents the future value at time t. The future value at the end of the second period, FV_2, is:

$$FV_2 = (1 + r) \times FV_1$$

Substituting for $FV_1 = (1 + r) \times P$:

$$FV_2 = (1 + r) \times (1 + r) \times P$$
$$FV_2 = (1 + r)^2 \times P$$

In a similar manner, FV_3 is computed:

$$FV_3 = (1 + r)^3 \times P$$

And in general, for any time period n, FV_n is computed as:

$$FV_n = (1 + r)^n \times P$$

The quantity $(1 + r)^n$ is called the *future value factor*. The future value factor represents the future value of one dollar at r percent (per period) for n periods. For example, the future value of $1,000 in 10 years at 10 percent (per year) is:

$$FV_n = (1 + r)^n \times P$$
$$FV_{10} = (1 + 0.10)^{10} \times \$1,000$$
$$FV_{10} = \$2,593.74$$

Alternatively, suppose that the present amount of $1,000 earns interest at the rate of 5 percent every six months, for 10 years or 20 semiannual periods. What is the future value?

$$FV_n = (1 + r)^n \times P$$
$$FV_{10} = (1 + 0.05)^{20} \times \$1,000$$
$$FV_{10} = \$2,653.29$$

This example shows the power of *compounding* the interest. The semiannual interest of 5 percent compounds to *$59.55 more* than the amount compounded at the annual interest of 10 percent.

Present Value

If you turn the future value "around" or invert the equation, you can calculate the present value. Thus computations for one period look like this:

$$PV = FV/(1 + r)$$

As an example, suppose a single lease payment of $25,000 is due at the end of the year. What is the present value of the amount today if the interest rate is 10 percent? The answer is:

$$PV = \$25,000/(1 + 0.10)$$
$$PV = \$22,727.27$$

The $25,000 to be received in one year is worth $22,727 today. In other words, the lessor is willing to trade the promise of $25,000 in one year for the $22,727 today. This assumes that the *appropriate discount rate* is 10 percent.

The formula for the present value of a cash flow in two periods is:

$$PV = FV_2/(1 + r)^2$$

What is a lease payment of $25,000 that is due at the end of two years worth today? The answer, assuming a 10 percent discount rate, is:

$$PV = \$25,000/(1 + 0.10)^2$$
$$PV = \$20,661.16$$

An alternative statement for this calculation is that a $20,661.16 investment today will compound to $25,000 in two years if the interest rate is 10 percent per year.

In general, the present value of a cash flow n periods in the future is calculated as:

$$PV = FV_n[1/(1 + r)^n]$$

The term in the brackets is called the *present value factor*. It represents the present value of one dollar discounted at r percent per period for n periods.

To illustrate the general formula, consider a lease with an expected residual value of $100,000 to be realized at the end of the lease or in ten years. The proper discount rate for this expected residual value is 15 percent. The present value is:

$$PV = \$100,000[1/(1 + 0.15)^{10}]$$
$$= \$24,718.47$$

Several Cash Flows

To determine the present value of several cash flows over time, the single cash flow formula is simply repeated for each cash flow and summed over time. Using the summation symbol, $\sum_{t=1}^{n}$, which stands for the "sum of the terms from t = 1 until t = n," a general formula for the present value of several cash flows can be expressed as follows:

$$PV = \sum_{t=1}^{n} \frac{CF_t}{(1 + r)^t} \qquad (A.1)$$

The symbol CF_t stands for a cash flow at time t (and could be zero for some periods).

Suppose there are five uneven cash flows over time: Time 1: $1,000; Time 2: $2,000; Time 3: $3,000; Time 4: $4,000; Time 5: $5,000. If the interest rate is 10 percent, applying the formula to these cash flows results in:

$$PV = \sum_{t=1}^{n} \frac{CF_t}{(1 + r)^t}$$

$$= \frac{\$1,000}{(1.10)^1} + \frac{\$2,000}{(1.10)^2} + \frac{\$3,000}{(1.10)^3} + \frac{\$4,000}{(1.10)^4} + \frac{\$5,000}{(1.10)^5}$$

$$= \$10,652.59$$

The present value sum of the five cash flows is $10,652.59.*

Annuity

Most lease payments are periodic cash flows over time; furthermore, most lease payments are even, periodic cash flows for a fixed

---

* All the financial calculators and popular spreadsheets available for personal computers have the present value formulas built in. They are simple to use.

number of periods. In fact, this is the definition of an *annuity*. The mathematical formula for the present value of an annuity is almost the same as equation A.1:

$$PVA = \sum_{t=1}^{n} \frac{CF}{(1 + r)^t} \qquad (A.2)$$

You will notice that the difference between the annuity equation A.2 and the general present value equation A.1 is simply removal of the subscript t from the cash flow notation (CF) in the numerator. The purpose of the notation change is to indicate that the cash flows, whether receipts or payments, are all the *same* for an annuity.

Mathematically, equation A.2 can be manipulated to take a slightly different form:

$$PVA = CF \left[\sum_{t=1}^{n} \frac{1}{(1 + r)^t} \right] \qquad (A.3)$$

$$= CF \left[\frac{1}{r} - \frac{1}{r} \times \frac{1}{(1 + r)^n} \right]$$

Both of the terms in the brackets are known as the *present value factor for an annuity of $1*.

Suppose a lease calls for five years of annual payments of $25,000. What is the present value of these lease payments if the discount rate is 8 percent? Applying equation A.3 to this problem results in:

$$PVA = CF \left[\frac{1}{r} - \frac{1}{r} \times \frac{1}{(1 + r)^n} \right]$$

$$= \$25,000 \left[\frac{1}{0.08} - \frac{1}{0.08} \times \frac{1}{(1 + 0.08)^5} \right]$$

$$= \$99,817.75$$

Suppose a lease has five years of *monthly* payments of $2,500. What is the present value of these payments if the discount rate is 1 percent *per month*?

$$PVA = CF\left[\frac{1}{r} - \frac{1}{r} \times \frac{1}{(1 + r)^n}\right]$$

$$= \$2,500\left[\frac{1}{0.01} - \frac{1}{0.01} \times \frac{1}{(1 + 0.01)^{60}}\right]$$

$$= \$112,387.60$$

Notice that the number of periods, n, for this problem is 60 months.

In general, the decision maker must adjust the present and future value formulas for non-annual compounding periods. If m is the number of compounding periods per year, the future value, present value, and annuity formulas appear as follows:

$$FV = PV\left(1 + \frac{r}{m}\right)^{m \cdot n}$$

$$PV = FV\left(\frac{1}{1 + \frac{r}{m}}\right)^{m \cdot n}$$

$$PVA = CF\left[\frac{1}{r/m} - \frac{1}{r/m}\left(\frac{1}{1 + r/m}\right)^{n \cdot m}\right]$$

Yield

Yields are calculated often in the leasing industry. The yield is calculated by using the present value formula to solve for the interest rate or the discount rate. Because the present value formula often involves polynomials, the solution for the yield is often difficult and can be solved only using trial and error or an iterative process. Again, these solutions are built into most financial calculators and spreadsheet software.

Suppose you want to know the yield on a lease that has annual payments of $25,000 per year for six years and a guaranteed residual value $20,000 at the end of six years. If the cost of the equipment is $120,000, what is the yield on this lease?

The formula to set up this problem is a present value formula with two components. One is a six-year annuity for the lease payments, and the other is the present value of the residual value. The present value is known: It is the cost of the equipment. So we want to solve the following equation for the interest rate or yield:

$$PV = \sum_{t=1}^{n} \frac{CF}{(1 + r)^t} + \frac{Residual}{(1 + r)^n}$$

$$\$120{,}000 = \sum_{t=1}^{6} \frac{\$25{,}000}{(1 + y)^t} + \frac{\$20{,}000}{(1 + y)^6}$$

By a tedious trial-and-error process, you might find the answer of about 10 percent. Or you could let a calculator or computer arrive at 10.045 percent for you.

Definitions of NPV

Net present value is defined as the present value of all future cash flows less the current cost of the investment. The following formula calculates NPV:

$$NPV = \sum_{t=1}^{n} \frac{CF_t}{(1 + r)^t} - COST_0 \tag{A.4}$$

The term "net" in NPV means "net the initial cost." A word of caution for those who apply spreadsheet software to NPV calculation. Popular spreadsheets define the NPV calculation to the first term *only* in equation A.4. That is, the spreadsheet software does not subtract the initial cost from what is called NPV. (It should probably be called present value, because the software does not net the initial cost.) Software packages, however, use PV for the standard present value calculation such as those presented in the section entitled present value above.

Continuous Compounding

For the option pricing model presented in Chapter 8, continuous compounding is often used. Continuous compounding is accomplished by taking the non-annual compounding formula and letting m approach infinity. This is defined mathematically as:

$$\lim_{m \to \infty} \left(1 + \frac{r}{m}\right)^{m \cdot n} = e^{rn}$$

For present value calculations using continuous compounding, the formula is:

$$PV = FV \times e^{-rn}$$

For example, if n is five years and r is 6 percent, the present value of $1,000 to be received in five years is:

$$PV = \$1,000 \times e^{-.06 \cdot 5} = \$740.82.$$

This number can be compared to the present value computed using annual compounding, $747.26, or monthly compounding, $741.37. There is one qualification in that the interest rate to use for continuous compounding is not necessarily the same one to use for discrete compounding. Of course, the assumption that was just made in the example assumes the same interest rate of 6 percent.

Summary

This appendix has reviewed the mathematics of present value calculations, including the topics of future value, multiple cash flows, annuities, non-annual compounding, net present value, and continuous compounding. For analysts of leasing contracts, present value calculations are absolutely essential—a tool that no financial decision maker can be without.

References

Finance and Economic Journals

Albert, Joseph D., and Willard McIntosh. "Identifying Risk-Adjusted Indifference Rents for Alternative Operating Leases." *Journal of Real Estate Research*, 4(3), 1989: 81–93.

Anderson, John C., and Barbara R. McIntosh. "An Analysis of the Tax and Incentive Considerations Involved in Employee Leasing." *Journal of the American Taxation Association*, 9(2), 1988: 19–30.

Anderson, Paul F., and John D. Martin. "Lease vs. Purchase Decisions: A Survey of Current Practice." *Financial Management*, 6(1), 1977: 41–47.

Ang, James, and Pamela P. Peterson. "The Leasing Puzzle." *Journal of Finance*, 39(4), 1984: 1055–1065.

Apland, Jeffrey, Robert N. Barnes, and Fred Justus. "The Farm Lease: An Analysis of Owner-Tenant and Landlord Preferences under Risk." *American Journal of Agricultural Economics*, 66(3), 1984: 376–384.

Athanasopoulos, Peter J., and Peter W. Bacon. "The Evaluation of Leveraged Leases." *Financial Management*, 9(1), 1980: 76–80.

Barone, Robert N. "Some Theoretical and Practical Problems in Leveraged Lease Analysis." *Business Economics*, 8(4), 1973: 15–19.

Baum, Clifford B. "Equity Lease Financing." *Financial Analysts Journal*, 25(3), 1969: 138–141.

Bayless, Mark E., and J. David Diltz. "An Empirical Study of the Debt Displacement Effects of Leasing." *Financial Management*, 15(4), 1986: 53–60.

Benjamin, John D., Glenn W. Boyle, and C. F. Sirmans. "Retail Leasing: The Determinants of Shopping Center Rents." AREUEA, 18(3), 1990: 302–312.

Bierman, Harold, Jr. "Buy versus Lease with an Alternative Minimum Tax." *Financial Management*, 17(4), 1988: 87–91.

Bower, Richard S. "Issues in Lease Financing." *Financial Management*, 2(4), 1973: 25–34.

Brandon, Dick H. "Computer Leasing Industry." *Financial Analysts Journal*, 24(3), 1968: 85–90.

Brealey, R. A., and C. M. Young. "Debt, Taxes and Leasing—A Note." *Journal of Finance*, 35(5), 1980: 1245–1250.

Brick, Ivan E., William Fung, and Marti Subrahmanyam. "Leasing and Financial Intermediation: Comparative Tax Advantages." *Financial Management*, 16(1), 1987: 55–59.

Burns, Jane O., Karen S. Hreha, and Suzanne M. Luttman. "Corporate Leasing versus Property Ownership under the Tax Reform Act of 1986." *Journal of the American Taxation Association*, 11(1), 1989: 105–113.

Callahan, J. "The Lease versus Purchase Decision in the Public Sector." *National Tax Journal*, 34(2), 1981: 235–240.

Capettini, Robert, and Howard Toole. "Designing Leveraged Leases: A Mixed Integer Linear Programming Approach." *Financial Management*, 10(3), 1981: 15–23.

Cason, Roger L. "Leasing, Asset Lives and Uncertainty: A Practitioner's Comments." *Financial Management*, 16(2), 1987: 13–16.

Cook, Donald C. "The Case Against Capitalizing Leases." *Harvard Business Review*, 41(1), 1963: 145–161.

Cooper, Kerry, and Robert H. Strawser. "Evaluation of Capital Investment Projects Involving Asset Leases." *Financial Management*, 4(1), 1975: 44–49.

Copeland, Thomas E., and J. Fred Weston. "A Note on the Evaluation of Cancellable Operating Leases." *Financial Management*, 11(2), 1982: 60–67.

Crawford, Peggy J., Charles P. Harper, and John J. McConnell. "Further Evidence on the Terms of Financial Leases." *Financial Management*, 10(3), 1981: 7–14.

Davidson, Sidney, and Roman L. Weil. "Inflation Accounting and Leases." *Financial Analysts Journal*, 31(6), 1975: 22–29, 57.

DeBrock, L. M., and J. L. Smith. "Joint Bidding, Information Pooling, and the Performance of Petroleum Lease Auctions." *Bell Journal of Economics*, 14(2), 1983: 395–404.

Dipchand, Cecil R., Arthur C. Gudikunst, and Gordon S. Roberts. "An Empirical Analysis of Canadian Railroad Leases." *Journal of Financial Research*, 3(1), 1980: 57–68.

Dyl, Edward A., and Stanley A. Martin, Jr. "Setting Terms for Leveraged Leases." *Financial Management*, 6(4), 1977: 20–27.

Fabozzi, Frank J., and Uzi Yaari. "Valuation of Safe Harbor Tax Benefit Transfer Leases." *Journal of Finance*, 38(2), 1983: 595–606.

Ferrara, William L., and Joseph F. Wojdak. "Valuation of Long-Term Leases." *Financial Analysts Journal*, 25(6), 1969: 29–32.

Findlay, M., Chapman, III. "Financial Lease Evaluation: Survey and Synthesis." *Financial Review*, 9(1), 1974: 1–15.

Finucane, Thomas J. "Some Empirical Evidence on the Use of Financial Leases." *Journal of Financial Research*, 11(4), 1988: 321–334.

Flath, David. "The Economics of Short-Term Leasing." *Economic Inquiry*, 18(2), 1980: 247–259.

Franks, Julian R., and Stewart D. Hodges. "Valuation of Financial Lease Contracts: A Note." *Journal of Finance*, 33(2), 1978: 657–669.

———. "Lease Valuation When Taxable Earnings Are a Scarce Resource." *Journal of Finance*, 42(4), 1987: 987–1005.

Fry, Maxwell J., and James Mak. "Is Land Leasing a Solution to Unaffordable Housing? An Answer from Fee Simple versus Leasehold Property Price Differentials in Hawaii." *Economic Inquiry*, 22(4), 1984: 529–549.

Galper, Harvey, and Eric Toder. "Owning Or Leasing: Bennington College, and the U.S. Tax System." *National Tax Journal*, 36(2), 1983: 257–261.

Gaumnitz, Jack E., and Allen Ford. "The Lease or Sell Decision." *Financial Management*, 7(4), 1978: 69–74.

Geltner, David. "Return Risk and Cash Flow Risk with Long-Term Riskless Leases in Commercial Real Estate." *AREUEA*, 18(4), 1990: 377–402.

Gilley, Otis, Gordon V. Karels, and Randolph M. Lyon. "Joint Ventures and Offshore Oil Lease Sales." *Economic Inquiry*, 23(2), 1985: 321–340.

Gordon, Myron J. "A General Solution to the Buy or Lease Decision: A Pedagogical Note." *Journal of Finance*, 29(1), 1974: 245–250.

Grimlund, Richard A., and Robert Capettini. "A Note on the Evaluation on Leveraged Leases and Other Investments." *Financial Management*, 11(2), 1982: 68–72.

Gritta, Richard D. "The Impact of Lease Capitalization." *Financial Analysts Journal*, 30(2), 1974: 47–52.

Harvey, Barbara. "The Leasing of the Abbot of Westminster's Demesnes in the Later Middle Ages." *Economic History Review*, 22(1), 1969: 17–27.

Heaton, Hal. "Corporate Taxation and Leasing." *Journal of Financial and Quantitative Analysis*, 21(3), 1986: 351–359.

Henderson, Glenn V., Jr. "A General Solution to the Buy or Lease Decision: A Pedagogical Note: Comment." *Journal of Finance*, 31(1), 1976: 147–151.

Hirschey, Mark, and James L. Pappas. "Market Power and Manufacturer Leasing." *Journal of Industrial Economics*, 30(1), 1981: 39–48.

Hochman, Shalom, and Ramon Rabinovitch. "Financial Leasing Under Inflation." *Financial Management*, 13(1), 1984: 17–26.

Hodges, Stewart D. "The Valuation of Variable Rate Leases." *Financial Management*, 14(1), 1985: 68–74.

Hollander, Abraham. "Quota Leasing as a Competitive Strategy: A Story of Chicken Feed, Laying Hens, and Eggs." *Canadian Journal of Economics*, 23(3), 1990: 617–629.

Honig, Lawrence E., and Stephen C. Coley. "An After-Tax Equivalent Payment Approach to Conventional Lease Analysis." *Financial Management*, 4(4), 1975: 28–36.

Hughes, John S., and James Vander Weide. "Incentive Considerations in the Reporting of Leveraged Leases." *Journal of Bank Research*, 13(1), 1982: 36–41.

Hull, J. C., and G. L. Hubbard. "Lease Evaluation in the UK: Current Theory and Practice." *Journal of Business Finance and Accounting*, 7(4), 1980: 619–638.

Hull, John C. "The Bargaining Positions of the Parties to a Lease Agreement." *Financial Management*, 11(3), 1982: 71–79.

Idol, Charles R. "A Note on Specifying Debt Displacement and Tax Shield Borrowing Opportunities in Financial Lease Valuation Models." *Financial Management*, 9(2), 1980: 24–29.

Ingberman, Monroe, Joshua Ronen, and George H. Sorter. "Lease Capitalization and Financial Ratios." *Financial Analysts Journal*, 35(1), 1979: 28–31.

Lancaster, Joe, and Ted D. Englebrecht. "An Analysis of the Availability of Percentage Depletion for Lease Bonuses and Advance Royalties." *Journal of the American Taxation Association*, 4(2), 1983: 44–51.

Lawrence, Edward C., and Robert M. Bear. "Corporate Bankruptcy Prediction and the Impact of Leases." *Journal of Business Finance and Accounting*, 13(4), 1986: 571–585.

Lease, Ronald C., John J. McConnell, and James S. Schallheim. "Realized Returns and the Default and Prepayment Experience of Financial Leasing Contracts." *Financial Management*, 19(2), 1990: 11–20.

Lee, T. K. "Resource Information Policy and Federal Resource Leasing." *Bell Journal of Economics*, 13(2), 1982: 561–568.

Lee, Wayne Y., John D. Martin, and Andrew J. Senchack. "The Case for Using Options to Evaluate Salvage Values in Financial Leases." *Financial Management*, 11(3), 1982: 33–41.

Leland, Hayne E. "Optimal Risk Sharing and the Leasing of Natural Resources, with Application to Oil and Gas Leasing on the OCS." *Quarterly Journal of Economics*, 92(3), 1978: 413–438.

Levy, Haim, and Marshall Sarnat. "Leasing, Borrowing, and Financial Risk." *Financial Management*, 8(4), 1979: 47–54.

Lewellen, Wilbur G., Michael S. Long, and John J. McConnell. "Asset Leasing in Competitive Capital Markets." *Journal of Finance*, 31(3), 1976: 787–798.

Loewenstein, Mark A., and James E. McClure. "Taxes and Financial Leasing." *Quarterly Review of Economics and Business*, 28(1), 1988: 21–38.

Long, Michael S. "Leasing and the Cost of Capital." *Journal of Financial and Quantitative Analysis*, 12(4), 1977: 579–586.

Maniatis, George C. "Promoting Industrial Investment in Developing Countries: Traditional Financing Methods vs. Industrial Leasing." *Oxford Economic Papers*, 23(2), 1971: 268–276.

Manning, Chris. "Leasing versus Purchase of Corporate Real Property: Leases with Residual Equity Interests." *Journal of Real Estate Research*, 6(1), 1991: 79–86.

Marcus, Robert P. "Residual Value and the Cost of Leasing." *Financial Analysts Journal*, 34(2), 1978: 58–60.

Marks, Barry R. "Calculating the Rate of Return on a Leveraged Lease—A Constant Leverage Approach." *Journal of Bank Research*, 13(4), 1983: 297–299.

Masse, I., J. R. Hanrahan, and J. Kushner. "The Lease versus Borrow Decision from a Public Sector Perspective." *National Tax Journal*, 40(2), 1987: 271–274.

McAdam, M. Bruce. "Equipment Leasing: An Integral Part of Financial Services." *Business Economics*, 23(3), 1988: 43–47.

McConnell, John J., and James S. Schallheim. "Valuation of Asset Leasing Contracts." *Journal of Financial Economics*, 12(2), 1983: 237–261.

McGugan, Vincent J., and Richard E. Caves. "Integration and Competition in the Equipment Leasing Industry." *Journal of Business*, 47(3), 1974: 382–396.

Mehta, Dileep R., and David T. Whitford. "Lease Financing and the M&M Propositions." *Financial Review*, 14(1), 1979: 47–58.

Miller, Merton H., and Charles W. Upton. "Leasing, Buying, and the Cost of Capital Services." *Journal of Finance*, 31(3), 1976: 761–786.

Morgan, Eleanor, Julian Lowe, and Cyril Tomkins. "The UK Financial Leasing Industry—A Structural Analysis." *Journal of Industrial Economics*, 28(4), 1980: 405–426.

Moyer, R. Charles. "Lease Evaluation and the Investment Tax Credit: A Framework for Analysis." *Financial Management*, 4(2), 1975: 39–42.

Mukherjee, Tarun K. "A Survey of Corporate Leasing Analysis." *Financial Management*, 20(2), 1991: 96–107.

Myers, Stewart C., David A. Dill, and Alberto J. Bautista. "Valuation of Financial Lease Contracts." *Journal of Finance*, 31(3), 1976: 799–819.

Nantell, Timothy J. "Equivalence of Lease vs. Buy Analyses." *Financial Management*, 2(3), 1973: 61–65.

Nickson, Jack W., Jr., and R. Bryan Grinnan III. "Should Banks Enter the Leasing Field?" *Financial Review*, 1(3), 1968: 181–190.

Niemira, Michael P., and Giela T. Fredman. "An Evaluation of the Composite Index of Leasing Indicators for Signaling Turning Points in Business and Growth Cycles." *Business Economics*, 26(4), 1991: 49–55.

O'Brien, Thomas J., and Bennie H. Nunnally, Jr. "A 1982 Survey of Corporate Leasing Analysis." *Financial Management*, 12(2), 1983: 30–36.

Ofer, Aharon R. "The Evaluation of the Lease versus Purchase Alternatives." *Financial Management*, 5(2), 1976: 67–74.

Olsen, Robert A. "Lease vs. Purchase or Lease vs. Borrow: Comment." *Financial Management*, 7(2), 1978: 82–83.

Owers, James E., and Ronald C. Rogers. "The Windfall of Safe Harbor Leasing: Evidence from Capital Markets." *National Tax Journal*, 38(4), 1985: 561–566.

Paddock, James J., Daniel R. Siegel, and James L. Smith. "Option Valuation of Claims on Real Assets: The Case of Offshore Petroleum Leases." *Quarterly Journal of Economics*, 103(3), 1988: 479–508.

Parker, James E., and Thomas P. Howard. "Leasing as a Means of Shifting Tax Savings to Non-Taxable Organizations." *Journal of the American Taxation Association*, 4(2), 1983: 14–22.

Parry, Robert W., Jr., and Stuart K. Webster. "City Leases: Up Front, Out Back, in The Closet." *Financial Analysts Journal*, 36(5), 1980: 41–47.

Perg, Wayne F. "Leveraged Leasing: The Problem of Changing Leverage." *Financial Management*, 7(3), 1978: 47–51.

Roberts, Gordon S., and Arthur C. Gudikunst. "Equipment Financial Leasing Practices and Costs: Comment." *Financial Management*, 7(2), 1978: 79–81.

Roenfeldt, Rodney L., and Jerome S. Osteryoung. "Analysis of Financial Leases." *Financial Management*, 2(1), 1973: 74–87.

Sartoris, William L., and Ronda S. Paul. "Lease Evaluation—Another Capital Budgeting Decision." *Financial Management*, 2(2), 1973: 46–52.

Schall, Lawrence D. "Analytic Issues in Lease vs. Purchase Decisions." *Financial Management*, 16(2), 1987: 17–20.

Schallheim, James S., Ramon E. Johnson, Ronald C. Lease, and John J. McConnell. "The Determinants of Yields on Financial Leasing Contracts." *Journal of Financial Economics*, 19(1), 1987: 45–68.

Schallheim, James S., and John J. McConnell. "A Model for the Determination of 'Fair' Premiums on Lease Cancellation Insurance Policies." *Journal of Finance*, 40(5), 1985: 1439–1457.

Scott, John T., Jr., and Franklin J. Riess. "Changing Technology and Lease Adjustment: Theory and Practice." *Land Economics*, 45(4), 1969: 400–405.

Smith, Bruce D. "Accelerated Debt Repayment in Leveraged Leases." *Financial Management*, 11(2), 1982: 73–80.

Smith, Clifford W., Jr., and L. MacDonald Wakeman. "Determinants of Corporate Leasing Policy." *Journal of Finance*, 40(3), 1985: 895–908.

Sorensen, Ivar W., and Ramon E. Johnson. "Equipment Financial Leasing Practices and Costs: An Empirical Study." *Financial Management*, 6(1), 1977: 33–40.

Srinivasan, V., Y. H. Kim, and P. J. Bolster. "A Framework for Integrating the Leasing Alternative with the Capital Budgeting Decision." *Advances in Financial Planning and Forecasting*, 3(1), 1989: 75–94.

Steele, Anthony. "Difference Equation Solutions to the Valuation of Lease Contracts." *Journal of Financial and Quantitative Analysis*, 19(3), 1984: 311–328.

Sunley, Emil M. "Depreciation and Leasing under the New Tax Law." *National Tax Journal*, 35(3), 1982: 287–294.

Sutinen, J. G. "The Rational Choice of Share Leasing and Implications for Efficiency." *American Journal of Agricultural Economics*, 57(4), 1975: 613–621.

Swenson, Charles W. "Some Preliminary Evidence on Tax-Exempt Municipal Leasing." *National Tax Journal*, 41(4), 1988: 573–578.

Taff, Charles A. "Developments in the Leasing of Motor Truck Equipment." *Southern Economic Journal*, 17(1), 1950: 50–54.

Taslim, M. A. "Short-Term Leasing, Resource Allocation, and Crop-Share Tenancy." *American Journal of Agricultural Economics*, 71(3), 1989: 785–790.

Vancil, Richard F. "Lease or Borrow—New Method of Analysis." *Harvard Business Review*, 39(5), 1961: 122–136.

———. "Lease or Borrow—Steps in Negotiation." *Harvard Business Review*, 39(6), 1961: 138–159.

Vancil, Richard F., and Robert N. Anthony. "The Financial Community Looks At Leasing." *Harvard Business Review*, 37(6), 1959: 113–130.

Weingartner, H. Martin. "Leasing, Asset Lives and Uncertainty: Guides to Decision Maketing." *Financial Management*, 16(2), 1987: 5–12.

———. "Rejoinder: Leasing, Asset Lives and Uncertainty." *Financial Management*, 16(2), 1987: 21–23.

Wiar, Robert C. "Economic Implications of Multiple Rates of Return in the Leveraged Lease Context." *Journal of Finance*, 28(5), 1973: 1275–1286.

Zises, Alvin. "Long-Term Leases: Case Against Capitalization; For Full Disclosures." *Financial Analysts Journal*, 18(3), 1962: 13–64.

Accounting Journals

Alderman, J. Kenneth, and C. Wayne Alderman. "Accounting for Leases." *Journal of Accountancy*, 147(6), 1979: 74–79.

Altman, Edward I. "Capitalization of Leases and the Predictability of Financial Ratios: A Comment." *The Accounting Review,* 51(2), 1976: 405–412.

Ashton, D. J. "The Reasons for Leasing—A Mathematical Programming Framework." *Journal of Business Finance And Accounting,* 5(2), 1978: 233–251.

Ashton, R. K. "Accounting for Finance Leases—A Field Test." *Accounting and Business Research,* 15(59), 1985: 233–238.

Baker, C. Richard. "Leasing and the Setting of Accounting Standards: Mapping the Labyrinth." *Journal of Accounting, Auditing and Finance,* 3(3), 1980: 197–206.

Beechy, Thomas H. "Quasi-Debt Analysis of Financial Leases." *The Accounting Review,* 44(2), 1969: 375–381.

———. "The Cost of Leasing: Comment and Correction." *The Accounting Review,* 45(4), 1970: 769–773.

Benjamin, James A., and Robert H. Strawser. "Developments in Lease Accounting." *CPA Journal,* 46(11), 1976: 33–36.

Benke, Ralph L. and Charles P. Baril. "The Lease versus Purchase Decision." *Management Accounting,* 71(9), 1990: 42–46.

Bierman, Harold, Jr. "Accounting for Capitalized Leases: Tax Considerations." *The Accounting Review,* 48(2), 1973: 421–424.

Bloomfield, E. C., and R. Ma. "The Lease Evaluation Solution." *Accounting and Business Research,* 4(16), 1974: 297–302.

Blum, James D. "Implicit Factors in the Evaluation of Lease vs. Buy Alternatives: A Comment." *The Accounting Review,* 49(4), 1974: 807–808.

———. "Accounting and Reporting for Leases by Lessees: The Interest Rate Problems." *Management Accounting,* 59(10), 1978: 25–28.

Bower, Richard S., Frank C. Herringer, and J. Peter Williamson. "Lease Evaluation." *The Accounting Review,* 41(2), 1966: 257–265.

Bowles, G. N. "Some Thoughts on the Lease Evaluation Solution." *Accounting and Business Research,* 7(26), 1977: 124–126.

Bowman, Robert G. "The Debt Equivalence of Leases: An Empirical Investigation." *The Accounting Review,* 55(2), 1980: 237–253.

Brief, Richard P., and Joel Owen. "Accounting for Leveraged Leases: A Comment." *Journal of Accounting Research,* 16(2), 1978: 411–413.

Burns, Jane O., and Kathleen Bindon. "Evaluating Leases with LP." *Management Accounting,* 61(8), 1980: 48–53.

Burrows, G. H. "The Lease Evaluation Solution: A Further Comment." *Accounting and Business Research,* 7(27), 1977: 208–210.

———. "Evolution Of A Lease Solution." *Abacus,* 24(2), 1988: 107–119.

Chamberlain, Douglas C. "Capitalization of Lease Obligations." *Management Accounting*, 57(6), 1975: 37–38.

Chasteen, Lanny G. "Implicit Factors in the Evaluation of Lease vs. Buy Alternatives." *The Accounting Review*, 48(4), 1973: 764–767.

———. "Implicit Factors in the Evaluation of Lease vs. Buy Alternatives: A Reply." *The Accounting Review*, 49(4), 1974: 809–811.

Cheung, Joseph K. "The Association Between Lease Disclosure and the Lessee's Systematic Risk." *Journal of Business Finance and Accounting*, 9(3), 1982: 297–306.

Clay, Raymond J., Jr., and William W. Holder. "A Practitioner's Guide to Accounting for Leases." *Journal of Accountancy*, 144(2), 1977: 61–68.

Cohen, Albert H. "The Future of Lease Financing under New Depreciation Rules." *Journal of Accountancy*, 98(2), 1954: 189–196.

Dieter, Richard. "Is Lessee Accounting Working?" *CPA Journal*, 49(8), 1979: 13–20.

Drury, Colin, and Steven Braund. "The Leasing Decision: A Comparison of Theory and Practice." *Accounting and Business Research*, 20(79), 1990: 179–191.

Duty, Glen L. "A Leasing Guide to Taxes." *Management Accounting*, 62(2), 1980: 45–50.

El-Gazzar, Samir, Steve Lilien, and Victor Pastena. "Accounting for Leases by Lessees." *Journal of Accounting and Economics*, 8(3), 1986: 217–237.

Elam, Rick. "The Effect of Lease Data on the Predictive Ability of Financial Ratios." *The Accounting Review*, 50(1), 1975: 25–43.

———. "Capitalization of Leases and the Predictability of Financial Ratios: A Reply." *The Accounting Review*, 51(2), 1976: 413–414.

Elliott, Grover S. "Leasing of Capital Equipment." *Management Accounting*, 57(6), 1975: 39–42.

Everett, John O., and Gary A. Porter. "Safe-Harbor Leasing—Unraveling the Tax Implications." *Journal of Accounting, Auditing and Finance*, 7(3), 1984: 241–256.

Fawthrop, R. A., and Brian Terry. "Debt Management and the Use of Leasing Finance in UK Corporate Financing Strategies." *Journal of Business Finance and Accounting*, 2(3), 1975: 295–314.

Felt, Howard M., and Donald T. Barsky. "Purchase vs. Lease: Computer Obsolescence." *Management Accounting*, 51(4), 1969: 29–32.

Ferrara, William L. "Capital Budgeting and Financing or Leasing Decisions." *Management Accounting*, 49(11), 1968: 55–63.

———. "Lease vs. Purchase: A Quasi-Financing Approach." *Management Accounting*, 55(7), 1974: 21–26.

————. "The Case for Symmetry In Lease Reporting." *Management Accounting*, 59(10), 1978: 17–24.

Findlay, M. Chapman, III. "Financial Lease Evaluation Under Conditions of Uncertainty: A Comment." *The Accounting Review*, 49(4), 1974: 794–795.

Finnerty, Joseph E., Rick N. Fitzsimmons, and Thomas W. Oliver. "Lease Capitalization and Systematic Risk." *The Accounting Review*, 55(4), 1980: 631–639.

Foss, Helga B., and Shaheen Borna. "Employee Leasing after the TRA." *Journal of Accountancy*, 164(3), 1987: 151–156.

Garrison, Ray H. "Methodology of Lease Capitalization." *The Accounting Review*, 43(4), 1968: 782–784.

Grant, Edward B., and Raymond C. Witt. "A Look at Leveraged Leases under FAS No. 13." *Management Accounting*, 60(8), 1979: 49–52.

Grinnell, D. Jacques, and Richard F. Kochanek. "The New Accounting Standards for Leases." *CPA Journal*, 47(10), 1977: 15–22.

Grinyer, John R. "The Lease Evaluation Solution: A Comment and Alternative." *Accounting and Business Research*, 5(19), 1975: 231–234.

————. "The Lease Evaluation Solution: Continued." *Accounting and Business Research*, 7(27), 1977: 211–214.

Gritta, Richard D. "Capitalizing Net Lease Rentals: A Comment." *Management Accounting*, 56(5), 1974: 37–39.

Hannon, John M. "Lease Accounting: A Current Controversy." *Management Accounting*, 58(3), 1976: 25–28.

Hanshaw, Nancy F., Thomas A. Ulrich, and Charles J. Hollon. "Save Time, Money, and Taxes—Lease Your Employees." *Management Accounting*, 67(10), 1986: 30–36.

Harmelink, Philip J., and Robert Capettini. "Income Tax Consequences in Leasing." *CPA Journal*, 49(3), 1979: 29–34.

Imhoff, Eugene A., Jr., Robert C. Lipe, and David W. Wright. "Operating Leases: Impact of Constructive Capitalization." *Accounting Horizons*, 18(1), 1991: 51–63.

Imhoff, Eugene A., and Jacob K. Thomas. "Economic Consequences of Accounting Standards: The Lease Disclosure Rule Change." *Journal of Accounting and Economics*, 10(4), 1988: 277–310.

Johnson, Sandra J., and Thomas M. Porcano. "The Safe Harbor Lease—Tax Implications." *CPA Journal*, 53(9), 1983: 20–29.

Kasper, Larry J. "Evaluating the Cost of Financial Leases." *Management Accounting*, 58(11), 1977: 43–51.

Loretucci, Joseph A. "Financial Leasing: What's the Best Replacement Cycle?" *Management Accounting*, 61(2), 1979: 45–48.

Ma, Ronald. "Comparative Analysis of Lease Evaluation Models: A Review Article." *Accounting and Business Research*, 11(42), 1981: 153–162.

Marston, Felicia, and Robert S. Harris. "Substitutability of Leases and Debt in Corporate Capital Structures." *Journal of Accounting, Auditing and Finance*, New Series, 3(2), 1988: 147–170.

Martin, John D., Paul F. Anderson, and Arthur J. Keown. "Lease Capitalization and Stock Price Stability: Implications for Accounting." *Journal of Accounting, Auditing and Finance*, 2(2), 1979: 151–164.

Munter, Paul, and Thomas A. Ratcliffe. "An Assessment of User Reactions to Lease Accounting Disclosures." *Journal of Accounting, Auditing and Finance*, 6(2), 1983: 108–114.

Murray, Dennis. "The Irrelevance of Lease Capitalization." *Journal of Accounting, Auditing and Finance*, 5(2), 1982: 154–159.

Nelson, A. Tom. "Capitalizing Leases—The Effect on Financial Ratios." *Journal of Accountancy*, 116(1), 1963: 49–58.

Nurnberg, Hugo. "Leases, Purchase Commitments, and Pensions Revisited." *CPA Journal*, 43(5), 1973: 375–389.

Orbach, Kenneth N., and William D. Samson. "An Open Letter to Congress: Leasing Little Lisa." *Management Accounting*, 64(9), 1983: 46–47.

Pierce, Happy. "Leasing and the Lessee." *Management Accounting*, 57(6), 1975: 33–36.

Richardson, A. W. "The Measurement of the Current Portion of Long-Term Lease Obligations—Some Evidence from Practice." *The Accounting Review*, 60(4), 1985: 744–752.

Ro, Byung T. "The Disclosure of Capitalized Lease Information and Stock Prices." *Journal of Accounting Research*, 16(2), 1978: 315–340.

Roenfeldt, Rodney L., and James B. Henry. "Lease vs. Debt Purchase of Automobiles." *Management Accounting*, 58(4), 1976: 49–56.

Russo, Joseph A., Jr. "Escalations in Commercial Leases." *CPA Journal*, 55(4), 1985: 28–35.

Ryan, Robert J., Jr. "Leveraged Leasing." *Management Accounting*, 58(10), 1977: 45–46.

Schall, Lawrence D., and Gary L. Sundem. "The Investment Tax Credit and the Leasing Industry." *Journal of Accounting and Public Policy*, 1(2), 1982: 83–94.

Schipper, Katherine, John R. Twombly, and Roman L. Weil. "Financial Lease Evaluation under Conditions of Uncertainty: A Comment." *The Accounting Review*, 49(4), 1974: 796–801.

Shanno, David F., and Roman L. Weil. "The Separate Phases Method of Accounting for Leveraged Leases: Properties of the Allocating Rate and an Algorithm for Finding It." *Journal of Accounting Research*, 14(2), 1976: 348–356.

Shaw, Wayne H. "Measuring the Impact of the Safe Harbor Lease Law on Security Prices." *Journal of Accounting Research*, 26(1), 1988: 60–81.

Shenkman, Martin M. "A Real Estate Leasing Checklist: Are Your Clients Making the Most of Your Services?" *Journal of Accountancy*, 166(2), 1988: 78–84.

Stickney, Clyde P., Roman L. Weil, and Mark A. Wolfson. "Income Taxes and Tax-Transfer Leases: General Electric's Accounting for A Molotov Cocktail." *The Accounting Review*, 58(2), 1983: 439–459.

Sundblad, Harry A. "Automobile Leasing." *Management Accounting*, 56(9), 1975: 53–55.

Taylor, Donald H. "Technological or Economic Obsolescence: Computer Purchase vs. Lease." *Management Accounting*, 50(1), 1968: 49–51.

Taylor, Peter, and Stuart Turley. "The Views of Management on Accounting for Leases." *Accounting and Business Research*, 16(61), 1985: 59–68.

Vaughn, Donald E., and Ronald W. Melicher. "Capitalizing Net Lease Rentals." *Management Accounting*, 55(7), 1974: 27–33.

Wilhelm, Maurice F., Jr. "Purchase or Lease: That is the Question." *Management Accounting*, 51(1), 1969: 43–46.

Wilkins, T. A. "A Behavioural Investigation of Alternative Methods of Financing Capital Acquisitions and Lease Capitalisation." *Accounting and Business Research*, 14(56), 1984: 359–366.

Wilkins, Trevor, and Ian Zimmer. "The Effects of Alternative Methods of Accounting for Leases—An Experimental Study." *Abacus*, 19(1), 1983: 64–75.

———. "The Effect of Leasing and Different Methods of Accounting for Leases on Credit Evaluations." *The Accounting Review*, 58(4), 1983: 749–764.

Wilson, Charles J. "The Operating Lease and the Risk of Obsolescence." *Management Accounting*, 55(6), 1973: 41–44.

Wojdak, Joseph F. "A Theoretical Foundation for Leases and Other Executory Contracts." *The Accounting Review*, 44(3), 1969: 562–570.

Wright, Ivor B. "Review of APB Opinion No. 27—'Accounting for Lease Transactions by Manufacturer or Dealer Lessors'." *CPA Journal*, 43(7), 1973: 563–566.

Wyman, Harold E. "Financial Lease Evaluation under Conditions of Uncertainty." *The Accounting Review*, 48(3), 1973: 489–493.

———. "Financial Lease Evaluation Under Conditions of Uncertainty: A Reply." *The Accounting Review*, 49(4), 1974: 802–806.

Wyman, Harold E., and Wesley T. Andrews, Jr. "Classifying the Receivable in a Lease Transaction: A Dilemma." *The Accounting Review,* 50(4), 1975: 908–909.

Young, Colin M. "The Competitiveness of Lease Markets: An Empirical Investigation of the UK Local Authority Lease Market." *Journal of Business Finance and Accounting,* 11(2), 1984: 189–198.

Index

A

AAA corporate bonds, 148–150
AAEL (American Association of Equipment Lessors). *See* Equipment Leasing Association (ELA)
ABC Warehouse Stores (fictional company)
bargain purchase option accounting and, 82–83
before- vs. after-tax discount rate and, 129–130
capital lease accounting and, 67–70
comparison of capital and operating leases and, 70–72
discount rate of interest and, 84–85
lease/purchase decision with AMT and, 130–131
NPV calculations for, 120–121, 127–128, 129–130
operating lease accounting and, 70
residual value accounting and, 78–79, 82–83
sale-and-leaseback transaction and, 86–87
yield analysis and, 137–139
Accelerated cost recovery system (ACRS), 50–51, 60, 62
Accounting profession, types of leases distinguished in, 18–19
Accounting rules. *See also* Statement of *Financial Accounting Standards (SFAS) No. 13*
bargain purchase options and, 82–83
bargain renewal options and, 83
for capital leases, 67–70
compared with tax rules, 89–90
comparison of capital and operating leases and, 70–72
definition of capital vs. operating lease and, 66–67, 85–86
definitions of key ratios and terms in, 76–77
disclosure requirements and, 89
discount rate of interest and, 84–85
executory costs and, 85
lease or buy decision and, 180, 183–185
residual value and, 77–82
sale-and-leaseback and, 85–87
yield analysis and, 139–140
ACE. *See* Adjusted current earnings (ACE)

ACRS. *See* Accelerated cost recovery system (ACRS)
Adjusted current earnings (ACE), 54
NPV analysis and, 131, 132, 133–134
ADR. *See* Asset depreciation range (ADR)
Alternative minimum taxable income (AMTI), 53–54, 130–131
Alternative minimum tax (AMT)
adjustments vs. preferences and, 53
lease or buy decision and, 130–134, 183
1993 rules and, 132, 133–134
tax effects of leasing and, 53–54
Altman, E. I., 150
American Association of Equipment Lessors (AAEL). *See* Equipment Leasing Association (ELA)
Ameritech, 70, 71, 74–75
AMT. *See* Alternative minimum tax (AMT)
AMTI. *See* Alternative minimum taxable income (AMTI)
Ang, J., 109
Annuity, 190–192
Apex Equipment Company, 170–171
Asquith, P., 150
Asset abuse problem, 13
Asset betas, 143–145. *See also* Residual value risk
calculations for, 158–163
by firm category, 161–163
portfolio theory and, 157–158
Asset cost, and NPV equation, 115–117
Asset depreciation range (ADR), 51
Asset life
criteria for operating vs. capital lease and, 66, 68
criteria for true lease and, 42, 43
economic depreciation and, 171–173
Asset risk. *See* Residual value risk
Asset type
beta calculation and, 161–163
financial leases and, 23–24
lease payments and, 27
residual value experience and, 163–167
residual value risk and, 27, 161–167

B

Bankruptcy
LS model and, 108–109
optimal capital structure and, 105

prediction of, 143
reasons for leasing and, 11–12
Banks. *See* Financial institutions
Bargain purchase option
accounting rules and, 82–83
tax rules and, 42, 43, 45
vs. fixed purchase option, 185
Bayliss, M. E., 110
Bierman, H., Jr., 131
Black, F., 168. *See also* Option Pricing
Model (OPM)
Black-Scholes option pricing model. *See*
Option Pricing Model (OPM)
Blum, M. E., 151
Boeing Corporation, 160–161
Borrowing, vs. leasing, 3–4, 93–99,
148–150
Bower, R. S., 113, 115
Bowman, R. G., 109
Brigham, E. F., 100
Brokerage commission, 27

C

Call option
defined, 20n
financial leases and, 20
pricing of, 169–171, 175
Cancellation
financial vs. operating lease and, 21
options and, 175–176
Capital acquisition budget, 12
Capital Asset Pricing Model (CAPM),
159, 177
Capitalization of leases, 67n, 74–75
Capital lease, 18, 19. *See also* Accounting
rules
accounting rules for, 67–70, 183–184
disclosure requirements for, 89
expense differences between op-
erating lease and, 70–72
qualification as true lease and, 89–90
SFAS No. 13 criteria for, 66–67, 68
Capital markets, perfect, 4, 101
CAPM. *See* Capital Asset Pricing Model
(CAPM)
Captive leasing companies, 17, 18
Case law, and lease/sale determination,
40–41, 45–47
Cash flows, 190
NPV analysis of, 121, 123
risks from, and yield analysis, 136–137
vs. accounting earnings, 10–11
C corporations, closely held, 52
Competitive equilibrium, 3, 117–119
Computer equipment, and residual
value, 153
Conditional sales contract, 4, 39, 40–41.
See also True lease
Continuous compounding, 193–194

Contract options. *See also* Option Pricing
Model (OPM); *specific option types*
asset abuse problem and, 13
lease or buy decision and, 181,
185–186
lease payments and, 23, 28, 31
net financial leases and, 19–20
renewal, 20
types of, 23, 28
Copeland, T. E., 175–176
Cost of funds, and lease payments, 25
Cost recovery, 50–51
Cross-border leases. *See* Double-dip
transactions

D

Day v. Commissioner, 41
DeAngelo, H., 102, 106
Debt capacity, 99–100, 101
Debt/leasing relation. *See also* Borrowing, vs. leasing
as complementary, 100, 105, 109–110
optimal capital structure and, 101–102
as substitution, 99–101, 110, 150–151
Debt ratio
calculation of, 7n
off-balance sheet financing and, 7
Debt-to-asset ratio, calculation of, 8n
Debt-to-value ratio, calculation of, 9n
Default. *See also* Bankruptcy
lease contract provisions and, 34–36
risk of, 25–26, 142–143
Depreciation
alternative minimum tax and, 53–54
calculation of, 50–51
debt tax shields and, 102, 104–105
monthly payment schedules and,
124–125
pricing of leasing options and,
171–173
types of, 171n
Diltz, D., 110
Direct financing lease. *See* Financial lease
Discounting. *See* Capitalization of leases
Discount rate of interest. *See also* Yield
analysis
accounting rules and, 66–67, 84–85
basic MDB model and, 119, 121, 122
before- vs. after-tax, in NPV analysis,
129–130
general NPV models and, 115
modified MDB model and, 126–128
Diversification, 14, 168
Diversification effect, 157–158, 161
Double-dip transactions, 57–58

E

Earnings
economic vs. accounting, 10–11

future, uncertainty of, 102
Economic Recovery Tax Act (ERTA) of
    1981, 50, 60–61
Efficient markets school
    capital vs. operating leases and, 66
    reasons for leasing and, 4, 6, 7–8,
        11–12, 15–16
ELA. *See* Equipment Leasing Associa-
    tion (ELA)
Employee leasing, 15, 23
Equipment Leasing Association (ELA),
    Survey of Industry Activity, 17, 18, 20
Equivalent loan
    concept of, 93–94
    defined, 95
    five-year lease example and, 98
    multiple lease payments and, 96–99
    NPV analysis and, 99, 119
    single lease payment and, 94–96
ERTA. *See* Economic Recovery Tax Act
    (ERTA) of 1981

F

Fair market value (FMV), 23, 31, 33
Finance lease, 62
Financial Accounting Standards Board
    (FASB), 65
Financial distress. *See* Bankruptcy
Financial institutions, 17–18
Financial lease
    characteristics of, 19–20
    distinguished from operating lease,
        18, 19, 21
    estimated vs. actual residual values
        and, 164–167
    leverage lease distinguished from, 21
    true leases and, 18
    types of assets for, 24
Firm size, 143
Foreign sales corporation (FSC) lease, 58
Full service lease. *See* Service lease
Future value factor, 187–188

G

Gapenski, L. C., 100
General Motors, 160
GPA Group Ltd., 13–14, 155, 168

H

Harper, C. P., 141
Harris, R. S., 110
Hedging, 14–15
High-yield bonds, 150–151

I

IFG Leasing, 168
Incremental borrowing rate, 84

Inflation, 14, 167. *See also* Interest rate
    risk
Information costs. *See* Transaction costs
Interest. *See also* Discount rate of interest
    deductibility of, 53
Interest rate risk, 25, 142
Internal rate of return. *See* Yield analysis
Internal Revenue Service (IRS). *See* spe-
    cific tax legislation; Tax rules
International leases
    tax advantages of, 57–60
    types of, 56–57
Inter-Regional Financial Group, 168
Investment tax credit (ITC), 51–52, 60,
    62
Itel Corporation, 21

J

Jaffee, J. F., 100
Japanese leveraged lease, 58–60
Johnson, R. E., 140, 141, 142–150, 161,
    163, 165, 167
Junk bonds, 150–151

K

Klein, D. B., 151
Kumiai-in, 60

L

Lambda factor, 172–173
Land, building, and equipment leases,
    88
Land and building leases, 88
Land leases, 88
Late fees, 31
Lease, R. C., 140, 142–150, 161, 163, 165,
    167
Leaseback. *See* Sale-and-leaseback trans-
    action
Lease contract. *See also* Contract options
    certificate of delivery and acceptance
        and, 31
    default and remedy clause in, 34–36
    financial information and, 36
    lessee as writer of, 30–31
    miscellaneous provisions in, 36–37
    structure of, 30–31
    termination provisions and, 32–33
    terms of, and taxes, 150
    terms of lease payments and, 31
    use, maintenance, and insurance of
        equipment and, 32
    warranties and, 33–34
Lease or buy decision. *See also* Net pres-
    ent value (NPV) analysis
    accounting rules for leases and, 180
    competitive equilibrium and, 117–119
    example decision-making sequence
        and, 181–186

options and, 181
residual value and, 180
rules for, 179
tax consequences and, 180
Lease payments
default risk and, 25–26
factors in determination of, 24–25,
141
late fees and, 31
lessor's cost of funds and, 25
maintenance and service provisions
and, 28–29
market competition and, 29
minimum, and accounting rules,
66–67
monthly payment schedules and,
124–125
NPV analysis and, 121, 122, 123, 134
option exercise price and, 46
options and, 23, 28, 31
periodicity of, 28
present value and, 183–184
target pricing and, 29–30
tax benefits to lessor and, 27–28
tax effects involving, 47–50
terms of, 31
transaction costs and, 26–27
type of asset and, 27
uneven, 48–50
yield determination and, 141, 142–145
Lease/sale determination
case law and, 40–41, 44, 46–47
intent and, 40–41, 44, 46–47
IRS advance ruling guidelines and, 41,
42–44
lessee and lessor benefits and, 47
Lease term, defined, 42
Leasing. *See also* Employee leasing
bankruptcy and, 11–12
compared with borrowing, 3–4, 93–99,
148–150
impact on earnings, 10–11
risk sharing and, 4, 5, 13–15
summary of reasons for, 3–6
tax savings and, 4, 5, 6, 14–15
transaction cost savings and, 4, 5,
12–13
Leasing market
competition in, 3, 29, 117–119
present value and, 3
pricing and, 2–3
segments of, 4
size of, 1–2
Lessee. *See also* Accounting rules
financial condition of, 25–26, 142–143
loan between lessor and, 42, 43, 45
residual value guaranteed by, 78–79
residual value partially guaranteed
by, 81

Lessor
cost of funds for, 25
type of, 17–18
Letters of credit, 26
Leverage, 143
Leveraged lease
characteristics of, 21–22
distinguished from financial lease, 21
FSC leases and, 58
Japanese, 58–60
Midland Cogeneration Venture and,
22–23
Lewellen, W. G., 117, 118
Lewis, C., 100–101, 105–109
Lewis and Schallheim (LS) model,
100–101, 105
empirical evidence for, 109–110
numerical examples of, 106–109
Limited-use property, 44
Liquidity, 143
Lloyds of London, 21
Long, M. S., 117, 118
Longterm lease, 49
LS model. *See* Lewis and Schallheim (LS)
model

M

McConnell, J. J., 117, 118, 161
pricing of leasing options and, 169,
171–173, 175
yield analysis and, 140, 141, 142–150
McGugan pricing formula, 29–30
MACRS. *See* Modified accelerated cost
recovery system (MACRS)
Maintenance. *See also* Service lease
in financial vs. operating lease, 21
leasing vs. borrowing and, 93
NPV analysis and, 125–128
Maintenance agreement, and lease pay-
ments, 28–29
Market (systematic) risk, 157
Market-to-book ratio, calculation of, 8n
Market value
residual value and, 13
vs. book value, 8
Markowitz, H., 157
Marston, F., 110
Masulis, R., 102, 106
Maturity, and operating leases, 20
MDB model. *See* Myers, Dill, and Bau-
tista (MDB) model
Midland Cogeneration Venture, 22–23
Miller, M. H., 101–102, 117
Minimum at risk requirement, 41–42
MM Theory, 101
Modified accelerated cost recovery sys-
tem (MACRS), 50–51, 131
Modigliani, F., 101

Motor vehicle leasing, 54–55
Mukherjee, T. K., 110
Mullins, D. W., Jr., 150
Myers, Dill, and Bautista (MDB) model,
94, 99, 181–182. *See also* Net present
value (NPV) analysis
assumptions in, 99–100, 101
basic NPV analysis and, 119–125
concept of equivalent loan and, 93–99,
119
debt capacity and, 99–100, 101
discount rate and, 115
marginal tax rates and, 101
NPV analysis with AMT, 131–134
NPV analysis with operating costs
and salvage value, 125–126
required input for, 120
yield calculation and, 136, 137–139

N

NAL (net advantage to leasing) analysis.
See Net present value (NPV) analysis
Net advantage to leasing (NAL) equation, 114
Net financial lease. *See* Financial lease
Net lease, 21
Net present value (NPV) analysis, 113,
180, 181–182
basic MDB model and, 119–125
calculation of yield and, 135–137
competitive equilibrium and, 117–119
concept of equivalent loan and, 99
definitions of net present value and,
193
factors in, 180
general models of, 113–115
mathematics of, 187–194
MDB model with operating costs and
salvage value, 125–126
monthly payment schedules and,
124–125
multiperiod loan example, 116–117
one-period loan example, 115–116
tax savings and, 6, 118–119

O

Oesterreich v. Commissioner, 44
Off-balance sheet financing. *See also* Accounting rules; Operating lease
debt ratio and, 7
IRS and, 7–8
stock prices and, 72
valid economic incentives for, 7–8
OFF-B Corp., 8–9
100 percent financing, 6–7
Operating costs. *See* Maintenance

Operating lease. *See also* Accounting
rules; Service lease
accounting rules for, 183, 185
analytical model for, 73–75
capitalization of, 74–75
characteristics of, 20–22
disclosure in footnote of balance sheet
and, 70, 71
disclosure requirements for, 89
distinguished from financial lease,
18–19, 21
expense differences between capital
lease and, 70–72
SFAS No. 13 criteria for, 66–67, 68
Operating leases, ownership and, 18–19,
66, 68
OPM. *See* Option Pricing Model (OPM)
OPM Leasing Company, 21
Optimal capital structure
DeAngelo and Masulis theory of,
101–105
interaction of leasing with, 100–101
LS model and, 100–101, 105–109
MM Theory and, 101
Option Pricing Model (OPM), 168–176,
181, 185–186
call option example in, 169–171
continuous compounding and,
193–194
general characteristics of, 168–169
pricing of leasing options and, 169,
171–176
Ownership, and operating leases, 18–19,
66, 68

P

Passive activity loss rules, 52, 53
Personal guarantee, 26, 36
Peterson, P. P., 109
Portfolio theory, and residual value risk,
157–163
Prepayments, and default risk, 26
Present value. *See also* Net present value
(NPV) analysis
criteria for operating vs. capital lease
and, 66–67, 68
defined, 3
matheematics of, 189–190
Pricing. *See* Lease payments; Net present
value (NPV) analysis
Processing costs. *See* Transaction costs
Profit
defined, 42
expectation of, and true lease, 42,
43–44, 45
Profitability, 143
Psychological school, 6–7, 10–11, 15–16,
66

Purchase option. *See also* Bargain purchase option
criteria for operating vs. capital lease
and, 66, 68
criteria for true lease and, 42, 43, 45
fixed-price vs. fair market value, 23,
31, 33
fixed vs. bargain, 185
Japanese leveraged lease and, 59
valuing of, 173–176
Pure financial cost savings, 4, 5, 6–9
Pure play firm, 160
Put option, 169, 175

R

Real estate leases
accounting rules for, 87–88
IRS rules for, 55–56
Recapture, 49–50
Related parties, 47
Renewal option
bargain, and accounting rules, 83
fair market value and, 33
Rental payments. *See* Lease payments
Rent payments (real estate), defined,
56
Residual value
accounting rules and, 77–82
asset type and, 27
expected vs. actual, 154–156, 163–167,
169
guaranteed, 78–79
guaranteed by third party, 82
lease or buy decision and, 180,
182–183
leasing vs. borrowing and, 93
minimum, for true lease, 42–43, 45
net financial leases and, 18
NPV analysis and, 125–128
operating leases and, 20–21, 185
ownership of, and true lease, 155
partially guaranteed by lessee, 81
unguaranteed, 80–81
Residual value risk
CAPM and, 159
contributing factors in, 155–156
expected vs. actual value and,
154–155
measurement of, 156-157 (*see also*
Asset betas)
portfolio concept and, 157–163
pricing of, 27, 158–163
risk sharing and, 13
yield determination and, 143–145
Revenue Procedure 75-21, 41, 42, 48,
60–61
Revenue Ruling 55-540, 40–41
Revenue Rulings, 40*n*
Risk sharing, 4, 5, 13–15. *See also* Default;

Interest rate risk; Residual value
risk
Ross, S. A., 100

S

Safe harbor leasing, 60–62
Sale-and-leaseback transaction
accounting rules and, 85–87
characteristics of, 22–23
disqualified, 49, 50
Salvage value risk. *See* Residual value
risk
Schallheim, J. S.
asset betas and, 161
LS model and, 100–101, 105–109
pricing of leasing options and, 169,
171–173, 175
residual value data and, 163, 165, 167
yield analysis and, 140, 142–150
Scholes, M., 168. *See also* Option Pricing
Model (OPM)
Security deposit, 26, 36
Service costs. *See* Transaction costs
Service lease, 12–13, 21, 28–29
Small business, 15
Sorensen, I. W., 141
Specialization, 168
Spreadsheet software, and NPV analy-
sis, 193, 194*n*
Standard & Poor's, 7, 73–75
*Statement of Financial Accounting Stan-
dards (SFAS) No. 13*, 65. *See also* Ac-
counting rules
disclosure requirements and, 89
discount rate of interest and, 66–67,
84
third-party guarantors and, 82
yield analysis and, 139–140
Stickney, C. P., 61
Systematic (market) risk, 157

T

Tax Equity and Fiscal Responsibility Act
(TEFRA) of 1982
depreciation calculation and, 50
motor vehicle leases and, 54–55
safe harbor leasing and, 61–62
Tax Reform Act (TRA) of 1984
accrual basis taxpayers and, 48
finance leases and, 62
motor vehicle leases and, 55
real estate leases and, 55
Section 467 rental agreements and,
48–50
Tax Reform Act (TRA) of 1986
finance leases and, 62
investment tax credit and, 52
passive activity loss rules, 52–53
real estate leases and, 55–56

Tax rules
  alternative minimum tax and, 53–54
  compared with accounting rules,
    89–90
  cost recovery, 50–51
  depreciation, 50–51
  guidelines for advance rulings, 41, 42
  interest deductibility and, 53
  international leases and, 56–60
  investment tax credit, 51–52
  motor vehicle leasing and, 54–55
  optimal capital structure and, 101–102
  passive activity loss rules, 52–53
  real estate leases and, 55–56
  rental payments and, 47–48
  true leases under, 4, 39, 40–47
  uneven rental payments and, 48–50
Tax savings. *See also* Tax rules
  lease or buy decision and, 180, 183
  lease payments and, 4, 5, 6, 14–15,
    27–28
  non-debt, sale of, 105
  NPV analysis and, 118–119
  as reason for leasing, 4, 5, 6, 14–15
  safe harbor leasing example and,
    60–62
  terms of lease contracts and, 150
Technological obsolescence problem,
  155–156
TEFRA. *See* Tax Equity and Fiscal Responsibility Act (TEFRA) of 1982
Terminal rental adjustment clause
  (TRAC), 54–55
Third-party lender, 21–22
Time value of money, 55
Tokumei-Kumiai Agreement, 60
TRA. *See* Tax Reform Act (TRA)
TRAC. *See* Terminal rental adjustment
  clause (TRAC)
Transaction costs
  lease payments and, 26–27
  reasons for leasing and, 4, 5, 12–13, 15
  yield determination and, 142–143

True lease
  accounting criteria for capital lease
    and, 89–90
  case law and, 44, 46–47
  guidelines for advance rulings, 41, 42
  IRS rules and, 4, 39, 40–47
  lease characterization and, 40–41
  minimum at risk requirement, 41–42
  net financial leases and, 18
  off-balance sheet financing and, 7–8
  ownership of residual value and, 155
  safe harbor leasing and, 60
  tax indemnities and, 28

U

Uncertainty, 6, 102
Upton, C. W., 117

W

WACC. *See* Weighted-average cost of
  capital (WACC)
Wall Street Journal, The, 61
Warranties, 33–34
Wear and tear. *See* Asset abuse problem
Weighted-average cost of capital
  (WACC), 126
Weil, R. L., 61
Westerfield, R. W., 100
Weston, J. F., 175–176
Wolff, E. D., 150
Wolfson, M. A., 61
Working capital, 12

Y

Yield analysis, 135–152, 179, 192–193
  calculation of yield and, 135–137
  determinants of yields and, 140–145
  empirical analysis and, 145–150
  examples of, 137–139
  high-yield bonds and, 150–151
  problems with, 136–137, 150
  studies of yields and, 141–142